Praise for *My 52 Weeks of Worship*

My 52 Weeks of Worship is a clever and unusual look at one woman's journey to regain her spirituality. Pamay Bassey has done what most people could never even imagine—spending one day each week in a different house of worship. That effort and commitment taught her the universality of community, the joy of sharing, the importance of respect, and the pride that people who are committed to religion feel about their churches, synagogues, and mosques. Most of all, she learned that there is dignity in worship—however you practice it—and that all people must find their own way to a more fulfilling life. We can all learn from her experience.

–Andrea Atkins

It takes a strong and courageous individual to launch herself into unknown territory in the midst of vast and devastating unfamiliarity. Yet, this is just what Pamay Bassey did when her world was transformed by a series of deeply impactful events. In the face of uncertainty, she commenced a search for God that took her into a variety of geographical regions, liturgical spaces and interfaith worship experiences. Her story is one of insatiable faith, holy curiosity and Womanist courage. Furthermore, there is nothing quite like hearing her story straight from her lips. Her telling captures how a season of personal loss and struggle was eclipsed by her discovery of God in the most unlikely locales, and how this discovery continues to enlighten her human experience. There is something for all to hear and learn from her story.

–Rev. Neichelle Guidry Jones,
Ordained elder in the Kingdom Council of Christian Churches
and Ministries; Associate Pastor to Young Adults,
Trinity United Church of Christ, Chicago, Illinois

D1040716

My 52 Weeks of Worship is a gem of a source of inspiration for anyone going through difficult times or pondering the big life questions. I'm completely taken with the way Pamay Bassey not only took a very personal experience of loss and channeled it into a journey of exploration, but more so with the way that she is now sharing her journey with others.

-Erin Mason, PhD,
Assistant Professor of Counseling, DePaul University

My 52 Weeks of Worship

LESSONS FROM A GLOBAL, SPIRITUAL, INTERFAITH JOURNEY

EKPEDEME "PAMAY" M. BASSEY

BALBOA.
PRESS
A DIVISION OF HAY HOUSE

Balboa Press books may be ordered through booksellers or by contacting:

Balboa Press
A Division of Hay House
1663 Liberty Drive
Bloomington, IN 47403
www.balboapress.com
1-(877) 407-4847

ISBN: 978-1-4525-4580-6 (sc)
ISBN: 978-1-4525-4582-0 (hc)
ISBN: 978-1-4525-4581-3 (e)
Library of Congress Control Number: 2012900705
Because of the dynamic nature of the Internet, any web addresses or links contained in this book may have changed since publication and may no longer be valid. The views expressed in this work are solely those of the author and do not necessarily reflect the views of the publisher, and the publisher hereby disclaims any responsibility for them.

The author of this book does not dispense medical advice or prescribe the use of any technique as a form of treatment for physical, emotional, or medical problems without the advice of a physician, either directly or indirectly. The intent of the author is only to offer information of a general nature to help you in your quest for emotional and spiritual well-being. In the event you use any of the information in this book for yourself, which is your constitutional right, the author and the publisher assume no responsibility for your actions.

Scripture quotations marked NKJV taken from the New King James Version of the Holy Bible. Copyright 1979, 1980, 1982 by Thomas Nelson, inc. Used by permission. All rights reserved.

Scripture quotations marked KJV taken from the King James Version of the Holy Bible.

Scripture quotations marked NIV taken from the HOLY BIBLE, NEW INTERNATIONAL VERSION®. Copyright © 1973, 1978, 1984 Biblica. Used by permission of Zondervan. All rights reserved.

The "NIV" and "New International Version" trademarks are registered in the United States Patent and Trademark Office by Biblica. Use of either trademark requires the permission of Biblica.

Scripture quotations marked NASB taken from the New American Standard Bible®, Copyright © 1960, 1962, 1963, 1968, 1971, 1972, 1973, 1975, 1977, 1995 by The Lockman Foundation Used by permission. (www.Lockman.org)

Scripture quotations marked NCV taken from the New Century Version. Copyright © 2005 by Thomas Nelson, Inc. Used by permission. All rights reserved."

Excerpts from the Bhavagad Gita taken from the English Translation from His Divine Grace A.C. Bhaktivedanta Swami Prabhupada Copyright (c) 1972 by His Divine Grace A.C. Bhaktivedanta Swami Prabhupada

Excerpts from the Holy Qur'an taken from the The Holy Qur'an, Yusuf Ali Translation.

Book Cover Image: Windows of Religious Symbols created by Kerry LaCoste, LaCoste Design, Inc.

Author Photo by Brian McConkey Photography

Edited by Elizabeth Schwaiger and Jenny Sullivan

Printed in the United States of America

Balboa Press rev. date: 02/27/2012

To my beloved father, my hero,
Ephraim Nseabasi Bassey.
Rest in perfect peace.
I miss you, today and always.
This one is for you.
Sosongo eti eti.
Abasi odiong fi.
Love, Ekpedeme Mfonabasi

To my grandmother,
Mama Mary Eigbe.
For all that you are to me,
and for all of you that is in me.
Obulu bulu.

And finally,
To CCB.
"Forgiveness is giving up the hope
that the past could have been any different."
—Oprah Winfrey[1]

But seek ye first the kingdom of God, and his righteousness; and all these things shall be added unto you.

—Matthew 6:33, King James Version

You will seek me and find me when you seek me with all your heart.

—Jeremiah 29:13, New International Version

TABLE OF CONTENTS

Acknowledgements xiii

Author's Note xv

Introduction xvii

The First Four Weeks 1

Week 5: From the 'Friend Zone' to the Golden Zone, Mi Iglesia Mexicana,
La Viña 3

Week 6: Super Bowl Sunday, My First Mass, St. James Church 8

Week 7: From Bayfield to the Big Easy and Back, Bayfield Presbyterian
Church 12

Week 8: Ashes to Ashes and Dust to Dust, Ash Wednesday, Old St. Mary's
Catholic Church 17

Week 9: Family, Forgiveness, and Fortitude, The Church of the Apostles . 21

Week 10: A Different Kind of Savior, Saviours' Day, The Nation of Islam 26

Week 11: Contemplating Compassion and Kindness, Vajrayana Kadampa
Buddhist Center 33

Week 12: Me and the Mormons, The Church of Jesus Christ of Latter-day
Saints 36

Week 13: Breathtakingly Beautiful Devotions, The Bahá'í House of Worship
for the North American Continent 43

Week 14: Grace under Fire, Sixth Grace Presbyterian Church 47

Week 15: Going Home, Anglican Church of the Nativity 54

Week 16: Cultural Immersion in the Niger Delta, St. Peter's Cathedral . . . 63

Week 17: Oh, Ye of Little Faith, Moody Bible Church 75

Week 18: Fighting Forward, Faith Community of St. Sabina 80

Week 19: Is that Michael Jackson Playing in the Lobby?, Church of
Scientology. 90

Week 20: Be Optimistic, First Church of Religious Science 99

Week 21: See You at the Crossroads, Old St. Patrick's Church 112

Mid-Day Meditation, Zen Buddhist Temple. 116

Week 22: It Takes a Village, Urban Village Church 120

Week 23: Seek Me With Your Whole Heart, Apostolic Church of God. 128

Week 24: Don't Play with Fire, Mountain of Fire and Miracles. 135

Week 25: The Beautiful Game, Our Lady of the Cedars, Maronite Catholic
Church. 144

Week 26: Get up and Eat, Fourth Presbyterian Church. 151

Week 27: Om. Peace. Amen, Ananda Church of Self Realization. 155

Week 28: Popsicles and Praise, Missio Dei Church 161

Week 29: Taking Time Out on a Tuesday, Shambhala Meditation
Center 167

Week 30: No Pre-Conceptions, Harvey Church of Christ 173

Week 31: Shabbat Shalom, Beth Shalom B'nai Zaken Ethiopian Hebrew
Congregation (House of Peace for the Children of the Ancient Ethiopian
Hebrews) 179

Week 32: Creating a Safe Space, New Life Community Church of Hope 189

Week 33: Remembering, Saint X Church 196

Week 34: Monks, Meditation, and Me, ISKCON, The Hare Krishna
Temple. 203

Week 35: Would You Like to See a Chaplain?, Northwestern Memorial
Hospital, Emergency Room 208

Week 36: Torah and Haftorah, KAM Israel Isaiah. 215

Week 37: Unsure, Seventeenth Church of Christ, Scientist. 219

Week 38: Atonement, Temple Sholom 222

Which Witches?, Mabon (Wicca) Festival, The Autumn Equinox, Sky Fire
Song Coven 227

An Evening Chant, "Kirtan" as a Spiritual Pathway, Lake Street Church. 236

Week 39: A Comfortable Silence, 57th Street Meeting of Friends, Quaker House. 239

Week 40: Faith, Culture, and the Importance of Language, Indo-Pak United Methodist Church 243

Week 41: Happy Sabbath, Shiloh Seventh Day Adventist Church. 251

Week 42: Memory Lane and the Mosque, Muhammad Mosque No. 2, Mosque Maryam, Nation of Islam Central Regional Headquarters 256

Week 43: Can I Get a Witness?, Discourse and Watchtower Study, Kingdom Hall of Jehovah's Witnesses. 269

Week 44: Happy Birthday to Me, All Saints Day Mass, Holy Name Cathedral 277

Week 45: Is You Is or Is You Ain't . . . A Catholic?, St. Mary of The Angels 279

Week 46: Giving Thanks, The Zoroastrian Association of Metropolitan Chicago 283

Week 47: Psychedelic!, Young Adult Worship, Kensington Temple, London City Church. 289

Jesus and Rugby, Lymm Methodist Church 294

Week 48: Denied, Humbled, Accepted, Atlanta Masjid of Al-Islam. 298

What's My Name?, Temple Sinai. 308

The Power of Words, Trinity Center for Spiritual Living 317

Week 49: The Simple Life, Rosewood Fellowship 323

Destination, Merita, The Earth Center 334

Week 50: Completely Out of My Element, Hindu Temple of Greater Chicago 337

Community and Hospitality, Anshe Sholom B'nai Israel Congregation . . 343

Week 51: Modern Mystics, Centers of Light. 347

Peace Be Still, All Saints Church. 354

Liberal Minds, Unitarian Universalist Church of Studio City. 359

Week 52: Last Worship Stop of The Year, Muslim Community Center . 362

In Closing 367

Notes 369

ACKNOWLEDGEMENTS

First, I give thanks to God. Experiencing God in so many wild and wonderful ways over my 52 Weeks of Worship was a blessing. I'm thankful for the life-changing journey.

Next, I would like to thank my family: my mother, Patricia, and my sisters, Idara, Emuata, and Maeyen. Words can't express how much I appreciate you all. Thanks to the Etomi and Eigbe families, who always surround me with love. Thanks to Roland, Anehita, and Akumbom Chie. To my cousins: Uduak Okeke, Uyai Ekpeti, Phillip, Anthony, and Eno Etuk, I know you miss Uncle, too. Thank you all for your love and support. I draw strength from our collective history and experience.

Special thanks to Andrés T. Tapia, who inspired me as I managed the publication process of his book, *The Inclusion Paradox: The Obama Era and the Transformation of Global Diversity.* He planted the seed that perhaps I could write a book, as well! And, to Dr. Jason Scott Henderson, whose blogtalkradio show, *Optimistic Radio,* kept my spirits up as I navigated the editorial and publication process of this book. He helped to nourish that seed when things got rough! Thanks for the encouragement, and for the opportunity to share my story with your listeners.

Additional thanks to *Women's Day Magazine, theroot.com, Ebony Magazine, Urban Cusp, vocalo.org's Morning Amp, SeeingGrowth.com, DrShannonReece. com,* and *Identity Magazine*—a few of the early media outlets that gave me a platform for sharing my story.

Thanks also to my52wow.com family. Your comments and responses to my blog postings continue to challenge and inspire me.

A hearty thanks to the countless friends and family who served as support and sounding boards throughout this process, too many to list! Some came with me to services; others provided a shoulder to cry on or a listening ear as I healed from my grief. Some read and reviewed my writing and provided feedback and detailed editorial support. Some provided information and guidance about their own worship traditions, so I didn't get things wrong! Some cheered me along, provided moral support, or prayed for me. I would like to thank you all. Without you—and you know who you are—you wouldn't be holding this book in your hand today.

Finally—I owe a debt of gratitude to each and every place of worship that opened their doors, and each worship community that opened their heart to me as I travelled through my 52-week journey. To the pastors, priests, preachers, teachers, reverends, rabbis, imams, monks, ministers, musicians, bishops, deacons, and worship leaders—thank you for sharing the wisdom from each of your worship traditions. To those strangers who became friends—who shared pews and sanctuary space with me, who prayed with me and sang with me, and laughed and cried with me, I will never ever forget you. I thank you from the bottom of my heart.

Thank you, thank you, thank you all. May God, however you perceive Him or Her to be, continue to bless you mightily.

AUTHOR'S NOTE

This book is in no way meant to be an exhaustive commentary or authority on the world's religions. It is merely an account of a personal journey through a small subset of faith traditions and communities. The experiences I share in this book were the result of a few hours spent in each place of worship, and could never encompass the totality of the beliefs and complexities of each religion.

Many have studied these religions in great detail; I have barely scratched the surface.

For those who are staunchly committed to one worship tradition or religion, this journey may seem to be a distraction from one particular truth. Nevertheless, I encourage all to see the beauty of a journey taken by one woman trying to learn as much as possible about different worship traditions, religions, and faith communities to strengthen her own spiritual foundation during a trying time in her life.

In making a choice to observe and participate in multiple faith traditions, I'm essentially celebrating faith in general.

I do hope that you are inspired, as I was during my 52-week journey, to step out of your comfort zone and truly explore your thoughts, feelings, and beliefs about spirituality and worship. Strength comes from knowledge of Self.

Visit www.my52wow.com for more information on my ongoing journey, sources of information about each worship tradition that I visited, and interfaith dialogue and discussion.

Blessings to you on your journey.

INTRODUCTION

At the beginning of 2010, I was moved to take a spiritual journey—to visit a different place of worship every week—whether that place of worship reflected my religious tradition or not. I visited sixty-one churches, temples, mosques, shuls, synagogues, living rooms, and gathering places in the United States, Mexico, the United Kingdom, Nigeria, and South Africa.

Why? Why spend time worshipping side-by-side with Jews, Catholics, Muslims, Protestants, Scientologists, Jehovah's Witnesses, Unitarians, Quakers, Mormons, Seventh-Day Adventists, Bahá'íans, Buddhists, Hindus, Methodists, Wiccans, Zoroastrians, Mystics, and Mennonites? Why spend countless hours in unfamiliar situations, with people I didn't know, experiencing traditions and rituals that I knew nothing about? Why share my pain and grief with strangers? What was the power of praying with others and for others in different divine spaces all over the world? What was I looking for?

The answers to these questions came down to three deep needs for me: Healing, Connection, and Remembrance.

Healing: Finding the Path Through My Pain

They say God never gives you more than you can handle. Well, 2009 apparently was my year to be tested. In April, my maternal grandmother died unexpectedly. In August, my father died of cancer-related complications after a long illness. As if this was not enough, when the year ended, the most significant romantic relationship of my life also ended. Saying goodbye to someone I loved a great deal in the middle of all this loss made everything worse. When the New Year began, I wondered how I could possibly heal from all my pain.

Given that life was so challenging for me in 2009, you might imagine that I spent ample time in church, praying and leaning on God. I didn't.

I was raised Christian. Admittedly, however, my walk as an adult was not the most committed or inspiring. My church attendance was inconsistent. My prayers were more of the "Thank you, God" kind before I drifted off to sleep, or the "Please, God" kind, followed by whatever I was hoping would happen in my life. I wasn't winning any awards for devotion or commitment. It was surprising to me that in such a challenging year, attending church was not more of a priority. I decided to do something that would encourage me to seek God everywhere so I could lean on Him as I navigated through my loss and disappointment. My spirit yearned to find out what the meaning of my life would be going forward.

Connection: Recognizing the Kindness of Strangers

I believe in the kindness of strangers. Throughout my journey, I soaked in it.

During a tragedy, it's often difficult to figure out what kind of support to ask for and how to accept it when it is offered. It was clear to me that my friends loved me, but when I was still struggling with missing my ex, or the loss of my father and grandmother, no part of me wanted to bother my friends or expected them to support me when I knew they were all doing the best they could to handle their own lives.

There was something wonderfully comforting about walking into a new place of worship, knowing that people were there on that day to stand before God, however and whomever they perceived Him or Her to be, to help them endure whatever challenges they faced that day, week, month, or year. They contributed their energy to fight their own battles and encouraged me to fight mine.

Oh, the love! In every single service, there was a time when visitors were welcomed, hugged, prayed for, and loved. The kindness of strangers sustained me, especially during times when my concern was that I was leaning on my friends too much or that my grieving process was taking too long.

Remembrance: Honoring My Father, Dr. Ephraim Nseabasi Bassey, My Hero

My father, Dr. Ephraim Nseabasi Bassey, passed away on August 24, 2009. He was my hero. He was a physician and a philosopher, a philanthropist and a proud family man. He was my father, and now he was gone. His funeral was on August 29, 2009. Writing a eulogy for my father was extremely difficult. In preparing to speak at his funeral, I thought about the things that made my father who he was. My remarks included the following:

> Certainly, he was a seeker of wisdom. He was a philosopher and a healer. His parents were pillars of the Catholic Church in their village in Nigeria, which is where he began his spiritual journey. **Throughout his life, he worshipped within a Christian context, but along the way, he scoured the earth and studied all manners of faith, religion, and creed to find out the meaning of this life and his place in it.** Many shared that they enjoyed having philosophical discussions with my father, and that they learned a great deal from him and how he viewed the world. Often, as we would close a phone conversation, he would remind me: "Don't forget to pray . . . make time to meditate." He once told me, "Ekpe, your life should be a prayer—all the choices you make should honor the Creator." Those are words to live by, words that he lived by. His quest for truth and wisdom was never ending . . . up until his last day on this earth.

Throughout my journey, I was able to live the meaning of my father's name, Nseabasi, which means, "I am looking to God." I honored my father's search for truth, as well as my own. Part of the joy and wonder of this journey were the many times a sign from my father appeared, letting me know that he was with me in spirit and in my heart, every step of the way.

Choosing the Places that I Visited

In some ways, I believe, the places that I visited chose me. In the early part of the journey, I did a lot of Internet searches. Along the way, I found great sources that helped me to think about the vast list of religions and worship traditions, like the Pluralism Project at Harvard University[2].

Because I live in Chicago, the majority of the places of worship that I visited were in the Chicagoland area. However, I also visited places of worship in Mexico, the United Kingdom, Nigeria, South Africa, and locations all over the United States.

Sometimes I ended up at a place of worship because the service fit my schedule for that week. More than once, grief-inspired-Sunday-morning oversleeping forced me to be creative and find an afternoon or evening service to attend. There was only one rule: if someone invited me to worship with them, I had to accept the invitation.

Before the Journey: My First Church Home

Prior to beginning my 52-week journey, for fifteen years, I attended a well-known church on the South Side of Chicago, Trinity United Church of Christ. My pastor was the Reverend Dr. Jeremiah A. Wright Jr.

During my first year in Chicago, I found myself challenged by the difficult experiences I was having in graduate school and working in corporate America. I discovered an article in an *Ebony* magazine that pointed me to a church where I might find some much-needed rest, rejuvenation, and inspiration. The article was entitled, "The 15 Greatest Black Preachers in America." It included this information about Reverend Wright:

> **The Rev. JEREMIAH A. WRIGHT JR.,** pastor, Trinity United Church of Christ, Chicago, represents . . . the first of a new generation of African-American preachers who blend a Pentecostal flavor with social concerns in their pulpit discourse."

A fellow preacher said, "He gives a contemporary, African-American, Afrocentric flavor to the traditional Black shout." A religious scholar said, "A Wright sermon is a four-course meal: spiritual, biblical, cultural, and prophetic.[3]

That description appealed to me. I hopped in my car and drove down to the South Side of Chicago to visit Trinity for the first time.

There, I found a brilliant, multi-faceted, African-American worship community. Sometimes the choir wore African attire, and the pastor did too! Having grown up in an African family, but without any level of comfort with my African heritage, I was able to come to church week in and week out and *get* comfortable with it. I began to be more curious about my large family in Nigeria. I started a meaningful dialogue with my father and my family, and traveled to Nigeria for the first time to see where my story began. I'll always be grateful to Trinity for helping me to see the value of knowing more about my roots and my ancestry, and for inspiring discussions that allowed me to connect with my father and develop what became a very close and meaningful relationship.

After hearing just one sermon, I became a member of Trinity. It was clear that this could become my church home, and that Reverend Wright was more than just an intelligent man. He was a well-travelled religious scholar with a strong sense of self and a true skill for communicating. He was a pillar in the community who was not afraid to speak his mind.

Reverend Wright baptized me on Easter Sunday, 1994. Before the ceremony, I tried to give him a cheat sheet to tell him how to pronounce my multisyllabic Nigerian name. This was my standard procedure before graduations and any other events where people had to pronounce my full name for the first time. He smiled, told me he didn't need a cheat sheet, and proceeded to pronounce my name beautifully without help. I was impressed. I wanted to know more about this man's educational, religious, historical, cultural, and philosophical background and perspectives.

I heard Reverend Wright preach countless times. His passionate delivery in the pulpit combined messages of biblical wisdom and social consciousness within a cultural context. Each sermon made me think. I was able to listen, decide what resonated with me, and determine what did not. I was inspired to do some of my own research—about theories, conflicts, and assumptions, and their relationship to scripture. I became a better, stronger person—spiritually, intellectually, and in relationship to my community and the world at large.

Trinity taught me about Christianity, culture, community, and Chicago. At Trinity, I was able to soak in a vibrant part of African-American culture—the Black church. I was able to round out my life experience, and share the gifts I had to give. I worked in two of the church's ministries that served the African-American community: the prison ministry, where I went to Cook County jail and prayed with men who hadn't made the best choices; and the high school counseling ministry, where I had the opportunity to work with teens who were on the brink of making important life decisions, and better choices!

Then, in an unfortunate political storm, my church was bombarded with media, negative energy, accusations, and half-truths during the 2008 United States presidential election. The beliefs and preaching of Reverend Wright, former pastor to President Barack Obama and his family, came under attack due to sermons that were deemed controversial and inflammatory.

During the election cycle, it saddened me to see the desecration of my pastor and my church home, a dynamic place of worship that often provided much needed spiritual boosts as I grew into adulthood. One of my main reasons for this journey was to heal, not just from the losses of 2009, but also from all the madness and mayhem at Trinity in 2008. This journey would help me to see if I could recover the feeling of safety in spirituality that was born out of a commitment to spirit and community which I had experienced—and loved—at Trinity, my first church home.

THE FIRST FOUR WEEKS

The first four weeks of this journey, admittedly, were a little slow.

On January 3, my friend Aneesah and I attended the 6:00 p.m. service at Trinity. I had not seen her in a while, and I was ready to honor my fresh resolution to be in a place of worship every week.

Then on January 10, I went to the 7:00 a.m. service . . . also at Trinity. It was wonderful and inspiring and familiar . . . and safe.

Given how much I loved my home church, I didn't undertake this journey lightly. But after attending two services at Trinity in the first two weeks in January, I said to myself, "Okay, am I going to do this 52 Weeks of Worship thing or not? Because worshipping at two different times at the same church doesn't really qualify." At that moment, I recommitted myself to the journey and made plans to visit a new church the next week.

On January 17, I attended church with my sister, Emuata, at Living Word Christian Center in Forest Park, Illinois. With its large, predominantly African-American congregation, her church felt very familiar. It was wonderful to share that experience with my sister—a woman whose faith and conviction I admire—but if I closed my eyes, I could have been right back at Trinity. The flow of the service, the songs, and the cadence of the sermon reminded me of my home church. I looked forward to experiencing new ways of worshipping.

Things picked up a bit on January 24.

My friend Mina invited me to visit her church, called the foglife4life ministry. They met at 6:00 p.m. at The Cornerstone Center, a community center in downtown Chicago.

1

As soon as the service began, my overarching thought was, "What in the world?" At the front of the sanctuary was a television screen that played Christian music videos with hip-hop tracks. The pastor starred in these videos (think MTV, not The 700 Club). When the music videos ended, the pastor showed a short video sermon. The intro to the sermon incorporated a Bentley, a little bling, and images of Louis Vuitton, Gucci, Chanel, and a private yacht. During the message, music played in the background while the pastor shared scripture and explained how life with Jesus Christ was, in fact, "the good life."

The service was entertaining. I found myself bobbin' my head to the hip-hop music that played throughout the service! It was not, however, an environment that could be spiritually nurturing to me in the long term. That said, I could only respect that I was witnessing an approach to worship infused with passion and commitment by the pastor and by those who were part of the congregation.

*   *   *

There was something about just starting this journey that filled me with hope . . . and apprehension. After the first four weeks, my heart's desire was to find the healing, connection, and remembrance that I so deeply needed. I wasn't sure, however, *what* I would find.

Week 5
From the 'Friend Zone' to the Golden Zone
Mi Iglesia Mexicana, La Viña

9:00 a.m. service, Mazatlan, Mexico

The "friend zone" is where I found myself at the end of the first month of my spiritual journey. It's that not-so-comfortable place where we sometimes land when we are not seen as "relationship material."

Here's the background: In an effort to distract myself from my troubles, I forced myself to go out and try to be social. On one of my outings, I met a charismatic man with an infectious personality. We hung out, we laughed, and we enjoyed each other's company. Both being single and available, naturally the thought crossed my mind—hey, maybe this could be a new ray of sunshine in my life. Maybe he might be a special friend, which I didn't think would be a bad thing, given the emotional dumps I was experiencing.

Then came that cold January day.

As we talked about the state of our respective love lives, he told me that he thought we should—wait for it—"just be friends." He also shared that he had gone on a date with a woman while I was out of town the previous weekend. He told me this because he had decided while I was gone that he wanted me to be his BFF—the kind he could tell anything, his wing woman. Yay! We could be best friends forever!

I felt like Queen Latifah's character in the movie, "Just Wright," who, after a date with an attractive man, had the following conversation:

    Man: I had such a great time tonight!

Woman: Oh, me too! You know, next time maybe we could catch a movie or . . .

Man: . . . I just . . . I just got out of a relationship, you know . . .

Woman: . . . You're not emotionally ready . . .

Man: Exactly! Man! But, you know, we can still . . .

Together: Hang out.

Man: Yeah, I mean you're . . .

Together: Good People.

Ugh.

Things went from possibility to train wreck in record speed. The whiplash was painful, and I had to shake my head while considering why the universe thought it was necessary for me to deal with this, along with the other challenges in my life. As my "new best friend" told me about this attractive woman he had met, it appeared that he wanted me to be happy about it—but honestly, I didn't really care. In fact, it was unclear to me why he thought I should care. Who did he think I was, Mother Teresa? Noticing my lack of enthusiasm, he asked, "What's wrong? Why aren't you excited for me?" Seriously? At the time, for some reason, through the Charlie Brown "Wah, wah, wah, wah" that was coming out of his mouth, my one clear thought was, "Wow, I need a vacation."

January in Chicago is no joke. West African blood runs through my veins. I grew up in Atlanta and went to college in California. Every winter, I wonder, "What the heck am I doing in Chicago?" To say that winter was cold is an understatement. We were seeing wind chills registering at negative twenty degrees. The cold was getting to me, so I gathered my frequent flyer miles and made plans to head to Mazatlan, Mexico.

4

Arriving in Mexico on a Friday, I began the process of defrosting, physically and emotionally. But just because I was in Mexico didn't mean that I was relieved of my promise to visit a place of worship. I was committed, but I had a decision to make—would I attend a Spanish service or English service? One of the reasons I like visiting Mexico is because I'm able to call up my three years of high school Spanish and practice mi Español. But speaking slowly to native Spanish speakers (Donde . . . esta . . . la playa?) is one thing; understanding an entire worship service in Spanish is quite another.

Calls to a few different churches confirmed which service was in English. I made sure that my Saturday night celebrations didn't end too late and set my alarm. Surprisingly, I didn't need it. I woke up before it went off. It felt like the first day of school!

After leaving my hotel, I flagged down a pulmonia, a glorified golf cart that served as a taxi. I told the driver, in my not-so-great Spanish: "Conoces la iglesia La Viña Mazatlan? Do you know the church, La Viña, Mazatlan?" I asked. "Si, lo conoces. Yes, I know it," he said nodding. "I'll take you there." The church was not far from Mazatlan's Golden Zone—a touristy section of Mazatlan where you can find Señor Frogs, lots of restaurants serving tall fruity drinks, many hotels, and persuasive people trying to lure you into a timeshare presentation.

The church was a sizable yellow stucco building with a palm tree out front and a "Taco Time" restaurant next door. Clusters of purple grapes decorated the outside of the building, and the name of the church appeared in purple cursive letters on the church's façade: La Viña, Vineyard Church.

A wooden cross under a yellow arch decorated the entrance of the building. Inside the spacious church sanctuary, white folding chairs were lined up in rows, as if they were set up for a revival. Before the service, some churchgoers asked me if it was my first visit to the church. Many of them were Canadians and Americans who travelled to Mexico every year during the winter months. (Some call them snowbirds.) They considered La Viña to be their church home away from home. They told me that the church served the surrounding community, working with other branches of the Vineyard Ministries of Central Mexico and in the United States, to provide services and support to residents of Mazatlan and other Mexican cities. Awesome!

Surprisingly, there were very few people of color there. I didn't see any Black people there at all. I chuckled to myself as I thought—I'm having a chocolate chip experience. I stood out because I was the only Black person there. It was obvious that I was new.

I did see some Mexican people on the stage. The praise team was a mixture of Mexicans and Americans with various instruments—the ever-present guitar that signified that some homegrown church music was forthcoming, someone with a tambourine; and a Casio keyboard on its stand.

Because my worship journey was still new, I felt myself experiencing a disconnect in this environment. I asked myself, "What in the world am I doing here?" I quickly received an answer that humbled and amazed me, touched my heart, made me cry, and immediately made me feel that I was in the right place at the right time.

The praise team fired up their instruments and started to sing the initial selection—the call to worship—which was the hymn, "To God Be the Glory." This was one of my father's favorite hymns.

He used to sing it all the time, his deep voice booming as he sang the chorus. We sang it at his funeral, and I cried then too. A portion of the song lyrics are as follows:

> To God be the glory, great things He has done;
> So loved He the world that He gave us His Son,
> Who yielded His life an atonement for sin,
> And opened the life gate that all may go in.
>
> CHORUS
>
> Praise the Lord, praise the Lord,
> Let the earth hear His voice!

Praise the Lord, praise the Lord,
Let the people rejoice!
O come to the Father, through Jesus the Son,
And give Him the glory, great things He has done.[4]

As musicians and the congregation sang on that morning in Mexico, a feeling of calm and purpose came over me. Tears were streaming down my face as I realized that I was not there alone. I truly felt through the music selection that my father was saying, "It's not at all weird that you are in this place. You are in the right place at the right time and God's house is your house, no matter where it is. Don't worry about anything. Seek God's face. Everywhere. I'm here and will always be with you."

The song ended and the service started. I remember it being pleasant and inspiring, but the true message from that service came directly to me through that song.

*   *   *

Comfort came unexpectedly this week. Healing came through a trip to a beautiful location where I connected with others. Remembrance was my main take away from this service. I was reminded that the people you love stay in your heart, and near your spirit even after they are gone from this earth.

WEEK 6
SUPER BOWL SUNDAY, MY FIRST MASS
ST. JAMES CHURCH

11:30 a.m. Mass, Chicago, Illinois

Super Bowl Sunday. The New Orleans Saints versus the Indianapolis Colts. This year, I cared about the game. My college alumni association was having a Super Bowl party, and I'd volunteered to host it, which ensured my full participation in this football ritual.

First, however, I had to find a place to worship. I needed to find a worship service that didn't start too early and didn't last too long, and that is how I ended up at my first Catholic Mass of this journey. Catholic Masses, I found, are wonderful. They are held several times a day, and they are relatively speedy.

As my 52-week journey continued, I found myself, more than once, in bed on a Sunday morning trying to motivate to go to a service, and fighting the urge to say, "Well, I can always go to Mass this evening." Often, I had to remind myself not to make this journey "52 Weeks of Catholic Masses."

Family and friends had introduced Catholicism to me throughout my life.

My parents were raised Catholic. Growing up, my mother shared colorful memories about Catholic school. The stars of those stories were the nuns who taught at her boarding school—and the contradictions she saw between what they told her to do and believe and what she saw other Catholics doing and believing. Based on her experiences, she chose not to practice Catholicism as an adult.

My father frequently told me the story about how he purposefully gave me a Nigerian name. He wanted to ensure that no church confirmation would replace my Nigerian name with any other name. That had been my parents' experience. Their names, Patricia and Ephraim, were the names given to them during their confirmation. They would use those names throughout their adult lives—instead of the Nigerian names they were given at birth.

Even with this perspective, my father still cherished his memories from his time as a practicing Catholic. A few times in my life, I recall attending Latin Mass with my father. I don't speak Latin, but my father did. Attending Latin Mass was nostalgic for him, and although I couldn't tell a *Deus vobiscum* from a *lorem ipsum*, I enjoyed it through his eyes.

My aunt, my father's sister, has been a nun for her whole adult life. Hanging out with her as a child gave me another perspective on Catholicism. If you have never hung out with a nun, you should. Amazingly, people will go out of their way to be kind to a nun, no matter what. Once, during a holiday visit from my aunt, we went shoe shopping. She asked to try on almost every pair of shoes in the store. The patience with which the store personnel treated her was almost comical. It was as if they thought their treatment of her would somehow get back to heaven and they would get some celestial points for being nice to a nun. More than likely, a request from anyone else to try on one hundred pairs of shoes wouldn't have resulted in the same treatment. The habit matters. I have seen it with my own eyes.

Finally, I remember attending the wedding of a dear friend, Felicia, who is Catholic. Throughout college, my good friend, cheerleading buddy, and one-time roommate would say she was going to Mass. Although we never really talked in depth about her faith at the time, I knew it was important to her. Her wedding included a full Catholic Mass, and I remember being very aware that I didn't understand the rhythm and flow of a Catholic Mass. When and why did I have to stand up, sit down, kneel, and make the sign of the cross? It was all a mystery.

With those experiences in my memory, I prepared, for the first time during my 52-week journey, to attend a Catholic Mass.

The church was under construction. The scaffolding around the building made it impossible to enter the church, leaving me stumped. Luckily, another parishioner noticed my confusion, and directed me around the back of the building, down a Chicago-style icy path, to the temporary location for Mass. It looked like an auditorium of some sort. It was full of folding chairs and people, just like La Viña in Mexico. This week, I was not a chocolate chip. There were people of all races there. When I arrived, service had already started—that was disappointing because I didn't want to miss anything.

In spite of the initial awkwardness of trying to find a seat without drawing attention to myself, I was able to find a place. Before long, I felt pretty comfortable.

As the service began, I joined in the call and response when I could (Peace be with you . . . and also with you . . .). It wouldn't be until many visits to Catholic churches later that I came to enjoy the standing, sitting, and kneeling, the familiar liturgy, cadence, and the call and response that are part of every Mass. Even at this early stage of my journey, I could see that there certainly could be comfort derived from the Mass rituals.

Communion time arrived. One of the things I knew (or thought I knew) about Catholic churches is that if you are not Catholic, you are not to take communion. This was the first time during my 52-week journey where I chose to respectfully pass on participating in a religious tradition so as not to offend other participants or disrupt the flow of worship. When communion began, and everyone stood to partake, I stayed in my seat.

It was then that I looked over at the elderly lady who was sitting next to me. She was wearing a sparkly elephant pin. She was an African-American woman, so I thought it was a good bet that she was my sorority sister. Members of my predominantly African-American sorority, Delta

Sigma Theta, often collect elephants and wear jewelry, accessories, and clothing with elephants on them.

During collection time, I leaned over and introduced myself, and she confirmed that she was indeed my sorority sister. She delightedly linked her arm in mine and asked me if I was new to the church. I told her I was. She immediately took the role of guide, pointing out people in the congregation. ("See that person there—that's the priest. That choir, that's not our normal choir—they are special for this service today, etc.") She whispered to me throughout the rest of the service, like an old girlfriend, telling me what events were coming up, and generally doing her best to make sure I was comfortable. I appreciated her effort and our connection made me feel even more welcome.

After the service, this lovely lady walked me around introducing me to the priest and other parishioners. She was especially enthusiastic, sharing that this church was committed to celebrating different cultures, and letting me know that the next week would be the Black history month celebration, complete with a gospel choir.

When it was time for us to say goodbye, unfortunately, I had to do something that I didn't particularly enjoy. She asked me, expectantly, "Are you going to come back next week?" I had to tell her no, that I wouldn't be back next week, but that I did enjoy the service and enjoyed her company. Throughout the year, I had to get used to finding creative ways to say, "No, thank you, I won't be back." Surprisingly this was one of the most difficult parts of my 52-week journey. Sometimes, I wanted to say, "Yes! I will be back!" But I knew I had more travelling to do. In this case, however, it was clear to me that I could be very happy coming back here, and I wondered if or when in life I might return.

*   *   *

A new friend—my sorority sister—provided a connection that made this Catholic worship experience special. Attending this Mass provided me with the opportunity to remember friends and family before me whose lives had been shaped by their Catholic faith.

11

Week 7
From Bayfield to the Big Easy and Back
Bayfield Presbyterian Church

10:00 a.m. service, 11:00 a.m. fellowship, Bayfield, Wisconsin

For President's Day weekend, my friend Ethan and I made plans to go on a winter sporting outing in Bayfield, Wisconsin. This proposition promised to be fun-filled and relaxing. It would allow me to spend some quality time with a dear friend who I have known since college, rather than obsessing about my ex, or what I didn't have planned on Valentine's Day, which fell during that weekend. I decided it would be preferable to relax in the easy-chair comfy conversation and company of someone who has known me since I wore MC Hammer pants to dorm parties, rather than ruminating about woulda-coulda-shoulda scenarios while watching eHarmony commercials on TV. I considered myself blessed to have an option.

When he asked if I wanted to hike to the ice caves near Lake Superior, I said yes. Even though I had no real concept of what I was signing up for, I was really up for anything that felt like living out loud.

As we were planning our trip, I shared with him that it was important to me to keep my commitment to my worshipping experiment. He was very supportive, and agreed to find a church for us to attend. We chose the Bayfield Presbyterian Church—which was on the way to our icy hiking adventure.

Contemplating the implicit trust I had for my friend, I went to REI and bought all the cold-weather gear that I could find. Ethan is a pro who grew up in Minnesota; I didn't want my being cold (or more importantly, complaining about the cold) to stand in the way of our adventure.

I arrived in Minnesota on Friday, spent time with Ethan's family on Saturday, and then we headed to the 10:00 a.m. worship service in Bayfield on Sunday morning.

Snow covered the exterior of the church, making for a winter wonderland effect. It was a small congregation and, like the church in Mazatlan, was full of Caucasian people except for us(two chocolate chips!). Because we were slightly late, we missed some of the initial liturgy, but heard the small choir sing the first song, "Morning Has Broken."

This is a song that I heard every Sunday when my family and I would watch Robert Schuller's Hour of Power on television. Every Hour of Power service at the Crystal Cathedral began with that song. My mother and father would sing together in harmony as me and my sisters sat huddled on the couch together, enjoying the show. I had a moment of religious remembrance that morning in Bayfield—my religious upbringing had many different inputs. One of the nice things is that, during my 52-week journey, I had the privilege of reflecting on and honoring the different stepping stones that built my spiritual foundations.

The intimate service had a real community feel. Some of my favorite parts of the service included the Passing of the Peace, and the Prayers of the People, during which I asked this random congregation in a little town in Wisconsin to pray for my mother. Her birthday was coming up, and I knew that she was really missing my father, her companion of fifty years. I found such comfort knowing that these people whom my mother would never meet or know were in good faith going to pray for her and her well being. I truly do believe in the kindness of strangers, and the power of prayer.

The pastor impressed me—his confident, measured tone revealed that he was a thoughtful man. The sermon further delighted me. As the pastor warmed up, he used the now-Super Bowl-champion New Orleans Saints as an example in his sermon. He asked how many people had seen the pre-show tribute by Wynton Marsalis to the Saints. Few people were in the congregation and even fewer raised their hands, but I did (and enthusiastically!). I marveled as I sat in this Bayfield, Wisconsin congregation (whose population was 611 at the 2000 census), and listened to the pastor quote from "The Spirit of New Orleans," which had really struck me the week before as I watched the Super Bowl pre-show commentary.

The pastor began reciting the Marsalis tribute:

> "New Orleans, N'Awlins, the Crescent City, the Big Easy, the northern capitol of the Caribbean, Groove City. Man, they have things down there you wouldn't believe. A mythic place of Mardi-Gras and mumbo, Voodoo and the moss-covered, alligator-spiked pathways of back-country swamp drained and sprinkled with gris-gris dust to house a wild, unruly population."[5]

Really? Was this Wisconsin pastor talking about Mardi-Gras and mumbo from the pulpit? Sitting up straighter and looking around, I wondered if this pastor was reaching his congregation, or just me, a stranger who had wandered into his church on this random Valentine's Day Sunday. He had my heart when he quoted a portion of the Marsalis tribute which had hit me square between the eyes the previous Sunday:

> "You ever wait for something so long that waiting for it becomes the something?"

I understood this quote at the core of my soul. When I heard it for the first time on Super Bowl Sunday, it made me think about the different areas of my life where I have been waiting so long for a specific something to happen, change, or manifest. Questions swirled in my mind:

Will I spend the rest of my life alone? Will I get married? Will I have children? When? If not, what will I spend the rest of my life doing? What is my purpose in life? Am I living it? If not, what should I change? What should I do differently?

My ex and I had talked about marriage. We had talked about kids, and even talked about names for our children. It was, apparently, just talk. Now, all of that was over, and I was left to wait and wonder what my future would hold. It was not easy.

My personal losses intensified my struggle to remain faithful to believe that God's plan for me isn't for me to just wait and wait and wait. I had to encourage myself to pray and be faithful, to remember that God knows the desires of my heart and will make sure that I don't live a life of waiting and wanting.

I found myself wishing that I had a pen during the sermon (and in subsequent weeks, I began carrying a pen and took notes on the various bulletins that I collected from each worship service). The pastor's choice of words and references reached me in a unique, spiritual-teaching manner—not just because he used the unexpected Marsalis tribute as the context for the lesson, but also because I learned something new, and the sermon touched my spirit.

The service ended with a powerful benediction. When the benediction started, it appeared at first to be a common benediction based on one of my favorite Bible verses, Numbers 6:24-26 (KJV):

> The Lord bless you and keep you;
> The Lord make His face shine upon you,
> And be gracious to you;
> The Lord lift up His countenance upon you,
> And give you peace.

But it was not. It was, in fact, an alternate version of the benediction, and the words spoke to me:

> Now, may the Lord bless you and keep you.
> May the Lord's face smile upon you and be gracious to you.
> May God give you grace
> Never to sell yourself short;
> Grace to risk something big for something good;
> Grace to remember
> That the world is now too dangerous for anything but truth
> And too small for anything but love.
> So may God take your minds and think through them.
> May God take your hearts and set them on fire,
> Through Jesus our Savior, Amen.[6]

I enjoyed the benediction so much that after the service, I sought out the pastor and asked him to give me a copy, which he did.

After the service was over, many of the congregants stopped by to talk to me and Ethan. They surrounded us with conversation, welcome, and love. One woman, as she greeted us said, "Nobody ever comes by here, so it is really great to see you!"

She invited us to have coffee with them in the basement, and we accepted. We found ourselves eating homemade cinnamon buns and drinking coffee with the people of Bayfield. Wisely, Ethan, who grew up in a small town, commented on this as we walked downstairs to break bread with the members of the congregation. He said, "When you take the time to stop in someone's neighborhood, and to stop by their church, that means something."

Apparently, it did, because by the time we were done with coffee, we had received information about our upcoming hiking trip. No, the lake was not frozen enough for us to hike on. We would have to hike on land (which was probably more my speed, as I was a winter-hiking newbie). A family from the congregation offered to lend us snowshoes if we needed them ("Just stop by," they said, "and knock on the door."). The kindness of strangers was in full effect, and it was truly touching.

*   *   *

Without the support of old friends like Ethan, there's no way I would have made it through this year of healing. Additionally, the unexpected gift of connecting with members of this small community of worshippers in Bayfield, Wisconsin (and the fact that I physically survived my icy Wisconsin hiking adventure) gave me hope that unexpected gifts and blessings would continue to appear, providing the strength I needed to survive my year of personal rebuilding. The people of Bayfield Presbyterian were different than me in many ways, but they opened their arms and welcomed me. What a gift.

Week 8
Ashes to Ashes and Dust to Dust
Old St. Mary's Catholic Church

Afternoon visit, Chicago, Illinois

Ash Wednesday. Since high school, I have observed Lent, forty days of sacrifice leading up to Easter Sunday. This year, I located a Catholic church nearby that was dispensing ashes all day.

Old St. Mary's Catholic Church is in Chicago's hip South Loop neighborhood, where I have lived for many years. I strolled down the street to the church, grateful that I could stop by, grab some ashes, and be on my way.

When I entered the church, I saw a small administrative area to my right. A woman in a glass-encased office in the lobby of the church building was administering them. Little did I know what would happen next. The ash-bearing woman looked into my eyes. She dipped her finger in a small container of ashes, used the ashes to make the sign of the cross on my forehead, and quoted a portion of Genesis 3:19(NASB):

> You are dust, and to dust you shall return.

To my surprise, my legs became weak and began swaying beneath me. The woman who administered the ashes was looking at me a little strangely. Much like I used to look at the individuals who would sway and fall down at the Ernest Angley ministry gatherings that my mother used to take me and my sisters to when we were young.

Yes, Ernest Angley. One of the diverse spiritual inputs in my life was a stint in my childhood when my mother would pack up her four girls and

17

drive to Atlanta's Civic Center to see this televangelist. The day-long service was complete with testimonies and healings—the blind seeing, the deaf hearing, the mute speaking, and the lame walking.

Time passed slowly during the long healing services. I remember staring at the sound gear on the ceiling, which looked like potato slices, and being scared to fall asleep, even though I was just a kid. What kid can sit still for hours in the dark while preaching is taking place?

The services consisted largely of the laying on of hands. Ernest Angley would put his palm on someone's forehead and say, "YOU ARE HEALED!" That person would fall to the floor, then get up crying and claiming their healing. The fall was often dramatic—with people fighting the fall, swaying, praying, crying, and *then* falling.

For me, during the Ash Wednesday ash dispensation experience at Old St. Mary's, the reason for the weakness in my legs was not because of any spontaneous healing, but because—with one phrase—I was taken back in an instant to my father's death, service, and cremation.

Ashes to ashes and dust to dust.

Throughout my father's life, he made it clear that his desire was to be cremated after death, rather than being buried. It wasn't until we were faced with actually fulfilling his request that the reality of what this meant set in.

The first thing that we had to deal with was the varied reaction from family members when we told them that my father wanted to be cremated:

"Cremation is a blasphemy!" said some of the more traditional Christian members of the family.

"You mean he won't be transferred back home for a proper burial?" said others, who expressed disbelief that his body wouldn't be sent back to his home country, Nigeria, for a traditional burial.

"Ah-ah! Who made this decision? When was this decided?" said some of those who questioned whether my father made this request when he was of sound mind and body.

The unifying feature of all of this commentary was that certain family members expressed their thoughts in a very loud and not very diplomatic tone. Given that we had just lost someone we loved very much, these verbal exchanges piled on top of the grief we were feeling and made everything worse.

With every discussion about it, I felt a stronger need to insist that we honor my father's wishes. I found myself standing, at the crematorium the morning after my father's funeral service, with the courage that only comes when you have no other option.

The experience was surreal. And that is an understatement. I had no idea what to expect. We all stood in what looked like a warehouse surrounded by large, industrial fixtures. I stared at the cremation chamber, where intense flames and heat of over 1,500 degrees Fahrenheit would reduce my father's body to ashes. We prayed. I remember my uncle saying during his prayer that, ". . . no one should suffer any mental or psychological damage as a result of participating in this ritual." That's how traumatized I think he, a devout Christian, was about the whole thing. In spite of this, our family stood together—even those who didn't understand why my father had made this choice.

The professionalism and composure of the gentleman who was conducting the cremation comforted us, allowing us to pray and to say goodbye. Even so, a numb feeling remained after it was clear that the process was over.

There was nothing particularly good about saying goodbye. A year prior, I'd watched my ex bury his mother. The feeling I had as her casket was lowered into the ground was no more or less final than the feeling that I had that morning at the crematorium—the realization that nothing will ever be the same, and that a loved one who had been present for your whole life was now gone forever.

All of these memories came rushing back in the instant that the Ash Wednesday ashes were placed on my forehead. It took enormous effort to pull myself together. Somehow, I made it back to my apartment.

*   *   *

A quote of unknown origin states:

> You never know how strong you are, until being strong is the only choice you have.

Words can't express how difficult it was for me to attend my father's cremation. Courage came only through remembering how much he meant to me and what he stood for as a man. I thought of these things after my time at Old St. Mary's Catholic Church—and long after the ashes on my forehead were washed away.

WEEK 9
FAMILY, FORGIVENESS, AND FORTITUDE
THE CHURCH OF THE APOSTLES

10:30 a.m. service, Atlanta, Georgia

On a sunny Sunday afternoon, about six months after my father passed away, my sisters and I piled in a car with my mother and headed to a church that was right around the corner from our high school, The Westminster Schools, in Atlanta's Buckhead community.

This church was not there when we were all Westminster Wildcats. I don't even recall what stood in the space where this enormous church now stands. Nevertheless, it was a familiar drive to a place that we thought might be a new church home for my mother—a woman who was determining how to create a life without the man she had been with for fifty years.

My mother and father met when my mother was an eighteen-year-old finishing up her first round of schooling, and my father was a new pharmacist in Benin City, Nigeria. As the story goes, my mother had a botany project that was due after Easter Break. She procrastinated, and as Easter approached, she realized that she was going to need some help to finish the project. She approached her friend, appropriately named Grace, and Grace said she should go and ask the "Safeway Chemist," my father, who apparently was well known not only for his good looks, but also for his intelligence. He helped her, and when their tutoring session was over, my mother knew that she had met the man she would marry.

She went home to tell her mother as much. Her mother told her to keep it to herself, as they both knew that if her grandmother found out, my father would be in trouble. Apparently, her grandmother—my great grandmother—was well known for making sure the boys in the neighborhood knew that her granddaughter was not to be messed with. My mother told us stories about how, as she and her sister went to school or to the market, her grandmother would follow with a pail of water. If any boy should be so bold as to whistle or even call out to my mother, her grandmother would throw the pail of water on them, thus ending that attempt at a love connection.

My mother didn't tell her grandmother she had met her husband-to-be. What she also didn't do, apparently, was thank my father for his help, even though she ended up getting a good grade on the botany project. My father told their mutual friend Grace that "that girl," my mother, had not been considerate enough to follow up and thank him, or even let him know how the project went. He asked Grace for my mother's contact information (which was probably more the point), wrote my mother, and that is how their correspondence started. Soon after, my mother and father began "courting." When my father found out that he would be leaving Nigeria to go to Germany for medical school, they then began their long, long-distance relationship. They dated across continents—from Africa to Europe—then married, came to the United States, and built a life and family together.

My mother dated no one else in her life. From the age of eighteen, my father was her companion, and then later, her husband. Now, fifty years later, she was faced with the prospect of life without my father; and my sisters and I were left to help her try to determine "what now?"

In trying to help my mother transition from life as a wife to life as a widow, we wanted to locate a church where my mother could feel at home and at peace as she figured out what her "new normal" would be.

The energy of The Church of Apostles was high, yet familiar. There was a great deal of movement, from figuring out how to park the car, to figuring out how to navigate from the parking garage to the sanctuary. Greeters welcomed us, pointing out a place for us to get our "visitor" nametags.

We sat in the huge sanctuary and settled in to listen to the message. The sermon for the day was very family focused. The pastor talked about how family was the primary congregation, and emphasized the importance of taking care of family. In discussing the importance, biblically and culturally, of taking care of elders, the pastor mentioned how Jesus wanted to take care of his mother even from the cross—that even when he knew he couldn't take care of her, he wanted her to be taken care of. This was quite relevant given that by simply visiting this church, we wanted to make sure our mother was taken care of.

In continuing to talk about Jesus' last moments on the cross, the pastor discussed the concept of forgiveness, mentioning the scripture, Luke 23:34 (KJV):

> Then said Jesus, Father forgive them; for they know not what they do.

He also talked about the human propensity to make promises, and then get busy breaking those promises. He urged us to stop running from God, stop running from making a commitment, and stop making and breaking promises. Given the amount of bargaining that I did as it became clear that my father was dying, or that my relationship was ending, this held special significance for me.

Once again, there was a "coincidence" where the pastor shared that his favorite song was "It Is Well with My Soul," by Horatio Spafford. This was another song that we sang at my father's funeral:

> When peace, like a river, attendeth my way,
> When sorrows like sea billows roll;
> Whatever my lot, Thou has taught me to say,
> It is well, it is well, with my soul.
>
> It is well with my soul,
> It is well, it is well, with my soul.[7]

The pastor shared the story of the song, which my Uncle Fred also shared at my father's funeral. The Job-like story of the song is equally as inspiring as the words of the song:

> Horatio Spafford (1828-1888) was a wealthy Chicago lawyer with a thriving legal practice, a beautiful home, a wife, four daughters and a son. He was also a devout Christian and faithful student of the Scriptures. His circle of friends included Dwight L. Moody, Ira Sankey and various other well-known Christians of the day.
>
> At the very height of his financial and professional success, Horatio and his wife Anna suffered the tragic loss of their young son. Shortly thereafter on October 8, 1871, the Great Chicago Fire destroyed almost every real estate investment that Spafford owned.
>
> In 1873, Spafford scheduled a boat trip to Europe in order to give his wife and daughters a much-needed vacation and time to recover from the tragedy. He also went to join Moody and Sankey on an evangelistic campaign in England. Spafford sent his wife and daughters ahead of him, while he remained in Chicago to take care of some unexpected last-minute business. Several days later, he received notice that his family's ship had encountered a collision. All four of his daughters drowned; only his wife had survived.
>
> With a heavy heart, Spafford boarded a boat that would take him to his grieving Anna in England. It was on this trip that he penned those now famous words: "When sorrows like sea billows roll; it is well, it is well with my soul."[8]

The pastor's message about family touched me, as did the message from the song. The pastor talked about submitting to the will of God even though you may not understand it, and talked about times when you may be puzzled at circumstances in your life. He talked about developing, ". . . the ability to trust the Lord when it costs so dearly." He noted that there will be times in your life when you feel like you are going uphill with the wind blowing in your face, but you should remember that ". . . all things work together for good to them that love God . . ." (Romans 8:28, KJV).

Given all that we had been through as a family in 2009, with the loss of my father and my grandmother, this message was relevant. And, being in the midst of processing the loss of a relationship that I really did think would be a lifelong connection, this was additionally impactful to me. Thoughts of what I'd imagined my family would look like, and how those images were no longer going to come to pass, brought tears to my eyes. Figuring out how to let go of those who are gone, for whatever reason, isn't easy.

After the service was over, there was a visitor reception and we fellowshipped with members of this church. We talked, played the do-you-know game, and, in the end, discovered a new location where a little peace and familiarity could serve as a new home for our mother.

*　　*　　*

Sometimes it's nice to take family with you to new places. This week, I connected with my family—and we walked this leg of our healing journey together. In one of my last conversations with my father, he requested that I "take care of my mother." This week, that request was priority number one. In contributing my energy to help take care of my mother, I was honoring my father's memory.

WEEK 10
A DIFFERENT KIND OF SAVIOR
SAVIOURS' DAY, THE NATION OF ISLAM

All day, The United Center, Chicago, Illinois

From the moment I parked my car a few blocks from the United Center, an atmosphere of helpfulness and respect engulfed me. "Are you going to the United Center?" asked a parking attendant as I walked by. "Don't park your car over there, Sister," she cautioned, "It's permit parking. They'll run your plates and give you a ticket. There's lots of free parking one street over," she said, "You can cut across this lot and make it over faster than walking around."

I thanked her, reparked my car, and then started what turned out to be a long day: attending Saviours' Day, the yearly event that celebrates the birthday of Wallace Fard Muhammad, founder of the Nation of Islam.

Also walking toward the United Center with me were women in white head garments, long white dresses down to the ground, and white shoes. Some women appeared to be dressed as royalty, with intricate outfits and headdresses. The majority of the men were in suits, and I saw a fair number of bow ties.

I was wearing a black dress and opaque black tights, but due to the length of my coat, I appeared to be wearing *only* a red coat and black tights. Initially, I felt self conscious about that. I don't typically worry about the appropriateness of my attire. Generally, I'm pretty astute in figuring out what to wear. But I found myself wondering if I should have taken more care in selecting my outfit. That is, until some young ladies appeared wearing tight, skimpy outfits. There were also some young men in attendance wearing sagging pants and blingy accessories. There was a wide spectrum of fashion choices. The phrase "come as you are" did certainly apply.

I joined a line heading in the direction of the United Center, but soon discovered I was in the line for the men. Several helpful men directed me to the line for the women. This was the first time that day I would be made aware of the distinction between genders. Growing up with three sisters and my mother—my father was the lone man—I'd become very good at fending for myself. There were rarely opportunities for me to have a man fix something for me, or help me with my luggage, or solve my problems. We were raised to do for ourselves. That day, I found myself feeling very feminine and worthy of protection. This was a different but enjoyable experience.

There were many "officials"—men with Fruit of Islam hats, and women who were dressed in red and white—who obviously had security and coordination roles. They kept shouting, "No cameras at all in the building!" I turned off my iPhone and stashed it in the side pocket of my purse. My response to this request was a matter of respect for the sanctity of the religious experience I was about to undertake. Respect was a term that I considered repeatedly throughout the day.

After buying my ticket, I saw that women were to enter through one door and men through another. While we stood in line, the women in white and red were pulling pregnant women and women with small children out of the line to allow them to enter first. "Sister, you shouldn't be standing in line if you're pregnant," said one of the ladies in white and red. "That's the next generation you're bringing forth. That's new life." There was certainly an air of cultural order and chivalry that was refreshing. It appeared that the culture of taking care of women and children was strong.

As the line moved toward the entrance to Gate 7 of the United Center, I looked to my left and found it significant that I was looking at the sign for Malcolm X College. Given the history of the Nation of Islam and Malcolm X, I wondered if anyone else noted the significance.

I found myself thinking of a young man named Rashid who I dated in my early twenties. Rashid was a gifted lyricist and a conscious rapper. In some of our initial conversations, as we got to know each other, I shared with him that my father was a physician and that my mother was a small business owner. His response was that "my family was like the Cosby Show." In reality, my family was nothing like the Cosby show, although I understood the surface resemblance. When I explained to him that my life was very different from that show, his response was, "It's okay, as long as you are down for Black people, we're cool."

I thought of that phrase as I stood waiting to enter the United Center. In this sea of Black people, I did feel like I was in a soup full of folks who were "down for Black people"—a place where everyone spoke the same language and no translation or explanation was necessary. As with Rashid years before, this was cool with me.

As I approached the door to the arena, it became clear that the separation of women and men was mostly to facilitate the security check, where the ladies in white and red patted me down and checked my purse. My iPhone made the cut, and I entered the United Center.

I found myself being extremely aware of the racial mix of the people inside. After being the chocolate chip in many of my early worship experiences, today, most of the people I saw were Black, with a few exceptions. An Asian woman in white and red helped with the security. I wanted to ask what her story was, how she ended up serving the Nation of Islam, but I didn't have the chance.

In the large stadium, instead of ads by Coca Cola, Nike, or Home Depot showing on the screens around the arena, quotations scrolled throughout the service on each of the billboards, such as a version of the Marcus Garvey quote: "Up you mighty nation, accomplish what you will."

The experience was culturally powerful, and inspired thoughts about the interplay between culture and religion. I wondered if and how it really is possible to separate one from the other.

This is something that I have been thinking about since my freshman year at Stanford, when I sat, among pizza boxes and popcorn, having my first real late-night philosophical college discussion with a friend, Becky. She told me that she was Jewish, but didn't believe in God, and my young brain just couldn't understand what that meant. We had an in-depth conversation about how Judaism was a culture as well as a religion. Having attended a high school lacking in cultural and religious diversity, it was hard for me to process that. Now, I understand completely. My worship journey pointed out examples time and time again where culture was front and center, or at least side by side, with religious beliefs.

Here at the United Center, I considered that interplay of culture, community, religion, and experience once again.

There were several performances before the keynote speaker. A Christian pastor, along with various imams and Muslim leaders, led opening prayers.

Throughout the day, these individuals recited familiar Bible verses. It's clear that Biblical scholars from different religious traditions find significance in the Old Testament and the New Testament. I found myself thinking about the fact that the majority of the Black people in this arena probably came from a Christian background and likely found comfort in hearing familiar Bible verses. One favorite verse of mine, Psalm 27:1(KJV), was mentioned repeatedly in various portions of different people's commentary:

> The LORD is my light and my salvation; whom shall I fear?
> The LORD is the strength of my life; of whom shall I be afraid?

After about an hour of preliminary speakers, announcements, and even some singing, The Honorable Minister Louis Farrakhan approached the podium.

The man spoke for about *three and half hours*! He just kept going like the Energizer bunny. Given that there had been some rustlings about his health in previous years, it was even more amazing that he just kept talking with power, enthusiasm, and authority.

My ignorance about the Nation of Islam on more than a surface level made some of his discussion very confusing. Some of it was religiously confusing, and some was historically confounding. I found myself at times saying, "Why is that important?" when The Minister clung to a specific point. For example, he repeatedly insisted that Elijah Muhammad was alive for longer than they said he was. Why is this important, I wondered? It made me want to do research.

There was an abundance of talk about the end of days. This was scary— especially when it was put in the context of natural disasters that had just occurred: the January earthquake in Haiti, and the February earthquake in Chile, for example.

Minister Farrakhan spoke for some time about visions that he had, including one intricate vision that involved a wheel-shaped spaceship. As he described this vision in detail, I had to consider my ambivalence about believing in visions. Few religious people these days talk about visions in the same way that was done in the Bible or the Qur'an. Farrakhan was talking about prophesy and visions with a high level of conviction.

Coming from a West African family, discussions about visions, premonitions, and evil are nothing new to me. There's a good amount of experience-based story telling about these topics in the Nigerian culture. For instance, when someone is ill, there are stories about certain animals showing up (a crow or a snake), and the caretakers must pray that animal away. Often, people have dreams about things, both good and bad, before those things happen. Generally, when I hear about this realm of spirituality, I just listen—sometimes with skepticism, confusion, or a sense of disbelief. I find myself thinking, "Good gracious! There's enough to consider in the world without thinking about enemies of the spiritual realm, voodoo, or juju."

I thought the same while Minister Farrakhan talked about the wheel-shaped spaceship.

Say what you want about Louis Farrakhan, but one thing is clear: his confidence and self-assuredness are powerful. I found myself jotting down some of his more striking quotes:

- I don't know anything about backing down.
- I have been questioned by the best minds that they got—and none of them could handle me.
- Kings seek my council, but I can't even get a meeting with a congressman if the white boys are watching . . . .
- There are some things that you must say, despite what the people think.
- If you want this world, go get it. But if you want the Kingdom of God, be ready. There will be a separation coming because the righteous and the wicked cannot coexist.
- I don't think more of myself than I should, but it would be wrong of me not to think as much of myself as I should.

The man's got swagger.

He spoke a great deal about his love for the African-American community. He shared how he often had to swallow his ego and remain quiet in the face of a situation where he might say or do something that he felt would negatively impact his community. He spoke specifically about David Dinkins' 1989 campaign for mayor in New York, and the presidential campaigns of Jesse Jackson in 1984 and Barack Obama in 2008. He pointed to these times as examples of times when he showed that, for him, it was not about ego, it was about his love for his people. He preferred in those situations to stay silent on some issues lest his words end up bringing negative attention to those aspiring candidates. This included staying silent when he was being denounced, vilified, or otherwise "thrown under the bus."

To be frank, half of the time that I listened to Minister Farrakhan speak, his specific historical and cultural references to the Nation of Islam confused me. But, the other half of the time, I found myself nodding my head yes, and standing and applauding—particularly, when he talked about cultural self reliance, and standing up as a great nation of people of color who need not be afraid of their own power, contribution, and ability to help themselves. At one point, he mentioned that he was talking to, ". . . the forty million people of color in America, the four billion people of color in the world, and some Caucasians as well . . . ." He is very clear on his purpose.

It was a long day, unexpectedly long and draining.

But it was a good day.

*   *   *

This was my first non–Christian worship experience of the year. I chose to attend Saviours' Day mostly because I wanted to hear Minister Farrakhan speak live, something I had never done. That alone was an experience. But after the experience was over, I realized that my 52-week journey would really be an interfaith journey. I looked forward to the lessons that I would learn from those who worshipped in many different ways.

Week 11
Contemplating Compassion and Kindness
Vajrayana Kadampa Buddhist Center

7:00 p.m. meditation and service, Oak Park, Illinois

The first time I visited the Vajrayana Buddhist Center, a friend of mine suggested that I attend after we discussed the value of meditation for creative minds. She, a former alcoholic, shared that a friend of hers from Alcoholics Anonymous had told her about the Buddhist Center and the positive experience she had there. On my initial visit, a man shared his testimony with me. He had been hooked on drugs and alcohol and had only begun to get his life back together when he started regularly attending meditations at the Buddhist Center.

As I processed my own personal grief, I developed a profound interest in finding ways that people walk through the most difficult times in their lives—including, of course, the religious practices that people choose when life gets difficult.

How do you make it through the storm?

Step by step.

It has always been clear to me that meditation could be helpful. I'm a ruminator—always thinking about things, turning them over incessantly in my mind, and trying to see if I can figure them out. Sometimes this works, and sometimes it drives my family, friends, and even myself, crazy.

The day I visited the Vajrayana Kadampa Buddhist Center had been that sort of day, preceded by that sort of weekend. I spent most of the day banging my head against a wall, trying to figure out how to communicate with a poor communicator. My ex was the type to say nothing when he was bothered, and then brood about it, sometimes to the point of disappearing for days rather than discussing what was bothering him. I did a terrible job of dealing with this. He was now refusing to talk at all about anything. I was distraught and unhappy. The non-communication was driving me crazy.

If that was not enough, I'd spent most of that morning discussing topics with my mother which, let's just say, didn't contribute to me feeling super about my life or myself. Popular topics between us throughout my adult life included my weight (why it was not lower than it was) and where my husband and children were (or why I was not more focused on finding them).

I knew she was grieving, and I have always known that she wants nothing but the best for me. On this day, however, her grieving and her motherly concern collided mightily with my lack of emotional clarity, and I was just exhausted with all of it.

I hopped on the highway and headed to Oak Park, the first suburb west of Chicago. It was time for some meditation.

I parked in front of the Center, entered, removed my shoes, and headed into the meditation room, which was full of folding chairs and a few people who, like me, were ready for a little silent contemplation.

The teacher entered; we all stood. When she moved to the front of the room, we all sat down. She welcomed us and started by telling us we made the right choice by coming. She knew that sometimes we hemmed and hawed, but ultimately we made the right choice. She reminded us that in meditation, we could find the tools that we needed to learn to rid ourselves of anger, frustration, hatred, and other negative emotions. By using those tools, we could find happiness.

I was not in the best mood. I felt very cynical and stressed. My internal voice certainly was not very gracious. "Yeah," I thought, "Bring on the tools."

We started with a breathing meditation. This exercise invited us to be silent and simply focus on our breath—on breathing in and out.

It was hard for me to concentrate, not just because meditation is sometimes challenging, but also because I was so unhappy. Banging one's head against a wall tends to hurt. I'd been hurling voice and text messages at the brick wall of my ex's impenetrable emotional bunker for about twenty-four hours. I was exhausted and sad. I was not feeling very compassionate (nor were the contents of the messages I sent).

Guess what the theme of the second meditation was?

Contemplating the kindness of your mother.

"Seriously?" I thought.

It seems the Universe had a sense of humor that day. It must have known that I'd been having difficult conversations with my mother about my life. Through my sadness and stress, it reminded me that there's always an opportunity to learn from the challenges we experience.

*　　*　　*

I didn't win any awards for focused meditation during my visit to the Vajrayana Buddhist Center that day. During my journey, sometimes I just felt sad. This was one of those days. However, the value of meditation was also clear to me. The messages of compassion and kindness I understood—intellectually. But my heart was heavy.

Week 12
Me and the Mormons
The Church of Jesus Christ
of Latter-day Saints

8:30 a.m. Sacrament meeting, Lost Mountain Ward, Powder Springs, Georgia

This week found me back in Atlanta to help my mother out with some house-related tasks. When Sunday rolled around, my mother invited me to join her for church—but to fulfill my promise to myself, I also needed to go to a new church. I needed to find a church with an early service, and a shorter service, so I could go to that church first, and then make my way to my mother's church to attend a second service with my mother and my sisters.

Yes, a bit of worship overload. Whaddya gonna do?

As I researched, it became clear that this week would involve a visit to the Church of Jesus Christ of Latter-day Saints.

Mormons.

My ignorance about Mormons was staggering. First, I needed to research whether I could attend a Mormon service without actually being a Mormon. The answer: a Mormon Church and a Mormon Temple are not the same thing. If a service is taking place in the Church, everyone is welcome to attend. Church buildings are always open to the public. Mormon Temples are not. I had to research terminology. I kept seeing information about specific "wards," but didn't know what that meant. I learned that a ward is the larger of two types of local congregations (the smaller being a branch). A ward is presided over by a bishop, who is the equivalent of a pastor in other religions.[9]

Finally, for my own personal comfort, I had to research whether there were Black Mormons. I wanted to avoid any awkward situations. It turns out that not only are there Black Mormons, but they have quite a history within the denomination. I found "A Web Site Dedicated to Black Members of The Church of Jesus Christ of Latter-day Saints."[10]

Who knew?

Armed with all of this information, I located a ward near my mother's house, and not far from her church. I prepared for my Mormon experience.

I found myself dealing with a certain level of apprehension. I considered the reality of a Mormon worship service versus my perception of a Mormon service. It is safe to say that there are many ideas swirling around out there about Mormons and what they believe; I had to push those aside.

With these thoughts in mind, I opened my spirit and went to the service. It was the first time I was really nervous. I had had the chocolate chip experience before, but even with the strength of my research about Black Mormons, I felt like I would certainly stick out like a sore thumb, and wasn't sure how I would be received.

I shared these concerns with one of my sisters, who—ever the wise woman—said, "If it's a church of God, you'll be okay."

And I was.

When I arrived at the service, a now-familiar thing happened. People smiled and greeted me heartily. I asked for directions to the sanctuary and everyone was very helpful. This put me at ease, sort of. I was as at ease as I was going to get.

At the service, there were families and many young people. The youth were a prominent part of the service, and community leaders made announcements about socials for various segments of the community.

There were members of the congregation who were selected for what they called their "Talks." A married couple spoke about obedience, and their experiences trying to be obedient to God and the tenets of their belief. The wife spoke first, then the husband. Both were extremely nervous. They shared that the only reason they could make it through this public-speaking opportunity was because they understood the importance of obedience.

The woman shared the story of how she joined the church as a young teenage girl, despite the fact that her friends didn't really agree with her choice. She also shared how she told her now-husband that if he didn't join the church, then they had no future. So he joined. Now, some might find that primitive or extreme, but her depth of conviction was clear. I contemplated the sense of self worth that someone must have to approach an intended partner and say, "This is what I need; can you get with the program?" This is something that has always been especially difficult for me: to figure out how to be fully myself while trying to accommodate someone that I love. I welcomed the opportunity to hear this woman state that this was part of her process, and that the result was a union within the church she had come to love and commit herself to at such a young age.

This brave woman went on to explain that her strong belief in the church had sustained her through the loss of a child. As she shed tears at this remembrance, I also shed my own tears—in sorrow for her loss and in memory of my father and grandmother, so recently lost, as well.

When her husband shared his part of the story, he was so nervous, he started to cry.

Profusely.

He was not the most articulate speaker, but what was clear was that he loved the church, he loved his wife, and he loved his family. Through his very emotion-filled speech, he shared a touching song that I'd never heard before. It was called "Help Pour Out the Rain," by Buddy Joel. The chorus was:

> Daddy, when we get to Heaven, can I taste the Milky Way?
> Are we goin' there to visit, or are we goin' there to stay?
> Am I gonna see my Grandpa? Can I have a pair of wings?
> An' do you think that God could use another Angel,
> To help pour out the rain?[11]

As I listened to the lyrics, and contemplated the thought that when I get to Heaven I might see my father and my grandmother again, more tears began to flow.

The lyrics also affected the man giving his "Talk." He choked through it, likely thinking about the loss of his child, and then sat down.

There were references throughout the service to the Book of Mormon. Many religions seem to have their own "last" prophet or messenger. I'm woefully ignorant about many of them. I don't think I know enough about the prophets within my own religious tradition, including Jesus, and precious less about any other "most recent" prophets or books. There's much to learn—not just from an academic perspective, but also from a heart perspective.

It is precisely for this reason that this journey was not a religious shopping expedition for me. I'm happy worshipping within my religious tradition. However, I have miles to go before I understand the heart of Jesus and what he has in store for me. Continuing down my path of enlightenment didn't and shouldn't prevent me from wholeheartedly investigating other worship traditions with an open mind and an open heart. I don't see a contradiction at all.

As the service continued and the "Talks" concluded, there was a portion dedicated to giving the sacrament. This was communion, and as I'd committed to respecting others' sacred rituals, I didn't partake in it. In this case, however, I was curious. In past communions, there was bread and wine (or grape juice). In this case, there was bread, but the accompanying liquid was clear. I really wanted to know if it was water or something else (vodka? I thought, chuckling to myself, doubting that was the case), but let it pass by me to be respectful. Later, I Googled this and found out that the liquid was water.

Mormon's don't drink alcohol.

Although initially I thought that the service was only an hour, it turned out that the true Mormon experience at this church was a three-part project, where each section lasted an hour. First, there was a sacrament meeting in the main sanctuary, then there was a Sunday School in smaller groups, and finally, in the third part, the men and women separated. The men went to a meeting called "Priesthood" and the women went to a meeting called "Relief Society."

I, of course, didn't know this when the Sacrament meeting began. I found out after the Sacrament meeting. A member of the congregation told me about the three-part service and invited me to come to the Sunday School.

This was a challenge, since I'd planned to meet my family at my mother's church. Nevertheless, I wanted to have as authentic a Mormon experience as I could, given my time constraints. I went to the small Sunday School group.

Due to the size of this group, it was even more evident there that I was a visitor. The Sunday school instructor had my brand new friend introduce me to the group, God bless her. She didn't even know me, but she shared the few pieces of information we had exchanged just a few minutes before. She told everyone that I Googled them and that is how I found them. Well, that sounded a little silly, I thought, but it was the truth and they say the truth will set you free, right? Anyway, I thanked everyone for having me and the lesson commenced.

The topic for discussion was "Marriage in the Covenant," which actually made me feel like there was some level of synchronicity about the topic for the day. As a single woman in her thirties, I've been open to advice that might help me determine if, when, and why I might be married, and if I do approach matrimony, what would it look like?

The lesson started with a joke about a woman and a man in the kitchen. The man continually made suggestions about how the woman should cook various dishes, and complete her cleaning chores. When the woman asked the man why he was bothering her so much, the man said, "Just wanted to let you know how it feels when I'm driving with you in the car."

This joke made me think, especially as I had become quite the student of myself in the wake of the loss of a relationship that I thought might be lifelong. I wondered if there were annoying things that I'd done or said that made my relationship end.

Quickly, I recognized the futility of that line of thinking. I tucked those thoughts away and kept listening.

This is when things became a little uncomfortable for me.

The discussion focused on a story in Genesis 24, where Abraham is looking for a wife for his son, a wife who is "within the covenant." The teacher asked a question about what that meant. Instead of being silent and observing like I should have, I put forth my two cents worth. I said something about Abraham wanting to find a wife for his son who had the same cultural perspective and background as he and his family. It seemed like a non-controversial observation when I was thinking it in my head. The Sunday school leader was kind and gracious and told me that I had a good point, but I realized, almost as soon as I opened my mouth, that it wasn't for me to talk. This was a small-group session discussing the concept of marriage within a specific faith tradition—and one that I knew nothing about.

Nobody told me to shut up. Nevertheless, I felt uncomfortable. Shortly after, two fathers took their infant children out of the room. I left as well. I didn't feel supremely rude, as I'd already told my new "friend" that I couldn't stay for the whole hour. Before I left, she and I exchanged information. Later, she sent me a follow-up note and a Bible, which I thought was kind. It showed me that I didn't say or do anything that was perceived as unforgivable, which made me feel a little better.

* * *

Stories of how faith had helped others through their grief have always impacted me. I connected with the married couple who shared their experience of losing their child. I took heart from the fact that their faith sustained them through that difficult time in their life. As they cried tears of love and remembrance, I cried with them.

In some ways, my initial apprehension about visiting a Mormon service became a self-fulfilling prophecy. My visit ended on somewhat of an awkward note, but I learned a valuable lesson that day about how I needed to continue to conduct this experiment—be humble, shut up, and listen. I had much to learn.

WEEK 13
BREATHTAKINGLY BEAUTIFUL DEVOTIONS
THE BAHÁ'Í HOUSE OF WORSHIP FOR
THE NORTH AMERICAN CONTINENT

12:30 p.m. service, Wilmette, Illinois

I arrived in Chicago in the early nineties, young, wide eyed, and ready for a new adventure. After four years of California dreaming, I headed to "the Chi," the Windy City, kind of.

I spent two years in graduate school in a city just north of Chicago, Evanston, which was a little less big city and a little more college town. It was the next chapter in my story. One of the first things that I discovered when I was tooling around in my little red Volkswagen Golf was the Baha'i Temple in Wilmette, Illinois, a suburb just north of Evanston. I knew nothing about the Baha'i faith then. The magnificence of the temple, however, stayed in my memory.

As my 52-week journey progressed, I often asked friends for suggestions about places to visit. Many suggested that I visit this temple, as the exterior had affected them in the same way it had affected me.

On a morning when I was beating myself up for not being prepared to run an 8K that I'd planned to run, I decided to hop in my car and drive about an hour north of where I live and finally visit this temple.

I'm glad I did.

As I drove north of Evanston on Sheridan Road, the temple rose up to meet me in a way that cannot be ignored. It's a breathtakingly beautiful edifice—a white, nine-sided temple surrounded by gardens and fountains with a long flight of stairs from the street to the entry. The temple's intricate architectural styling is striking.

I arrived early and spent some time just driving around the building and trying to take pictures from various angles. I parked across the street and walked to the entrance of the temple.

Inside the enormous sanctuary existed a quiet serenity so calming you could feel the spiritual truths of the Baha'i faith: the oneness of God, the oneness of humanity, and the oneness of religion. The feeling of peace and unity and divinity within the temple was palpable.

The services, apparently, took place every day, and they had the Catholics beat in terms of speed. Although a congregant told me that the service would take an hour, after thirty minutes, the service was over. I mulled over how useful it might have been to know, when I was a young graduate student, that these peaceful services were a short drive away. A lunchtime ritual of sitting in peace in this temple could have helped the hustle and bustle of my life at the time. Among the seemingly important stresses of graduate school and my early twenties, I never made time. I should have.

During the service, there was no clergy, no sermon, just members of the church reading from the *Prayers and Meditations by Bahá'u'lláh*, which I assumed was a religious text. There was no preacher or translator to interpret the readings. It felt like these church members were presenting the word directly to the congregation to do with it what they would.

The first reading in the service was in Arabic. Even though I didn't understand it, I experienced a serene feeling during the reading. The second reading was in Spanish. This spoke to a love I have for the language that was born in my high school Spanish class and nurtured through travelling as an adult to Spanish-speaking communities and countries. Periodically, throughout the service, there were choir selections. I couldn't see the choir. It was not in front of us, but hidden away in the balcony of the temple. Their music was enchanting. I found myself closing my eyes just to experience the music more fully. Next, there was a reading selection in English. I noted a specific accent from the reader that was not an American English accent, but some type of British accent. After the choir selection, another selection in English, and another non-American accent. This was a true multicultural, multinational congregation.

The service on Sunday was over quickly. I found myself wondering: what is the true walk for someone of this faith? Attending Sunday service is one thing, but what happens during the week really informs how you grow in your faith.

Later, at home, I did some research, and learned this about the Baha'i Faith:

> The Faith's Founder was Bahá'u'lláh, a Persian nobleman from Tehran who, in the mid-nineteenth century, left a life of princely comfort and security and, in the face of intense persecution and deprivation, brought to humanity a stirring new message of peace and unity.
>
> Bahá'u'lláh claimed to be nothing less than a new and independent Messenger from God. His life, work, and influence parallel that of Abraham, Krishna, Moses, Zoroaster, Buddha, Christ, and Muhammad. Bahá'ís view Bahá'u'lláh as the most recent in this succession of divine Messengers.
>
> The essential message of Bahá'u'lláh is that of unity. He taught that there is only one God, that there is only one human race, and that all the world's religions represent stages in the revelation of God's will and purpose for humanity. In this day, Bahá'u'lláh said, humanity has collectively come of age. As foretold in all of the world's scriptures, the time has arrived for the uniting of all peoples into a peaceful and integrated global society. "The earth is but one country, and mankind its citizens," he wrote.[12]

As in many faiths, this religion had a respect for all of the world's great prophets, but it also had a final messenger, Baha'u'll'ah.

Without more investigation, I wouldn't fully know about the faith. Of course, that would be the case for each worship tradition that I experienced throughout my journey.

*   *   *

If there is a beautiful place of worship nearby that you have always wanted to visit, you should go. Soon. The short service that I attended at the Baha'i temple was one of the most memorable of my journey. Just to sit in the peace and serenity of that temple did my soul a world of good.

WEEK 14
GRACE UNDER FIRE
SIXTH GRACE PRESBYTERIAN CHURCH

11:00 a.m. Palm Sunday Service, Chicago, Illinois

They say time heals all wounds, but I wasn't convinced. Sometimes, it appeared that time was just passing. After many months, I still felt very sad sometimes about the losses I'd suffered in my life. Some days, I was unsure how I would ever feel like myself again.

This Sunday, I felt especially despondent. I'd made plans to share this service with two friends, Jackie and Akeshia, but was feeling extremely alone in spite of those plans. I was antsy, cranky, and feeling scattered. All of these feelings were intensified by the fact that my friends were running late that morning. One of the things that I really tried not to do during my 52-week journey was to be late for church. Some of the most enjoyable pieces of church for me were the initial pieces—the songs, the initial call and response portions of the service, the liturgy, and the establishment of the rhythm of the service.

I contemplated the irony of wanting to have company, but being irritated by the choices and timing of the company that I wanted so much. Why did I find it difficult to adjust my actions to accommodate others? Was that the reason why my ex was now an ex? Had I lived so long on my own that I'd become difficult to live with or to deal with? Did I really need to spend more time cutting myself and others some slack and manage my expectations so that I was easier to be around? Was the way that I was getting grouchy about my friends being late indicative of the lessons that I needed to learn to be a better friend, a better woman, a better partner? Were there lessons that I needed to learn, not just about spirituality and religion, but about my life and the kind of person I am versus the kind of person I needed or wanted to be?

For anyone who has experienced the end of a relationship, it is common knowledge that ruminating on the whys and what-ifs can quickly take you down a dark and destructive path.

This Sunday morning, I was sprinting down that path toward the flames of an unproductive personal meltdown.

Luckily, my friends arrived just before full combustion occurred. We made it to the church, and I tried to put that rumination on the back burner. Although it was simmering in the back of my mind throughout the whole service, I did my best to focus on the experience I was having.

The moderately-sized church appeared to be a tight-knit community. It was small enough that when a member's death was announced, there was an audible gasp, which suggested to me that the majority of the congregation knew who the dearly departed was. During the passing of the peace, I received a hearty welcome from those who sat around me, not because I was a chocolate chip (this was a majority Black congregation), but because it was clear in this smaller congregation that I was a visitor. When people asked me how I ended up choosing the church, I pointed out that I was there with my friend Akeshia, who many people appeared to know.

Small versus large. A lot versus a little. These themes resonated deeply with me that day.

People who have lost a loved one often have to go through a process where they think about the life of the one that they loved. My father— he never stopped working hard. He was a physician first and foremost, but he was also a businessman. He invested in real estate, and in the years prior to his death, he was working on several development deals. I had no idea why, at that time, he just didn't choose to rest, relax, play golf, chill. He worked hard until he couldn't anymore. As someone who has been ready to retire since I started working, we often had discussions about, "How much was enough."

I was raised to concentrate on hard work and achievement with a singular focus. Nothing but the best was expected, and there was always something I could be achieving, acquiring, actualizing—if not for my own good, then because I could use my achievements and assets to help others. But how much is enough? How big is too big? Being in my thirties without a family of my own to speak of, I'd begun thinking that sometimes you have to put your foot down and say enough. Enough achievement and acquisition, because without someone to share it with, or a family to work for, it means nothing. Enough stress about doing more, working harder, because sometimes doing too many things brings about an unsustainable pace that ends up being counterproductive.

I wish my father could have spent his last days relaxing, surrounded by family and the books that he loved to read. I wish that he could have met his yet unborn grandkids. I wish that he didn't feel like he had to keep working, keep achieving, keep acquiring, even after I told him that he was enough for us, that he had done enough for us, and that he didn't need to do anymore. He provided my sisters and me with the education and the experiences that served as the foundation upon which we could build *any* kind of life.

I don't think he ever thought it was enough.

It was more than enough.

I sat in that church of about 150 members—a smaller church than my home church with a membership of more than 8,500—and contemplated the concepts of small versus large. Of just enough versus never enough.

To say I was distracted during this service was a bit of an understatement. Through my distractions, I was able to focus on remembrance, which was one of the points of the whole journey. As I looked around at the congregation and saw many elderly Black men, they all reminded me of my father.

Oh, how I missed him.

Even with my mind moving in a million different directions, I tried to find some time and energy to focus on the message for the day. The sermon focused on "the price of a missed opportunity." As the pastor warned that, ". . . once an opportunity has passed, it's hard to get it back," I found my mind wandering back to the unproductive ruminations of what-ifs and whys that I'd started the day with. Clearly, thinking about the sermon was going to make me think about my ex, and that was no good. I did stay focused enough to hear the pastor share that I needed to "feed my spirit, just like I feed my body and feed my imagination."

True. And my imagination wouldn't stop working during this service.

The pastor was dressed in a gown that looked much like one I recognized from the many times I watched Robert Schuller preach at the Crystal Cathedral in Orange County, California. The Crystal Cathedral was another one of the diverse spiritual inputs that left an indelible mark on my spiritual development. Its special brand of "possibility thinking" was part of my life for many years. My parents supported the ministry with many monetary contributions, and were part of the church's Eagles club. I remember a house filled with these eagles. They all had inspiring quotations on them, many related in some way to Isaiah 40:31(KJV):

> Those who wait upon the Lord shall renew their strength,
> They shall mount up on wings as eagles,
> They shall RUN and NOT grow weary,
> They shall WALK and NOT faint.

There were big eagles and little eagles. Eagle coins and eagle statues. There were many books, all with inspiring titles like, *Tough Times Never Last, But Tough People Do!* and *Turning Your Stress into Strength!* There was never-ending possibility and positivity, and we steeped in it. Until one day when my parents went to an event where they actually met Robert Schuller.

As the story goes, my father—who was ever the proud African man—asked Dr. Schuller when he would take the ministry to Africa. At this question, Dr. Schuller stated that if my father would consider donating funds, he could consider making a trip to the African continent. As my father had already supported Dr. Schuller and his ministries financially for years, he didn't find this to be a satisfactory response; in fact, he found it offensive. The ministry became less and less omnipresent in our lives, and although the power of positive thinking continued to be a family mantra, the trickle of eagle deliveries to the house slowed, and then stopped.

Time was passing as my imagination worked, and soon the Sixth Grace sermon was over. I heard the familiar comments made that signified that it was time to invite visitors, non-members, and those who were not "born-again" to join the church. A song began playing, and familiar words were spoken: "Doors of the church are open."

It was invitation time.

The altar call is familiar to many who have worshipped in the Christian tradition. It's the time when you can heed the pastor's call to join the church if, in fact, you don't have a church home. It's the time when you are asked to stand up wherever you are in the sanctuary, walk down the aisle to the front of the room, and ". . . give your hand to the preacher, but give your heart to Christ." It's the time when you look into your heart, determine whether you are saved, and then decide if you can afford to stay in your seat during this very highly emotional portion of a worship service.

In my time at my home church, Trinity, in the early years, the altar call served another purpose. I was dating a young man named Rashid who came to church regularly, but often came only for the sermon. Because of this, and my desire to see him every Sunday, I would sit in an aisle seat in the enormous church. Whenever I heard "doors of the church are open," I would jump out of my seat, but instead of walking toward the front of the church, I would head to the back and into the lobby of the church, where Rashid would invariably be. That would afford me the opportunity to act as if I just happened to run into him on my way to the restroom, or to my car, as I could pretend that I valued only the singing and the sermon, and not the altar call, as he did.

I know. Trifling.

Once, after our relationship hit a rough patch, I used this opportunity to get up, leave the sanctuary, and then walk out of the church with Rashid calling my name, wondering why I was not speaking to him. I remember hearing him call: "Pamay . . . Pamay . . ." as I purposefully walked straight out of the church, angry at something he had done or not done, most likely. This, I suppose, felt like some sort of victory at the time.

I know. Ridiculous.

I remember telling my pastor this story years later, and he thought it was equally ridiculous. He just shook his head. Then we had a good laugh. Thank goodness for personal development, and moving past such juvenile actions in general.

At this moment at Sixth Grace, with my imagination running through this memory, I could see and enjoy the fact that altar calls have affected my life in many different ways.

The pastor wrapped up the service, telling us to read the passion narrative and contemplate religious scripture, in preparation for Easter.

It was probably a good idea that we were instructed to complete this at home—given how scattered I was feeling. Sometimes it's like that.

*   *   *

Sometimes you go to church feeling less than optimal, your mind wanders during the service, and then you still feel less than optimal when you leave. But it's okay. Go back next week, or go somewhere else.

My feelings this weekend had nothing to do with the church, it's message, or the kind friends who had asked me to join them. It was just because I had a great deal on my mind and was distracted throughout the service.

I counted myself lucky that journeys all have beginnings, middles, and ends. They have high points and rough patches. I looked forward to the next week, when I would take a long trip that would reveal new opportunities for connection and remembrance.

WEEK 15
GOING HOME
ANGLICAN CHURCH OF THE NATIVITY

11:00 a.m. service, Easter Sunday, Diocese of Lagos, Park View Estate, Ikoyi, Lagos, Nigeria

Home.

The word home means many different things to me. I was born in New York and raised in Atlanta, but have lived most of my life in Chicago. Depending on where I am, I could be talking about any number of places when I reference "home."

If I'm in Chicago and talking about where I'm going for Thanksgiving or Christmas, saying "I'm going home," clearly means Atlanta.

When I get to Atlanta, if I tell someone "I'm going home on Sunday," I clearly mean Chicago.

Sometimes I clarify by saying "Going home to Chicago" or "Going home to Atlanta," but people who know me well can usually suss out the context and make the right deduction.

Going home could refer to Nigeria, the West African country where both of my parents were born and raised, and the location where the lion's share of my extended family still lives.

Nigeria is Africa's most populous country. It is located in West Africa, bordered by the Republic of Benin in the west, Chad and Cameroon in the east, and Niger in the North. My father was from the Ibibio ethnic group; for those who know, my name gives that away. My mother was born in Lagos, the country's former capitol. She is from the Esan ethnic group. Nigeria is part Christian, part Muslim, part indigenous religions, and part "other" religious traditions.

Being in Nigeria on Easter Sunday held great meaning. It was on Easter Sunday in 1960 that my mother and father met for the first time. Fifty years had gone by since that day. Not only was I travelling home and thinking of my father every step of the way, I was extremely aware of the timing of the trip. My emotions were deep and plentiful. I flew from Chicago to Atlanta to Lagos, and spent a few wonderful days there with family. Cautious types may have their own warnings and admonitions about the need for prudence when travelling to Nigeria. Although I won't contradict this advice, I've always felt quite safe flying into the Lagos airport. My loving and supportive family descends on the airport, gathers around me after I clear customs, and shepherds me safely, every time, to waiting vehicles that take me to homes full of love and reminders of where I come from and what I'm made of.

This time, I stayed with my Uncle George and Aunty Efe. I shared with them that it was important for me to visit a church in Lagos before we left for Abuja, the location for a conference where I would be presenting. They said no problem.

I attended their family church, the Anglican Church of the Nativity. We arrived at the tail end of Sunday School, when the pastors were doing questions and answers with the congregation. The question for the day was: why is it not right for a man to have more than one wife?

Lord, I thought. This should be a fun discussion.

The first person to answer this Sunday School question was a woman. As she began trying to communicate her perspective, a gentleman cut in and said, "It's not right for a woman to answer, because of course she is going to say it's not right for a man to have more than one wife."

Good gracious.

One of the topics, for some reason, that always comes up when discussing African cultures and traditions is polygamy.

I suppose I have a slightly different perspective on this idea of one man, many wives. My mother comes from an expansive family. My maternal grandfather had multiple wives, and fathered more than thirty children. As a result, my cousins number in the hundreds, and once we all start having kids, we will approach the "salt of the earth" numbers. For me, this has been a wonderfully supportive environment within which to conduct family and cultural research as I learn, every day, about my Nigerian heritage. The first time I went home to Nigeria, I met so many family members that I began to assume that someone was an aunt, uncle, or cousin, unless someone told me otherwise.

That is my mother's family.

In contrast, my father had one brother and two sisters. I don't need both hands to count the number of cousins on his side of the family with whom I am in contact.

Family comes in many configurations. My family is proof of that.

Back at the Anglican Church of the Nativity, my experience took a little bit of a weird turn. I found myself wanting to take pictures of the service, from within the service. I wondered if this journey was turning me into a worship tourist, instead of someone who could be fully present and participating in the service. Not necessarily what I was trying to accomplish.

There's a difference between documenting and participating. I was reminded, at that moment in church, that I wanted to make sure I participate in all of the worship services, rather than spending my time trying to document them. It was a fine line, and I struggled with walking it every time I visited a new place of worship.

I refocused on the service. I was honored to watch my uncle being commissioned as the Vicar's Warden that day. In the Anglican tradition, the Vicar's Warden is one of the senior lay leaders of a Parish. The

Vicar appoints him or her. There's also a People's Warden, who the parishioners appoint. Both are part of the Church Council in the Anglican church.[13]

As part of my uncle's swearing in at the church that morning, he had to promise that he was not part of any secret cults or societies.

This reminded me of my mother. She was very specific and insistent about what I was and was not supposed to do when I left for college. One of the commandments was that I was not, under any circumstances, to join any "sororities or cults."

The reason for the command is that, apparently, there is a very robust community of secret societies, cults, and other underground groups that flourishes in Nigeria. Many of these groups are campus based, and they historically have wreaked political and cultural havoc. In addition, their activities are not always consistent with Christian values and practices.[14]

When my sisters and I said sorority, my mother heard, "Secret Society." She wasn't having it. She scared me so much that I didn't pledge a sorority until my senior year of college. After I pledged, I didn't tell my parents that I was in a sorority for ten years. I was undercover. That was the power of African parenting.

Her commandment was rooted in the experiences that my parents had while growing up in Nigeria. Her commandment not to join a cult or a sorority almost made me miss out on one of the best experiences that I have had in my life—that of being a member of Delta Sigma Theta Sorority, Inc., one of the few historically African-American sororities founded in the United States.

If the oath that I watched my uncle take was any indication, the concerns about cults and secret societies had not changed in all these years.

My musings about these issues were interrupted as the hymn for the day began. They sang the song, "Christ The Lord is Risen Today," which was one of my father's favorite Easter hymns. I remembered hearing it often during our many viewings of The Hour of Power at the Crystal Cathedral:

57

Christ the Lord is risen today, Alleluia!
Earth and heaven in chorus say, Alleluia!
Raise your joys and triumphs high, Alleluia!
Sing, ye heavens, and earth reply, Alleluia![15]

After the singing, it was time for prayer. I have never heard prayers like the ones that I hear when I'm at home in Nigeria. The "everything AND the kitchen sink" prayers. The "leave no stone unturned" prayers. The prayers that ask God to protect us from every possible, probable, and improbable enemy or obstacle.

On my first trip to Nigeria, I heard these prayers for the first time, and I was in awe of them. "How can people pray one prayer for twenty minutes? Thirty minutes?" I thought.

One prayer I remember was from a friend of the family who was also a pastor. During a visit to her house, she learned that myself and all of my sisters were single. At the time we were all in our twenties. Although I didn't realize she tucked that fact away, she revealed it in the prayer that she prayed when we left her house and prepared to journey out to another area of the country. We were travelling by road, which, at the time, required a great deal of prayer and faith.

Her prayers were 1/10 "travelling mercies" and 9/10 the hope that God should be so gracious as to help us find husbands: "And in Jesus' name, please have mercy on each of these young women, that God should help them find a maaaaaaaaaan to be a husband to each of them . . ." she said, repeatedly, in different ways, as she put her palm to the sky and begged God on our behalf.

My sisters and I laughed about that story many times in the years to come.

Another favorite prayer came just as we were leaving Nigeria at the end of my first trip. At the time, the Lagos International Airport was challenging to navigate. It was in our best interest to arrive at the airport hours in advance so that we could go through all the security and drama that we had to go through to get checked into our flight home.

But first, we had to pray.

And since we were travelling for a long time, the prayer had to be all-inclusive.

I remember the prayer taking so long that after about twenty minutes, my father just said Amen in the middle of something, announcing that if we kept praying, we would miss our flight.

I found this hilarious.

I guess he figured we had covered our bases enough.

The everyday life of the average Nigerian is full of many challenges. Prayers like this probably help you to keep your equilibrium in situations that are often frustrating and exhausting. When life is challenging, prayer helps. The more challenging, perhaps, the more prayer is necessary or helpful.

Back to the service. Time for the sermon.

The pastor focused on John 20:1(NIV):

> Early on the first day of the week, while it was still dark, Mary Magdalene went to the tomb and saw that the stone had been removed from the entrance.

A good solid Easter scripture.

The service continued, and it included many of the relevant themes from Easter services that I'd attended over the years.

I smiled to myself as I remembered Rashid, and a discussion that we had about religion years ago. He was interested in my African heritage and was doing a little soul searching himself. He had been a member of my home church also since he was a boy. He had stopped eating pork, was reading the Qur'an and learning more about Islam, although as far as I know he never converted. We discussed the familiar themes

59

in an Easter service. He observed that every Easter service basically said the same thing, "Christ died, he rose again—yeah we know that. What else?"

He was, at the time, as we all do, struggling to make his faith more active, more relevant, more in tune with his life experiences.

Which I understood.

The pastor talked about how the stone was removed from the entrance of Jesus' tomb, and how it had been rolled away. He related that to the removal of obstacles and hindrances from your life. He referred to this as "Resurrection power," saying that the same power that removed that stone was available to me, and I could use that power to remove issues, obstacles, or hindrances from my life.

A useful message given all that I was trying to make sense of during this particular year. "Could this power make me heal and move on with my life?" I thought.

A quote that the pastor used caught my attention. He said, "Mary was hot for the Lord." He discussed her enthusiasm and faith—and, boy, she must have had strong faith to believe that she, who had never had relations with a man, was to have a baby, and not just any baby, but the Son of God.

"That's a whole lot of, 'Not my will, but the will of God.'" I thought, "So, yes, I'm a Christian, but have I ever been hot for the Lord?"

I'm not the most evangelistic Christian, nor do I think I ever will be. Maybe, I thought, I'm warm for the Lord. I struggle with the idea that I need to convince others to worship the way I do or believe what I believe. This journey of worship alone flies in the face of that. I truly believe you can worship in your own way and stand shoulder to shoulder with someone who believes something else just as strongly as you believe (or even more strongly). But, that might be a cop-out. Maybe it takes more energy, commitment, and passion to be "hot for the Lord" or "hot for Allah" or "hot for Jehovah."

The pastor mentioned this himself—he brought up the discussion of Islam versus Christianity. "Muslims pray five times a day," he said, "what is your commitment to Christianity?"

He had a point.

Religion in Nigeria, I found, was just more evangelistic than my experience in the United States. The pastor talked about evangelism and asked, "Are you ashamed of the gospel of Jesus Christ?"

Was I?

Did my interest in learning about other faith traditions mean that I had watered-down beliefs about my own?

Was there a difference between how I was currently approaching my faith and true belief?

Visiting a different place of worship every week for 52 weeks was bringing me a specific type of blessing. But when this was all over, I wondered, would I be ready to accept the challenge of selecting one place of worship and committing to the community and the experience, to receive that kind of blessing?

Perhaps.

The pastor continued by reminding us that it isn't good to come to church without a Bible. He said that the congregation had been spoiled since Bibles are in the pews, people "stroll in with their hands in their pockets, like they are going to the club."

I contrasted this with the Anglican Church I went to in Atlanta in February. The church provided Bibles. The pastor told you the chapter and verse he was focusing on, as well as the page number in the Bible where the scripture could be found. This seemed like it went too far to the other side—not even requiring people to familiarize themselves with the Holy Book of the faith they claimed to profess.

Perhaps there was a balance to be struck?

Service wrapped up, my family and I left the church, and we left Lagos. We were on our way to Abuja, the capital city of Nigeria.

*   *   *

Each time I visit Nigeria, I learn a little more about who I am and who my family is. Every step of this trip reminded me of my father. My connection to Nigeria is strong. My father was a very proud Nigerian man and taught me to be proud of my Nigerian heritage as well. I felt blessed to spend part of my 52-week journey on Nigerian soil.

WEEK 16
CULTURAL IMMERSION IN THE NIGER DELTA
ST. PETER'S CATHEDRAL

11:00 a.m. service, Diocese of Okrika, Nigeria

As a part of my trip to Nigeria, I visited a place called Okrika for the first time. Okrika, Nigeria is in the Niger Delta area—a place that many know simply as, "where the oil is."

> Okrika is a port town in Rivers State, Nigeria, capital of the Local Government Area of the same name. The town is situated on a small island just south of Port Harcourt, making it a suburb of the much larger city . . . . Formerly a small fishing village of the Ijo (Ijaw) people in the mangrove swamps of the eastern Niger River delta, Okrika became the capital of the Okrika kingdom in the early 17th century and actively dealt in slaves. It served as a port for the exportation of palm oil after the abolition of the slave trade in the 1830s . . . . The local Kirike language is part of the Ijoid group.[16]

My travelling partners for this trip were my twin uncles on my mother's side, Uncle George and Uncle Mike. They grew up in this area and were well known. I accompanied them to Port Harcourt for a service commemorating the tenth anniversary of the death of their mother, Mama Jane.

The Niger Delta area is often in the news, thanks to the joint blessings and challenges that come from the presence of oil in the area. Many of my friends, when I told them I was headed to the area, were concerned for my safety (although I was not). Their concern likely came from the many stories about kidnappings and violence that have dominated the news cycles in previous years.

My uncles told me that things had changed. I believed them and felt safe with them.

After we landed in the airport in Port Harcourt, we went directly to the church where their mother's remembrance ceremony would take place. As we travelled to Okrika, my uncles shared with me how things used to be. The appearance of the town was very different than the serene and peaceful village that my uncles described, and where my mother had spent significant time when she was a little girl.

I saw many dilapidated oil trucks. They appeared to be abandoned but were apparently still in use. Some of the brands stamped on the trucks were recognizable company names that I could see every day driving through Chicago looking for a gas station.

BP.

Shell.

Mobil.

Chevron.

Traffic packed the narrow roads, which were not in the best condition. Sounds of honking cars filled the air, as the motorcycles, or "okadas" as they are called, weaved in and out of the cars trying to make their way to their destination.

Pandemonium.

Piles of trash lined the streets. From the safety of our vehicle, I took pictures, so I could remember and share.

We arrived at my place of worship for the week, another Anglican church, St. Peter's Cathedral. I thought how notable it was that both churches I visited, on this trip that commemorated the fiftieth anniversary of my parent's meeting, were Anglican churches. The new church that we found for our mother to attend in Atlanta was also an Anglican church—the first one I'd ever been to.

Synchronicity.

As we arrived at the church compound, a sign hung on the gate. The sign said:

> Notice! Notice!! Notice!!! It is forbidden for any woman to enter the church compound/personage (sic) premises with: 1) trousers, 2) uncovered head, 3) Sleeveless dresses including men . . . Order by the Dean.

Well, it was Saturday, we had just taken a flight. I was wearing comfortable flying clothes—which included jeans, and didn't include a hair cover. With my jeans, I violated Notice! 1. With my uncovered head, I violated Notice!! 2. My comic sensibilities just didn't even know what to make of Notice!!! 3. Perhaps if I was wearing a sleeveless dress with a man attached to it, that would be a violation? Or, if I was with a man wearing a sleeveless dress?

And who was the Dean?

I never figured that out, but regardless, I needed to do something to comply with the Dean's order so that I could enter the church compound.

The church officials who met us provided a solution. They gave me a wrapper (a printed piece of cloth, which Nigerian women often wear in a skirt-like fashion) to wear around my jeans. They also gave me a white handkerchief to place on my head. Then we were ready!

My Uncle Mike thought I looked ridiculous, which I did. He really got a kick out of my improvised outfit. He was the one taking pictures this time.

Granted, my outfit didn't match, but it was okay with me. I had no problem complying with cultural regulations. I was flexible! Whatever was necessary—that day, and throughout my entire 52-week journey—to make sure I was honoring the place of worship in which I was present was fine with me. I sat to the side as I listened to the preparations for Mama Jane's service the next day.

After the consultation with the church pastor was over, as we headed back to the car to go to another uncle's house to retire for the day, we found ourselves in the middle of a funeral procession for someone from the village. There was a throng of mourners marching in a procession, carrying a casket on their shoulders, and dancing and playing drums—a celebration of the dearly departed. Loud, lively music played, and different people carried enlarged photos of the recently deceased.

There's a definite cultural precedent for the spirited funeral processions you might see in New Orleans.

I had a similar experience when I attended my grandmother's funeral in Benin City, Nigeria in June, 2009. On that day, there was a forecast for rain, but everyone prayed that it would hold off, and it did—until the service was over, and light rain began to sprinkle on us, like a gentle goodbye from my grandmother.

My aunts and uncles hustled and bustled as they completed final preparations for the ceremony. Purple and gold curtains and flowing materials decorated the whole house, transforming the home from being simply "my grandmother's house" to the scene of a final goodbye for a woman whose family loved her and thought her worthy of a royal farewell.

Savory aromas emanated from the kitchen, where food was being prepared for friends, family, and neighbors who would join in the remembrance. A full menu of jollof rice, fried rice, hot pepper soup, pounded yam, egusi soup, stewed beef, moi moi, suya, and fried plantains ensured that all would be fed after the funeral service.

The elders from my grandmother's village—a group of about five older African men wearing bright, regal outfits—came to my grandmother's house. My uncle made sure that they had food and drink so they could participate peacefully in the remembrance of my grandmother. Chairs and tents were set up outside of her home, and her final resting place had been prepared in front of the house, where she was to be buried.

Noises from outside heralded the arrival of the casket in a car. We all went out to meet the car. The pall bearers removed my grandmother's casket from the car, hoisted it on their shoulders, and walked and danced the rest of the way from the car to the house, where the ceremony would take place. At times, they would hoist the casket high above their heads, then bring it back to their shoulders—including my grandmother in the choreography of her last dance before her burial.

Joining the pall bearers were musicians playing drums and trumpets that signified it was time for a celebration of my grandmother's life.

Pictures and posters of my beautiful grandmother hung on the gate outside of her home and throughout her neighborhood, letting people know that she was gone, and inviting them to come and celebrate her life with her family from all over the world.

Funerals are big events in Nigeria.

As the processional in Okrika went by, I also found myself thinking about my father and his funeral—what it would have been like if it had happened in Nigeria. It would have been quite a production, because of the stature of the man he was and his accomplishments both as a man and a physician. He was a man who left his village to "do big things." One of the reasons why there was so much backlash about his desire to be cremated was because some members of his family thought it was a disgraceful way for a "Big Man" to leave this earth.

To be a "Big Man" living outside of his birth-country was something my father and I talked about often. He was an African man who had left home in search of his destiny. Along the way, he had a family and made choices that resulted in him living, working and dying in America—a country where he became a citizen, but a place that he never, in his true heart, called home.

Often, I thought that he gave up so much for us by staying in the United States. He gave up growing old in a country that he loved, surrounded by family and friends. In leaving Nigeria, he made some choices that changed the trajectory of his life and of his family, including me. Did he truly do it for us, or for himself? What regrets did he have? Should I spend time considering moving to Nigeria or living here for some time? Is that even something I could do or wanted to do? Is my destiny intertwined with that of Nigeria? Or was I trying to force the issue?

I should have talked to him more about all this. We did discuss it. But never enough. Now he is gone, and there is no more time.

Tears.

Should I do something in Nigeria—some sort of memorial service in his village or with his family? Could I, even if I wanted to? These unresolved questions filled my mind as I watched the processional in Okrika.

One day, I imagined, they would be resolved. But not today.

The next day, Sunday morning, my aunt took mercy on me and gifted me with a lovely outfit of maroon and gold African attire with a matching head tie. I was in compliance with the Dean's order early in the morning, and in stylish fashion!

As we entered the church, I immediately focused on familiar elements. The logo on the pulpit reminded me of my high school logo:

When I was in high school, I remember thinking that the letters in the center looked like they spelled out the word "The." After seeing this symbol in a few different churches that I visited, I engaged the help of some friends from high school. After some spirited discussion and some research, we located this description of the image from the church logo and in my school seal:

> The sun is a Messianic symbol of Christ. This symbol is based on a phrase in Malachi 4:2, "But unto you that fear my name shall the sun of righteousness arise with healing in its wings . . . ." The monogram represents the first three letters of the name "Jesus" in Greek, with Gothic-style letters. The circle surrounding the monogram represents eternity. The rays, which are alternatively straight and wavy, indicate glory. The seal, then, represents the fact that Jesus, the eternal sun of righteousness, is the heart and center of the school.[17]

I quietly acknowledged the tie between my experience on this day and the school back in Atlanta, thousands of miles away, where I'd spent my formative years.

Then, I turned my focus back to the service.

It became clear very quickly that this was going to be a special experience. After about five minutes, I leaned over to my Uncle and said, "Is any of the service going to be in English?" He shrugged and said, "I guess not!"

Uncle Mike takes things in stride.

Most of the service was in the Okrika dialect, Kirike, the language of the Nigerians in the area. It was my first experience of many in my 52-week journey where I didn't understand much more than God, Jesus, and Amen!

Because I didn't understand most of the beginning of the service, I was able to think instead about the importance of the preservation of culture as it was being displayed before me. I was seeing a community that valued their history and culture even as they worshipped within a Christian context that may or may not have been familiar to their ancestors of generations before.

Amazing.

As part of the service, a young Nigerian man sang "Hosanna in the Highest" in a traditional operatic fashion. I was seeing and hearing the result of cultural transfer happening in front of my eyes. This inspired many questions: How do the people merge multiple cultures? Do they realize what is happening? They must, since they felt the need to conduct the service in their mother tongue. They must have realized the importance of sharing heritage, culture, experiences, and stories, before they were lost in the transfer to a new way of living, a new way of worship.

Later, my Uncle Mike explained that it was his maternal grandfather, Chief W.W. Peters, who translated the hymns and the elements of the service into the language of the Okrika people. Chief Peters was halfway through the translation of the Bible before he died. He was also the church's first organist.

Even as he and his contemporaries started to become Christians in Africa, Chief W.W. Peters realized that if they didn't speak their language when the community gathered weekly for church, then the language would be lost. In the face of extreme religious change, there was a realization that the preservation of culture was important.

A humorous moment in the service came when the pastor announced the unison scripture. He stated that the verse was in the "fifth book of Moses." There was rustling and discussion as people seemed to challenge him.

"The fifth book of Moses?" some said. "What is that?"

The pastor was referring to Deuteronomy, which is the fifth book of the Old Testament, but is also—biblically—the fifth book of Moses, although perhaps not often referred to as such.

People were shouting out, "The fifth book of the Old Testament!" seemingly trying to correct the pastor. This annoyed him, and he explained that he was, in fact, referring correctly to Deuteronomy as the fifth book of Moses. As the rustling continued, I found myself trying to recite the books of the Old Testament in my head (Genesis, Exodus, Leviticus, Numbers, Deuteronomy . . .). At one time in my life, I could recite all the books in order from Genesis to Revelation, but on this day, after I reached Deuteronomy, I stumbled.

My inability to rattle off all the books in the Bible in order made me once again think about how well I knew my own religious text. I found myself wondering, "How does one really know God?" There's going to church and then there is knowing God. When my father died, I knew beyond a shadow of a doubt that he knew I loved him. I made a specific effort over the years to connect with him, learn from him, and honor him. We talked frequently about our mutual interests—sports, Africa, reading, and philosophy. We talked about our hopes, dreams, and the challenges we faced. He shared his wisdom with me.

In contrast, I wonder if God really knows how I feel about Him.

Maybe not, because I'm still determining how I feel. Although I know I love God, I know I don't always take the time to show Him, or show others how I feel about Him.

Perhaps I needed to make some sort of change in my intentionality regarding my relationship with God, and how I interact with Him. If I want God to know beyond a shadow of a doubt how I feel, it might be necessary for me to make the same concerted effort to connect with Him, honor Him, and learn from Him—as I made with my father.

When the pastor asked the question, "What part of your day is reserved for serious prayer?" I had to make a mental note to really think about that after the service was long over.

"Understanding the Times" was the theme of the sermon.

The sermon was the only part of the service that was in English, there was then a translation into the Kirike language. It included all of the drama and comedy of any speech that is first spoken in one language, and then translated into another. The pastor seemed to speak—going on and on for about ten minutes—then the translator got the job done in a fraction of the time. I found myself wondering what in the world was the pastor really saying? Was something being lost in translation?

Since I didn't understand the language, I could just revel in the humor of the moment.

The sermon talked about how we are already in the "last of days," also known as the "end of times."

I'm not a big fan of "last days" talk. I find it frightening. I remember as a child reading a book by the evangelist Ernest Angley called *Raptured*. It was about the end of days and the mark of the beast and how God would sweep his people up into the heavens and everyone else would fend for themselves as society degenerated into a lawless mess.

It freaked me out.

Even though the pastor in this church in Nigeria talked about how the Bible says in the last days, "knowledge will increase," I felt unable to process all the talk about the end of time.

Other parts of the sermon were equally discomforting. There was a section where the pastor prophesied, calling out certain people in the congregation and telling them what lay ahead for them. At one point during this section, he mentioned: "three men here have three years added to their lives."

I looked around, as did others in the service, and wondered. Hmmm . . . who are the three men? I hope they enjoy the bonus years.

Fortunately, there were also parts of the sermon that were familiar and comforting. The pastor spoke on the parable of the talents, one of my favorite parables.[18] He also quoted Philippians 3:12-14(NIV), one of my favorite verses:

> Not that I have already obtained all this, or have already arrived at my goal, but I press on to take hold of that for which Christ Jesus took hold of me. Brothers and sisters, I do not consider myself yet to have taken hold of it. But one thing I do: Forgetting what is behind and straining toward what is ahead, I press on toward the goal to win the prize for which God has called me heavenward in Christ Jesus.

Given what I was going through regarding trying to forgive and forget my ex and my failed relationship, I called upon the portion of the verse that instructed me to ". . . forget what is behind and strain toward what is ahead," often and with varying success.

Philippians continues to be one of my favorite books in the Bible thanks to an off-the-cuff challenge from one of my New Testament teachers, Mr. Bob Neu. Mr. Neu was saved and convinced, and he was one of my favorite teachers. As a prerequisite for graduation, we were required to take both an Old Testament and a New Testament class, and Mr. Neu facilitated my introduction to the serious study of the books of the New Testament.

In one class, he offered a challenge. Mentioning that the book of Philippians was a short book (only four chapters), he asked us to commit to reading a chapter a night for a month. When we finished, he said, start over. I took that challenge, and as a result, I read the book of Philippians many times and developed a love for many of the verses in it. I don't know that I accomplished what Mr. Neu intended, since I didn't immediately apply this one-chapter-a-night approach to other books in the Bible. It was not until years later that I actually read the Bible cover to cover. But, his challenge and the things I learned that month did stay with me.

What was staying with me as the service in Okrika continued was the fact that it was extremely hot. It was so hot that people were falling asleep. One of the pastors or deacons was going around tapping people and waking them up. As the power of 25 fans tried to keep everyone in the church cool, the pastor wrapped up the service on that special Sunday afternoon.

*   *   *

Just because an entire worship service is in a language that you don't speak doesn't mean that you won't understand what is going on. Although the majority of this week's service was in a language that I don't speak, I learned about the interplay of faith, culture, and community.

But, most importantly, my family provided me with a safe place to rest in remembrance.

Week 17
Oh, Ye of Little Faith
Moody Bible Church

5:00 p.m., Sunday Evening Connection, Chicago, Illinois

With April came the first anniversary of my grandmother's death. On April 22, 2009, she passed away.

She was the only grandmother I ever knew. I didn't see her often as an adult but her mere existence had an impact on my life. She was a strong, hard-working woman, who me, my mother and my sisters resemble. Many told me that my heart was large and kind like hers. I learned about her through my cousins, who grew up with her.

She didn't speak English, but when I met her, she danced and praised the Lord and told me, through my mother, that she had been praying for me and my sisters all her life. When I went to her funeral, I saw, in a corner of her home, a photo album of me, my sisters and my cousins that I'd sent her years before.

She saved it.

She knew me and she loved me, even though she rarely saw me.

After returning from Nigeria, I had a rough week. The week of the anniversary of her passing had me in a melancholy soup, not knowing what I was mourning on any given day.

I was weary. I had an emotional meltdown that found me, one night, crying in my car and driving toward my ex's house.

It's never a good idea to be outside your ex's house in the middle of an emotional meltdown. Or for any reason.

I remember hearing something on Oprah once—this might not be an exact quote, but she basically said, "If you find yourself driving toward your ex's house to 'get some answers,' just keep driving to the nearest psychiatrist instead."

Sound advice.

I ignored it.

After arriving at his house and parking my car, I decided to just lean into my crazy, walk up to the house, knock on the door, and take whatever consequence of shame may come. I ended up getting lied to by a senior citizen—his uncle—who told me where I could find him (although I think he was just tickled that the crazy lady had reappeared at the house). He sent me on a wild goose chase to another suburb and back again.

Hours later, I found myself again sitting outside his house in my car, asking God, "Why in the world am I here and why can't I shake this man?" As I was starting the car to vacate the premises, my ex drove up.

Shaking on the inside and outside, I exited my car and went to talk to him. To talk to the man who I had once considered the love of my life—a man whom I hadn't seen in six months. It was excruciating and wonderful and soul crushing.

As we talked, it felt like we still cared about each other. Upon reflection, though, it was clear to me that he loved himself far more than me. It was also clear that I was still fighting a battle to learn how to love myself again, after all of the pain and loss of the previous year.

Excruciating.

When the weekend began, I was still reeling from that interaction. I was unable to convince myself to get up early, so my worship choices were restricted to evening services. I went to one church that I'd been meaning to visit, but there was no service, so I drove to the second—the Moody Bible Church in Chicago's Old Town Neighborhood. I don't feel that anything happens randomly. I entered the sanctuary, wondering what the Lord had in store for me. As I sat down, a familiar calm feeling came over me.

"This matters," I thought.

It quickly became very clear why I was led to this service, at this time, on this day.

At the beginning of the service, the youth choir performed a piece called Revolutions Cry.

"I could use a revolution," I thought.

The name of the service was the "Sunday Evening Connection."

"What was I desperate for, if not a connection," I thought.

The topic was "The Greatest Pain."

"Yeah," I reflected, "Great pain, I get."

The unison scripture was Mark 15:34 (NIV).

> And at three in the afternoon Jesus cried out in a loud voice, "*Eloi, Eloi, lama sabachthani?*" (Which means "My God, my God, why have you forsaken me?")

A whole sermon about excruciating pain, and feeling forsaken by God.

"Well, isn't that something," I thought, soaking in the relevance of the message.

The sermon actually started by explaining that the original meaning of the word "excruciating" was "of or by the cross." The pastor talked about the pain of Jesus on the cross. I thought about the excruciating emotional pain I was in and tried to put everything in context.

During that service, I became a student of the concept of pain. The pastor talked about the five aspects of pain—physical pain, emotional pain, the pain of abandonment, the pain of bearing sin, and the pain of bearing the wrath of God.

As I contemplated pain, I thought of a conversation that I had with my friend, Serene, who is a marathon runner. She was one of my inspirations as I trained for my first marathon—the Chicago Marathon in 1997.

One day I was complaining about how sometimes on long runs I would want to stop and walk, because I couldn't take the pain of exertion anymore. Serene, who was not especially religious, told me that when she felt like that, she liked to focus on how strong she could be, and on the fact that if she just kept taking the next step, she would eventually make it through. Her next comment humbled me. She said, "You're the one who is supposed to be religious—isn't that what faith is all about?"

Yes, it is, isn't it. "I guess you told me," I thought.

Why do I worry? If I say I'm a Christian, where is my faith?

The sermon asked the same question.

At that moment, I really had no idea at all where my faith was.

The pastor challenged us to think of the pain of Jesus on the cross when he thought his Father had forsaken him. "What pain did Jesus go through to save us?" he asked, "Much attention has been given to the physical suffering endured by Jesus. While this physical suffering was great, it is only a small part of a larger picture. Join us as we look at the pain of the cross—the greatest pain ever experienced."

Do I ignore the lessons of the crucifixion? What kind of Christian am I really?

"Not a very good one," I mused.

Verse after verse, he highlighted examples of Jesus' pain, and how he died to take our sins away. As the service ended, and the altar call came, the pastor said, "Maybe you are a doubter. Do you believe? Jesus calls us to believe."

The pastor mentioned the story of Doubting Thomas, found in John 20:27-28 (NIV):

> Then he said to Thomas, "Put your finger here; see my hands. Reach out your hand and put it into my side. Stop doubting and believe." Thomas said to him, "My Lord and my God!"

All I could think was, "Thomas, I feel your pain!"

* * *

Sometimes, pain, faith, and belief don't make the best bedfellows. My only hope after this week's worship service was that the next week would be better.

Week 18
Fighting Forward
Faith Community of St. Sabina

2:30 p.m. service, Chicago, Illinois

My best self cares about the children. Over the years, I have participated in many mentoring and tutoring programs: the Cabrini Green Tutoring Program, the Metro Achievement Program, and various other programs where I try, in my own herky-jerky way, to give back to my community.

One organization that I support is LINK Unlimited. LINK Unlimited is a wonderful organization that matches young students of color with sponsors. Those sponsors contribute to private school tuition for their students, and provide tutoring, mentoring, and a different perspective for students.

As part of the LINK program, sponsors and their students are invited to worship together periodically during the year. On this Sunday, my mentee, Bri, invited me to join her for this teen worship service. For the third time this year, my plan had been to attend the evening service at Chicago's Apostolic Church of God, but that plan didn't pan out. This turned out to be fine, as the teen service was at another well-known Chicago church, St. Sabina.

As I walked into the church, some young people greeted me and gave me the Teen Worship program. The theme for the service was, "Pressing into Maturity." As I entered the sanctuary, I pondered the irony of this theme—as the youth pastor and the teens probably thought it would be relevant only to them. Of course, any self-aware adult knows that we

80

are always pressing toward maturity, no matter how old we are and no matter how old we become.

Inside the sanctuary, I scanned the crowd. I saw a sea of faces of color, and a few white chocolate chips—since many of the sponsors for this organization are Caucasian, and many of the students and their families are African-American. I found my mentee in a group of her girlfriends. She made introductions, and then we found a seat to the right of the pulpit. I had fun watching her scan the church for her friends from different high schools, as this was one of the first gatherings of all the students since the beginning of the year.

One of the LINK students, Demarius, came to the microphone for the call to worship. He introduced himself as DJ Marvin. He was rapping the intro and reminded all of us that it was okay to have fun—even as you were preparing to hear God's word in God's house. He served as the MC for the service with a combination of confidence and composure that demanded you pay attention.

As he expertly spoke (or, rhymed) his piece, I contemplated the wisdom of youth. Each young person who approached the microphone to participate in the service spoke eloquently about his or her dreams and beliefs.

First, Jobari, a high school junior, did the opening prayer. Then came the gospel music, provided courtesy of Walt Whitman & The Soul Children of Chicago, a "world-class performance group with a single-minded purpose: to utilize music as the motivator and catalyst to inspire young people throughout the world to have faith in themselves, each other, and God."[19]

As I listened to the choir sing, I was shocked to realize I recognized one of the faces in the choir.

"Well, I'll be," I thought.

Front and center in the choir, singing his heart out was Rodney, one of my former students from an after-school program where I'd taught years before.

After studying improvisational comedy in Chicago for many years, I had the opportunity to co-teach a course with one of my acting and improv mentors, Dionna Griffin, Director of Diversity at The Second City. When she approached me and asked if I would like to teach an improv class with her, I jumped at the chance. I would be on The Second City's payroll (a dream come true for a wannabe comedian), but would be teaching for a nonprofit organization that offered Chicago high school teens innovative out-of-school activities. The classes would take place at a high school on Chicago's South Side.

I enjoyed it. Dealing with high school students was a challenge, but one that I welcomed. One of the first things I learned as an improviser and a performer was the importance of focus. I'll never forget my first improv class, where my fabulous instructor, Jean, very quickly let us know that this was a place where everyone's work would be respected. She made it very clear that we were required to focus both when we were performing and when others were. For a room full of people who were used to being the funny person in the room, always making commentary on whatever they saw around them, this was not the most natural way for us to operate. However, it was only by learning about focus and respect that all of us became better performers and team players, important lessons to learn if you aim to be on a stage creating great theater from scratch.

But the high school students we were teaching had complex issues on their minds. Focus and team playing wasn't always their priority or their strength.

Generally, it was a test of wills. Ms. Griffin and Ms. Bassey against the students. Who would win? When we encouraged them to focus, sometimes it worked and sometimes it didn't.

One afternoon, it really didn't work.

Rodney and his sister, Kina, were unhappy with another student, and throughout the whole afternoon, they were hurling insults at each other. Ms. Griffin and I were trying to be the mediators. At one point, I saw a fight breaking out. As I tried to restrain one of the students, I saw something out of the corner of my eye. In a split second, it hit me in the head.

Rodney had thrown a chair.

A hush came over the room. I was angry, sad, and tired. "Really?" I thought, "Was it okay to throw a chair and hit an adult in the head?" Why was I even in a place where that would happen?

All the students sat down and security arrived. They ushered me upstairs into a classroom and asked me what happened. I explained the sequence of events. One officer asked if I was okay, and I said yes. Another officer, who seemed like she did this every day, asked me if I wanted to press charges.

"Press charges," I thought, "Against a child?"

I started to cry right there—not because of the pain of being hit in the head by a chair thrown by a teen. But because I lived in a world where it seemed like it made sense to ask a grown woman if she wanted to press charges against a child for that action.

No, I didn't want to press charges.

This was not enough for the officer. "Are you sure?" she asked. "If you go home and change your mind, you can just call us and we will take care of it."

In no world, at any time, I thought, will I want to contribute to the entry of a child into the criminal system.

"I'm sure I don't want to press charges," I said.

"Please don't ask me again," I thought.

After this disturbing interaction, I was done for the day. When I went downstairs, I found that Dionna had dismissed the class. I talked with her briefly. We agreed that we were both going to go home and relax.

I remembered all of this as I listened to Rodney belt out gospel music in a prestigious children's choir. I thought about what a small world it was, and wondered what in the world he was doing in that choir?

I rubbed the back of my head in remembrance as the choir finished their selections, and a few students approached the microphone to share the unison scriptures for the service:

Angel, a high school sophomore, read one of my favorite scriptures, Philippians 3:13-14 (NIV):

> Brothers and sisters, I do not consider myself yet to have taken hold of it. But one thing I do: Forgetting what is behind and straining toward what is ahead, I press on toward the goal to win the prize for which God has called me heavenward in Christ Jesus.

La Mel, a high school junior, read John 15:16-17 (NIV):

> You did not choose me, but I chose you and appointed you to go and bear fruit—fruit that will last. Then the Father will give you whatever you ask in my name. This is my command: Love each other.

After they shared their chosen scripture, they each spoke a little of their truth. They explained what the scripture meant to them, and how it applied to their young lives.

I saw them, and remembered that I used to be them. I was always the youngest person in my classes at school, in activities, and in organizations that I joined. I often received recognition for my accomplishments, and became used to accolades that ended with the phrase, "especially at such a young age." Being the youngest, I suppose, became part of my identity.

Now, I am no longer the youngest. In fact, I'm older than many of my friends who have gone on to marry and start families. I receive no more age-based accolades.

What do you do when you cease to be the inspiring young person? How do you figure out how to adjust your self perception so that it does not rest on receiving recognition for what you have done at such as young age, but rather rests on who you are, how you deal with success and failure alike, and how you treat yourself and others?

How do you put age in perspective, realizing that you are always younger than some and older than others, and that you can be an inspiration at any age?

How do you change your life so that, "your life itself is a prayer," as my father always said it should be? What work did I need to do in my life so that I could sleep at night knowing that I was successful with that life goal?

All this contemplation, and the sermon hadn't even started.

A group of students presented a dramatic rendition focused on resisting peer pressure, and then Trina, a high school junior, approached the microphone to introduce the speaker.

The guest minister for the day was Reverend Will E. Hall. I was pleasantly surprised to learn that he was a youth minister at my home church, Trinity. By this time, I was beginning to miss Trinity quite a bit—it had been four months since I last attended a service there.

In introducing Reverend Hall, Trina explained that he had committed his life to helping others, sharing his belief that, "If he can help somebody every day, then his living is not in vain."

Anyone who has had to truly focus on living one day at a time may understand this approach. In getting through this, my healing year, I'd made a decision to do two things:

1) Breathe in and out every minute, every hour, until 24 hours passed and another day hopefully brought me closer to feeling better, and

2) Try to do something every day to help someone, a stranger, anyone, so that if anything happened and I should have to meet my Maker, I could say, "Yeah, I wasn't feeling my best, but I did try to do something to help someone, even through my pain."

I looked forward to hearing what Reverend Hall had to say.

The theme of his sermon was "Fighting Forward," and he shared that if we are in a time in our life where we are fighting with ourselves or with our situation, we might as well "fight forward."

He started with a scripture familiar to anyone who has ever been to my home church, Trinity, or any church in the African-American worship tradition, Isaiah 54:17 (NKJV):

No weapon formed against you shall prosper, and every tongue which rises against you in judgment you shall condemn. This is the heritage of the servants of the LORD, and their righteousness is from Me, says the LORD.

He shared that we are always fighting for something or against something. All of us are fighting to keep ourselves straight and balanced in the midst of everything that is going on. He also conceded, and I agreed, that some of us are really tired because we have been fighting for so long.

"I'm ALWAYS fighting with myself," I thought.

Fighting to achieve more and to work more effectively. Fighting to help others, fighting to help myself. Fighting to figure out how I could have done better, or done differently. Fighting to heal, and fighting to give myself a break.

No wonder I'm exhausted.

He shared the universal wisdom that everyone is longing for someone to listen to our stories in the midst of our fights and our struggles.

True.

He shared his experience, saying, "My God never leaves me or forsakes me when I'm going crazy."

Sounds like a good truth to lean on.

He shared that we would like to pick the time to fight, but that battles come at inopportune times.

Tell me about it.

Then came the thunderous words of encouragement:

"Don't run. God did not create us to run!"

People began to stand and applaud.

"Don't be scared. We should not be conditioned to be scared!"

More applause.

"Get your fight back! If you are fighting, it means you are valuable to humanity!"

Hands in the air, waving, testifying!

"Fight is about who is going to hold on the longest!"

Along with everyone else, I was on my feet, energized by his words. I was thinking, "BRING IT!" I'm here to get my fight back. I'm going to keep fighting and fight forward. I want to fight so I can be better.

"It is in moments of challenge that you find the courage to be yourself."

Amen!

"Thank you for the fight I'm fighting and thanks that the fight hasn't taken me out yet."

Thank you, Jesus!

"The biggest fight is about you and God. God is trying to pull you along and you are trying to stay back."

Yes, Lord!

"God is ready to give you what you are asking for, but you are stubborn in staying where you are."

Have Mercy!

As the sermon wound down, and the pastor moved from a spirit of loud encouragement to a quiet spirit of prayer, he reminded us all: "God is a God of progress. God moves at the right speed. Let God do what God wants to do."

Yes.

After the service, I went to say hello to Rodney in a room off the sanctuary where the choir members were gathering, changing back from their choir robes into street clothes, and preparing to leave the church. (I first scanned for any nearby chairs before approaching him.)

He immediately recognized me.

"Hi, Ms. Bassey," he said.

"You remember me?" I said.

"Of course," he said.

He went on to thank me for the influence I had on his life and admitted that he was a handful when he was in the after-school program that I'd co-taught.

"I was bad," he said, "And so were many of us in that after school program. But I have changed my life. I graduated from college, and now I'm focusing on my gift, my talent for singing."

I told him I was proud of him, and I was.

*   *   *

"Miracles do happen," I thought, as I left the worship service this week, "If you just keep fighting forward."

WEEK 19
IS THAT MICHAEL JACKSON PLAYING IN THE LOBBY?
CHURCH OF SCIENTOLOGY

11:00 a.m. service, Chicago, Illinois

The week before, as I sat in a very inspirational teen worship service in a church on the South Side of Chicago, I'd made a silent observation: I'd been leaning toward visiting churches that were very close to my own religious tradition. There was a reason for this. Because my grief was often preventing me from wanting to get out of bed early on weekend mornings, my worship choices were often limited to evening church services, many of which ended up being in traditionally African-American Christian churches. I'd made a mental note to expand my worship horizons. I needed to venture out and make a choice to worship somewhere that placed me farther from my comfort zone.

That's how I ended up at the Church of Scientology.

My many years in Chicago had found me living on the North Side, the Near West Side, and the Near South Side. I also spent a few years in Evanston. During some of my years, I was a member of a health club located not far from the storefront that houses the Chicago Branch of the Church of Scientology.

Today was the day that I would enter that storefront.

There were a few weeks during my 52-week journey, where I had to really clear my mind, open my heart, and approach an experience with as few pre-conceived notions as I could muster. This was one of those weeks. Anyone who has ever turned on the TV or surfed on the Internet has an opinion about the Church of Scientology.

The website for the Church of Scientology-Illinois invites everyone to, "Come in and find out for yourself what Scientology is and how you can use it to be happy and successful in life."

I decided to take a deep breath and do just that.

When I entered the storefront on North Lincoln in Chicago, there was a woman sitting behind a desk by the door. I told her I was there for the 11:00 a.m. service, and she looked at me confused, before saying "Oh! It's Sunday!"—suggesting to me that perhaps there wasn't really a regular service like in other places I'd worshipped.

Oh, boy.

She asked me to sign in and I did, but to be honest, I was hesitant to write down my full name and correct contact information (terrible, I know). I signed my name as "Pam Bass" (not proud of that, but it is what it is), left the contact information blank, reminded myself to keep an open mind, and walked in.

There was a flurry of activity in the location. It appeared as if they were setting up for something, which I assumed was the 11:00 a.m. service. Turns out, I was wrong. They were setting up for some other training or meeting in the front of the building, which I learned by reading a blackboard near the door.

Where was this 11:00 a.m. service going to take place, I wondered?

Not knowing exactly what to do next, I decided to make my way to the restroom as I waited for the service to begin. When I emerged, a man was waiting for me. He asked me if I was Pammy, which startled me a bit. How did he know who I was? He told me that he had spoken to me on the phone the day before when I called about the service, which made things a little less weird, but still . . . memorable. He told me that they would be starting shortly, and I could sit and wait in the outer room.

So I did.

As I entered the outer room, I found it amusing that Michael Jackson was playing on a radio somewhere nearby. "Why in the world is Michael Jackson's "Thriller" playing in the lobby of the Church of Scientology's building on the North Side of Chicago?" I thought.

"Wanna be startin' something . . . got to be startin' something . . ."

I chuckled, thinking, "Next time I go *so far* out of my comfort zone, I'm bringing a friend with me."

I was very aware that I was in a new, strange place by myself. I looked around to see where I could make myself comfortable and inconspicuous.

I spotted a couch covered in bags and jackets. A woman asked a young girl to help her move the stuff off the couch so I could sit down. Telling her I was fine, I perched on the edge of the couch. The young girl was about six or seven years old. She looked at me intently. (In my experience, sometimes young children who have not regularly been around Black people tend to stare. I generally give them a pass. They are kids, after all.) My hair was in long twists, which to some look like locs. I was imagining that perhaps she had never seen anything like that. But who knows why she was really staring at me.

I decided she would be my new friend. I introduced myself as "Pam" (again, the alias). I chatted with her. I asked her about her father, who was seated nearby, and her brothers, who were running around and crawling about the location. They were not much older than she was.

She was holding a book by L. Ron Hubbard, called *Learning How to Learn*. It appeared to be a children's book. "Children's books by L. Ron Hubbard?" I thought. I asked her if she liked the book. She said she was just looking at the pictures, which made me smile. Kids will be kids.

Whenever I enter a place of worship, or a community religious space, I'm always interested when I see kids. I assume that the parents responsible for them think that this religion, this way of life, is the best framework within which they can raise their kids. At every church, every family is doing the best they can by their children. I had to assume that this little girl's parents thought that the Church of Scientology was the best context within which their children could grow up to be productive, happy, individuals.

After some time, the little girl's mother—the woman who tried to clear the couch—came back and appeared to be somewhat frantically looking for someone to lead the service. Again, an indication that the service might not be as regular an occurrence as one might imagine. I wanted to say, "Hey, if there isn't really a service, I can go home," but I resisted the urge. I was there, and I wanted to know how this story would unfold.

Someone was located to lead the service. We were all guided to a small black room in the rear of the building, which looked like a film-viewing room. Inside the room was stadium-style seating so everyone could see the screen (which was not used during the service). There were about fifteen seats in the room, and about seven people in the service, including my young friend, her two brothers, her father, and myself.

The service started with the man at the front of the room saying, "What is Scientology? It is a new slant on life."

I buckled my virtual seatbelt, and prepared for the ride.

He continued by reading the *Scientology Creed*[20], which was written by L. Ron Hubbard shortly after the Church was formed in Los Angeles on February 18, 1954. It states what Scientologists believe.

When I was in the presence of a worship tradition that wasn't my own, I was careful about what I said, did, ingested, or professed. As I listened to the creed, I thought, "Well that sounds reasonable." I waited for what came next.

A discussion of personal integrity followed the reading. The sermon, titled, "What is Greatness," appeared to be a reading of a chapter out of a big black book. Upon later research, I discovered it was really an article called *What is Greatness,* by L. Ron Hubbard[21]. The article was read from beginning to end.

Much like my experience at the Saviours' Day event months before, some of what was being said made sense to me, and some parts were confusing.

For example, after the reading, the man leading the discussion shared a story about someone who was trying to help people by teaching them Scientology, but then somebody got killed, only it was not that person's fault.

I had no idea what that was about.

Then there was an invitation to love your fellow man, not hate them, and never desire revenge.

I thought, "That generally makes sense."

Suffice it to say, I was a bit perplexed by the whole experience.

At the end of the service, there was a prayer. I bowed my head and closed my eyes, but wondered if other's were doing the same. It appeared that the prayer was not a spontaneous one, but one being read from a Scientology text. In my heart, I said my own little prayer. I thanked God for the opportunity to be exposed to many different things, to seek his face, and to know that wherever I was, I was going to be safe, because God is everywhere.

Then, I listened to the *Prayer for Total Freedom*[22].

Nothing in the prayer seemed wildly out of the ordinary. I realized when I opened my eyes, that I was checking, "Hey is there anything about this prayer that I might not feel comfortable saying or praying?" When I came up with the answer no, I felt relief and contentment. I also felt slightly disappointed—mostly because I had not been able to immerse myself in the experience. Despite my best efforts, my guard was up.

I was very aware that this church had quite the reputation. I kept waiting for something out of the ordinary to happen. I kept waiting for someone to say something controversial.

After the speedy thirty-minute service was over, I was in the lobby looking over all the materials. The same woman asked if I had any questions. I really didn't. She asked if I was there to do a report or if I was there for myself. When I said I was there for myself, she lit up and asked me if I wanted to take a personality test.

Uh oh.

I'd heard about said personality test, and although I hesitated before deciding to complete it, I thought, "Well, what the heck?" Problems arose, however, where the test asked for my address, phone number, and other personal information, which I really didn't want to give to the Scientologists, or to anyone who wasn't my friend. I decided to start the test and make the decision later about the contact information piece. After twenty-five questions, I flipped over the document and realized there were hundreds of questions.

Too many questions.

I decided at that point I would take it with me and I might fill it out or I might not. As I left, I let the woman at the front desk know that I would take the questionnaire with me and fill it out at home. She said to me that I should just bring it back the next time I came, and that she knew I would be back.

I just nodded and smiled.

It is my understanding that further training would have been based on the result of that test, which, not surprisingly, I never ended up filling out. I imagine that is why I didn't really experience any of the stereotypically idiosyncratic behavior that one hears about Scientology in the media.

Few show you anything bad the first time you meet them. That, I think, is a pretty universal truth.

One thing that was a little curious was that directly after my time with the Scientologists, I made a decision to visit my home Church, Trinity, which I hadn't visited since January. I yearned for something familiar after the unfamiliar experience of visiting the Church of Scientology. I immediately drove South and caught the tail end of that Sunday's service at Trinity.

I would be remiss if I didn't share the reactions of others when I told them I visited the Church of Scientology in Chicago. As this year went by, I chronicled my journey on my Facebook page, posting only the picture of the church, the date, and the name of the church. Those who saw that I visited the Church of Scientology had some things to say:

- "Ooooh . . . details if you can. If there's a danger you'll go missing if you do share, I'll totally understand. Mum's the word."
- "Didn't know they actually had 'church.' Do tell."
- "Very interested in your thoughts on this experience!"

After I didn't post a response (as I generally didn't write much about each experience until I started writing this book in earnest), I received this comment.

". . . She's obviously still going through auditing."

Although I didn't know initially what auditing was, research revealed that "auditing is a unique form of personal spiritual counseling which helps people look at their own existence and improves their ability to confront what they are and where they are."[23]

The auditing comment prompted me to give a synopsis of my visit, which ended with the admission that I decided to visit my home church after my Scientology experience. The same friend posted the following response:

"Going back to your home church is a psychological response. Kinda like when you see something totally gross and feel like you have to shower. Be prepared to be hounded to the ends of the earth if you send the questionnaire in and also to just give them your wallet. Obviously I would be declared an SP."

I had no idea what an SP was (and heard no mention of it in my initial visit). Upon doing some research, I found out that an SP is a reference to "Hubbard's 'Suppressive Person' doctrine, in that any person that is perceived to impede—directly or indirectly—the expansion of Scientology is seen as 'criminal,' with no regard of how honorable are their motivations. If someone criticizes some intrinsically harmful Scientology practices, this person becomes a 'Suppressive Person' in Scientologists' worldview, regardless of how substantiated is their criticism."[24].

Another told me that his wife came close to being a cult specialist who worked with people trying to get out of cults, and she had told him numerous times that Scientology is a cult, nothing more or nothing less.

A favorite comment stated:

> "You gotta come to LA to really experience Scientology in its full flower. The temple they've constructed in Hollywood would put any mega-church to shame. And who knows, you might run into a celebrity . . . To be fair the woman that made my wedding dress is a Scientologist and she's totally normal. Apparently, the faith really helped her through a tough time and is really doing right by her kids. After hearing her account of it, I tried to be less quick to judge and give it more the benefit of the doubt. It still seems quacky to me, though."

The last comment took me from the City of Angels to Music City, where a friend posted:

> They have a huge building in Nashville and have cute college-looking people handing out sheets with questions like "Want a free personality test?" or "Want to know what you are really like?" or "How do other people see you?" during music festivals and football games, etc. Interesting techniques. Glad I had strong anti-cult psychology classes.

My response to the cult-related posts was this:

> I think when you are searching, any number of options can sound like a solution. It really takes knowledge of self, and knowledge of the people/organization/religion you are interested in so that you don't end up in a situation that ends up being wrong for you.

> I think the key for me during the whole 52-week journey was that I was not searching. I was not looking for a "replacement religion." I was not looking for a better way to worship, or a better way to be a better me, or the one true way to find God. I simply wanted to stand in as many places as I could where the people there believed they were in a place that was helping them to become who they were born to be, a place where they believed what they were learning or doing was helping them to move closer to God, and to deal with whatever hand life had dealt them—good, bad, or ugly.

*   *   *

Just because something doesn't resonate with me, doesn't mean that it can't resonate with many other people.

That may seem like a cop out, but I don't see any real value in adding my voice to the chorus of negative commentary about The Church of Scientology that already exists.

I did not comfortably find healing, connection or remembrance on my visit—despite my best efforts. I was too anxious about what I might find, or what might happen during the service.

It was clear, after my unique experience with the Church of Scientology this week, that it did not provide what I needed to help me through my life's challenges. But for others, apparently, it did. I hope they find what they are looking for.

Week 20
Be Optimistic
First Church of Religious Science

11:00 a.m. service, Chicago, Illinois

During my life, my parents sent me several daily devotional magazines as gifts. For years, my mother subscribed to the *Daily Word* for me, as well as the *Daily Meditation*. My father, however, subscribed to only one for me: the daily devotional for the Religious Science of Mind. Because this happened more recently (in the years just prior to my father's illness and subsequent death), I still have all of the issues that were part of that subscription, and still re-read them from time to time. On this Sunday, I was happy to visit the oldest Religious Science of Mind church in Chicago. This church started in 1919, and was housed in the same building as the well-known Water Tower Place mall. I walked in with my friend, Darnell, and he promptly sat down in a chair at the very back of the church—in a row of chairs on the wall. There were about ten rows of pews in the church, and there were about seven people in the entire church. I wondered why in the world we were sitting on the back wall like the church was packed to the gills, but I didn't want to rock the boat (as I was Darnell's guest). I sat back there feeling a bit ridiculous. Apparently, one of the pastors didn't understand our choice of seats either, and encouraged us to sit at the front of the church so, "we could contribute our positive energy to the service."

So we moved to the front.

I'm not really an optimist. A cynical optimist maybe. One of my favorite stories of how a friendship was forged came when I was playing a warm-up game during one of my improv classes at The Second City training center. We played a game called "I like people who." To start, we all sat in a circle of chairs with one person standing in the middle of the circle. The person in the middle would make a statement, such as "I like people who love chocolate," and everyone who also loved chocolate was required to get up and switch seats. There was always a spirited competition for seats, and in musical-chairs like fashion, there would be one person who was not quick enough to get a seat. Whoever was left standing had to make the next "I like people who" statement.

On this particular day, as we started the game, the person in the middle of the circle said, "I like people who are optimistic." Who doesn't, right? As that statement was made, everyone in the room stood up and began running around trying to switch chairs.

Everyone except me and one other young lady, Summer.

While everyone was running around, we made eye contact and started laughing. Not only were both of us not particularly optimistic, we were brave enough to admit it, in a world where optimism is heavily favored.

After that class, we started to chat, and we realized we had a great deal in common. To this day, Summer is one of the most hilarious, intelligent, wonderful people I have ever met—simply because we admitted that we were not unabashedly optimistic.

I grew up in a household that believed in positivity. One of the strongest religious inputs from my childhood was from Reverend Robert Schuller's ministry—and all he preached was positivity, power, and prosperity. I'm no stranger to it.

Much of it resonates with me. I do believe that you can create your own situation and that your attitude has an impact on your destiny. I am familiar with The Law of Attraction, and the idea that you can bring something into existence by thinking on it. I don't find it completely hokey.

At the same time, a little part of me is cynical to the point where I turn into a contrarian voice when I'm in the presence of those who believe it with no exception.

That is what was going on in the Science of Mind Church that Sunday morning. At first, the pastor seemed to me to be a bit of a caricature. He was elderly and had a great deal of energy.

A GREAT deal.

He moved around the sanctuary with high enthusiasm, speaking loudly, and gesticulating with his hands. Every once in a while he would perch one leg on a chair and look directly at someone in the audience, engaging with them in a one on one fashion.

I looked around to see if anyone else found this entertaining. I was certainly enjoying the showmanship of this extremely positive pastor.

The title of the sermon was "Subconscious Power. God loves you and so do I." The high energy delivery of the sermon was full of affirmations and meditations. For example, we all said, "I love God and God loves me" several times in unison. It reminded me of the days when I worked on Jesse Jackson's first presidential campaign and we all participated in the call and response:

> I am!
> Somebody!
> Up with hope!
> Down with dope!

And so on.

One affirmation in particular stated that, "God and I are unbeatable." I liked that one and repeated it to myself on and off in the weeks that followed the service.

And there were more. The pastor energetically shared the following thoughts:

- It's not a zero-sum game—you can be all that you can be, but others can also do what you do and become all they can be!

- You should say positive things to yourself! Write down all the positive things in your life and focus your thoughts and energy on those things! Take the highest thought you can think and concentrate on it!
- You have the ability to do whatever you want, but you have to make up your mind!
- It doesn't make sense to moan to Jesus about your problems. Jesus doesn't care! He has given us the tools to solve any issue, to make anything happen! Just make the command and the God within you will do the work!
- You need active right thinking, not just abstaining from wrong thinking!
- You should be actively constructivist and happy in your thinking!
- Nothing will keep you back except you!
- What we need is greater consciousness and greater power!
- Every time you think a thought, you are creating something!
- Let the triumphant joy within you surprise you!

None of these sounded far out and crazy. Some of these lifted my spirits! Although the message that every time you think a thought you are creating something can turn even a sane person into a basket case, (Oh no! I've thought so many crazy things. No wonder my life is full of dramedy!) for the most part, I can agree that these are positive teachings.

I listened to the pastor reminding us that we could do all things if we kept our consciousness on a high level.

We sang a Celtic Christian song that was familiar to me from my days as a member of the Fellowship of Christian Athletes in high school: "Lord of the Dance." The chorus sticks with you:

Dance, dance, wherever you may be
I am the lord of the dance, said he
And I lead you all, wherever you may be
And I lead you all in the dance, said he . . . [25]

After the song, we meditated.

Meditation is one clear spiritual practice in which I believe. Just saying the word reminds me of my father. He always asked that I try meditation, practice meditation, believe in meditation. This is mostly because he and I had very similar minds—always ruminating, always turning over something in our heads, always creating action/reaction models of whatever we happened to be thinking about at that time.

My father was the most brilliant person I have ever known. He remembered everything he ever learned. He could teach it to anyone, as well. I remember asking him questions just so I could be the student in his one-pupil classroom. With each lesson came diagrams. He would draw pictures upon pictures to help you understand the concepts he was trying to explain.

In one of the most difficult moments I remember as he was fighting the illness that would ultimately take his life, he was trying to explain to my mother and myself how he was feeling. In his typical fashion, he grabbed a piece of paper and a pen and started drawing one of his famous diagrams. Instead of one of his award-winning diagrams appearing on the paper, what he was drawing was gibberish. I think he thought he was drawing something intelligible, and my mother and I both allowed him to think that. It broke my heart, however, to see that the illness was taking not just his body, but also his brilliant mind. I still have that diagram, and I keep it to remind me that tomorrow is never promised.

When you have such an active mind, I humbly say, it is hard to get any rest. If you are always thinking about something, it's important to be able to find a moment to quiet your mind so that you can function in some realm of peace. Meditation, I believe, is one of the things that will afford me that kind of peace. It's a practice that isn't easy to start, continue, or commit to.

But it is worth it.

Anytime meditation was a part of a worship service that I attended, I thought of it as a gift, a treat, and a reminder of my father.

I began my foray into meditation in earnest while my father was still alive. I found a style of meditation called "Passage Meditation[26]," started by Eknath Eswaran, which requires that you memorize inspiring passages and repeat those passages as you meditate. This seemed a more likely way that I could successfully practice meditation. For me, meditating silently while focusing on my breath just left me chasing the ideas in my head like a kitten chases a ball of yarn.

The first passage I decided to memorize was Psalm 23 (KJV):

The LORD is my shepherd; I shall not want.

He maketh me to lie down in green pastures: he leadeth me beside the still waters.

He restoreth my soul: he leadeth me in the paths of righteousness for his name's sake.

Yea, though I walk through the valley of the shadow of death, I will fear no evil: for thou art with me; thy rod and thy staff they comfort me.

Thou preparest a table before me in the presence of mine enemies: thou anointest my head with oil; my cup runneth over.

Surely goodness and mercy shall follow me all the days of my life: and I will dwell in the house of the LORD forever.

The second passage that I memorized was a quotation from St. Teresa of Avila.

Let nothing upset you.
Let nothing frighten you.
Everything is changing.
God alone is changeless.
Patience attains the goal.
Who has God lacks nothing.
God alone serves every need.[27]

The final passage that I learned was the Prayer of St. Francis of Assisi:

Lord, make me an instrument of your peace.
Where there is hatred, let me sow love.
Where there is injury, pardon.
Where there is doubt, faith.
Where there is despair, hope.
Where there is darkness, light.
Where there is sadness, joy.
O Divine Master,
Grant that I may not so much seek to be consoled, as to console;
To be understood, as to understand;
To be loved, as to love.
For it is in giving that we receive.
It is in pardoning that we are pardoned,
And it is in dying that we are born to Eternal Life.[28]

I would repeat these three passages in my mind, and then start over with the first one, until forty-five minutes was up (yes, I used a timer). The idea was that the words and wisdom in the passages would then become part of my subconscious mind, and I would be able to call on them whenever a challenging situation came up in my life.

I committed to the daily forty-five minutes of meditation practice for a few months, and then tapered off. After my father passed away, I started again, and had a pretty good run of a few months until I began to take notice of the actions of some "takers" in my life. I had to ask myself—while contemplating why I kept meeting people who took more than they gave—whether it was wise for me to continue to meditate on a passage like the prayer of St. Francis of Assisi, which states, "For it is in giving that we receive."

I'm still working on this conundrum.

When the pastor at the First Church of Religious Science led us in meditation, he calmed down a bit. He caught my attention and earned my respect. I allowed myself to be blessed by his wisdom and the wisdom of the day. The pastor seemed to care. He said repeatedly, "I want to inspire you."

I wanted to be inspired.

After the meditation, the service continued. There were some familiar scriptures shared. First, John 16:33 (NIV):

> I have told you these things, so that in me you may have peace. In this world you will have trouble. But take heart! I have overcome the world.

Then, during the offering, the same verse, Luke 6:38 (NIV), that I have heard repeatedly at my home church, Trinity:

> Give, and it will be given to you. A good measure, pressed down, shaken together and running over, will be poured into your lap. For with the measure you use, it will be measured to you.

The whole morning reminded me of my father and my family, and it was a little surreal to be at the church with someone outside my family. All of it was familiar. It is what I grew up hearing. On one hand, I think it's great and I believe it all. On the other hand, it makes me feel like a failure because I'm unable to consistently implement all these tenets to create a life that is flawless and full of abundance, wealth, butterflies, and flowers.

I find a curious contradiction between messages that say, "God doesn't make losers," and the messages that I received over the years about my flaws, my need to fix them, and my need to generally achieve more. The result is a war between extreme positive teachings and severe inertia.

Does everyone experience this conflict?

Probably not, I thought. But this is my reality.

As I was contemplating this, the service took me to a very, very sad place. Emotional memories came rushing in as the pastor encouraged us to, "pray without ceasing," because prayer is the most practical way of healing. He reminded us that, "If you are sick, it is because you want to be sick."

Whoa.

Really?

Who wants to be sick?

Nobody.

Who wants to die of cancer?

Nobody.

What if you pray and pray and you remain sick . . . or if you die?

Then what?

What kind of comfort does this bring to someone who is sick or dying, or to someone who loves someone who is sick or dying?

None.

Apparently, on this day, unbeknownst to me, a highly publicized walk was raising money for an organization whose focus was to fight cancer. The pastor mentioned that he was not thrilled about the walk for cancer. He said first it should be on Saturday, rather than Sunday, so people could go to church and be inspired on a Sunday morning, rather than walking to raise money for a disease like cancer, which could be cured by means other than what traditional medicine could offer. Second, he mentioned his thoughts that raising money to fight cancer just meant that we were giving cancer power that it didn't deserve.

Well, my father died of cancer-related complications. This discussion just made me weary.

My father, I'm quite sure, didn't want to die of cancer. People don't choose holistic treatments over traditional Western medicine, or vice versa, because they don't want to live. They do their best to choose a treatment option based on the information that they have. Often it is complicated. In my opinion, to suggest otherwise is irresponsible and disrespectful to those who have to make these difficult decisions for themselves and their loved ones.

My father was a physician and my mother is a holistic health practitioner. My whole life has taken place at the crossroads of traditional and non-traditional methods of healing. Some of my favorite memories, in a post-traumatic stress syndrome kind of way, happened at these crossroads.

As the child of two very committed African parents, there was a laser focus on education and achievement, and less emphasis on social outings or development for me and my sisters. That played out in many ways, but one memorable arena where it played out was when it came to me or my sisters dating in any way, shape, or form.

During our teenage years, boys were the enemy, and that was something that was reinforced every which way, including when it came to our Junior-Senior Prom.

At our high school, the prom was open to all juniors and seniors, hence the name. My sisters and I were invited, but none of us were allowed to attend during our junior years. That was not okay with us, but what could we do?

What was I doing the day of prom my junior year?

Getting my first colonic with my mother.

I kid you not.

I remember being mortified on many levels. First, what fifteen-year-old needs a colonic? I have always been a little heavier than I needed to be, and I had very bad seasonal allergies when I was a child. I can't remember what the purpose of the colonic was—what ailment, perceived or real, was being addressed. As I lay on the colon therapist's table having an out of body experience, I just remember thinking, "All of my friends are getting their hair and nails done, and putting their final touches to their prom finery . . .

. . . and I'm getting a colonic."

That evening, I was inconsolable. My parents asked me what was wrong, and I just told them I didn't feel well, because what else would I tell them?

They were concerned, as parents are, and then had an impassioned discussion about what they should do to make me feel better. My father, coming from a traditional medical background, was suggesting specific medications that might help, and my mother was recommending herbal teas and vitamins.

I listened to this, flabbergasted in the way that only a teenager can be.

Hello! I just wanted to go to prom.

I ended up just going to bed and letting them work it out.

This is just a (somewhat) humorous memory from my adolescence, but this continued to play out into an arena where the stakes were much higher.

As my father's illness progressed, it became clear that there were many potential treatments. Prostate cancer is a very common disease, especially for Black men, and some believe that there is no reason why anyone should die from it.

My father lived with it for many years, and successfully. But when it became clear that the disease was progressing into more serious territory, there were many discussions about what approach should be taken—the more traditional medical approach, the more holistic non-traditional approach, or some combination of the two.

And what did I want?

I just wanted my father alive.

My mother thought healing was not out of the realm of possibility, "If we just did the right things."

And that is what the enthusiastic pastor of this church was saying, as well.

I don't know. My thoughts on the matter are complex. What I do know is that when a loved one is ill, everyone is trying to do the best they can by that person. The discussions that we had as a family about the decisions that needed to be made were difficult. Certainly, they were not as easy as the pastor of this church was making them out to be on this Sunday morning.

When all was said and done, I found myself thinking that when my 52-week journey was over, I may need to find more than one home church. A suite of churches? A church for every season? I'm amazed how each different worship service up until this point has spoken to the different sensibilities, experiences, and beliefs that I have, including the Religious Science of Mind church.

The choice of the solo music selection pretty much summed up how I was feeling as I left this service:

Day by day
Day by day
Oh, Dear Lord
Three things I pray
To see thee more clearly
Love thee more dearly
Follow thee more nearly
Day by day . . . [29]

*   *   *

Positivity has its place. Sometimes a message of "Get up and go!" can help. Sometimes the responsibility of making things happen for yourself can be so heavy that it keeps you in a place of inaction and despair.

Once I allowed myself to hear the messages of optimism shared in this week's Religious Science of Mind service, it did lift my spirits.

More importantly, this week reminded me that I need a balanced approach—understanding that I have the power to change my own condition, but remembering that the first step in claiming that power often requires me to be still, be quiet, and listen to inner wisdom.

WEEK 21
SEE YOU AT THE CROSSROADS
OLD ST. PATRICK'S CHURCH

11:00 a.m. Pentecostal Sunday Outdoor Mass, Chicago, Illinois

There is always something comforting about taking familiar streets back to your house. A gift is when you take a route that you've taken a million times, and you see something new—or something old in a new way.

Old St. Patrick's Church is a famous Chicago church. I'd heard of it before, mostly because they hold a giant street party every year, where, as legend goes, it is apparently a good place to find "the one."

On a late evening while driving home one day, I saw a sign outside the church that said, "Mass at the Crossroads." The sign gave a date and a time for the service. I pulled over to write down the information. When I arrived home, I made a note that I would have to come by and check it out.

I told my friend Darnell about this outdoor Mass. He had accompanied me on my visit to the church of Religious Science the week prior, and let me know that he wanted to come with me on another visit. His response was less than enthusiastic. "I went to a Catholic church growing up," he said, "My college was a Catholic university," he continued, "I've been to Mass a thousand times—the only thing that's different about this one," he concluded, "is that it's outside."

I disagreed, but respected his perspective. I decided that I would go to the Mass by myself, but that I would make this a two-service Sunday. We would meet after Mass to go to a service at a Buddhist temple.

On an unusually warm Chicago morning in May, I drove to Old St. Patrick's.

The streets around the church were blocked off, and at the crossroads of Des Plaines and Adams streets in Chicago was a huge stage, set off with what looked like thousands of flowers.

There were chairs in the streets south and east of the stage, and I claimed one for myself. My initial intuition about this outdoor mass was correct. There was something pleasing about watching the transformation of an intersection in downtown Chicago into a church. I was glad I had decided to come.

Taking it to the streets, indeed.

The beginning of the service was marked with songs and bells. As the liturgy for the Mass began, I had an epiphany:

I like the rhythm of a Catholic worship service.

Who knew?

The unusually warm Sunday morning turned into an extremely hot Sunday morning. This was especially ironic because the forecast for the day had been for rain. It had been raining all weekend. The congregation had prayed for the rain to stop so that weather wouldn't spoil the outdoor Mass. Well, it stopped raining—the power of prayer?—but then the heat was blazing!

Because I was excited to come out to the Mass, I'd neglected to bring my sunglasses. I found myself looking directly into the sun throughout the service—a powerful reminder that there are certain times in life when you realize you are not in charge. Sometimes, you just ask that it not rain and you end up with too much sunshine and too much heat. That's when you realize that God is in charge, not you.

If you are smart, you just try to roll with it. You welcome your lack of control.

Wearing a Chicago Blackhawks hat to celebrate our hockey team's recent Stanley Cup win—and to protect his bald head from the sun that was beating down on us—the pastor asked us repeatedly if we "got it." He explained the motivation for the outdoor Mass: to remind us that we need to take the church from within the four walls of the building out into the world.

I got it.

The pastor talked about how there was really nothing strange about an outdoor Mass, that we can be blessed by God's spirit in the most unusual and unexpected places. With that comment and the quote that followed, he articulated the reason why I embarked on this journey.

God is everywhere and there are people everywhere seeking his favor.

I had many weeks of proof that this was the case, and many more to go.

The homily for the day focused on the lessons from the story of Pentecost[30]. In the Christian tradition, in the days after Jesus ascended into heaven, there was a plentiful gathering of people praying, including Jesus' mother, family, and many of his disciples. As the story goes, there was an outpouring of the Holy Spirit. As the disciples preached to the crowds, by the miracle of the Holy Spirit, everyone heard the prayers in their own language. This caused quite a sensation, and thousands of people were baptized on that day.

With this story as a backdrop, we were encouraged to preach often—when necessary, in words. This message reminded me of the advice from my father that, "my life should be a prayer."

Throughout the service, the audio equipment was cranky. Sometimes we could hear clearly, sometimes not so much. The pastor did a good job of just moving things along regardless. In some ways, the service was more endearing because it didn't go off without a hitch.

Many shared their stories that morning. One woman talked about how, throughout her life, she craved the love of her father, who denied her. Then she found a surrogate father in the church, who gave her what her biological father couldn't. She talked about the love between a father and a daughter: how it can be taken away, but it appears in other ways.

In opening her heart, she took a risk, and it paid off.

One thing she said really spoke to me. She said, "Risk is God's aphrodisiac. If you want to get close to God, take really big risks," and that, "it's not about locking yourself in, it's not about keeping people out. It's about unleashing God's abundant love and God's abundant life in the world and in the lives of others."

We should welcome surprises.

Great advice.

*   *   *

As the service came to an end, I had a surprising thought. Although I find value in my 52-week journey, when I go to a temple or a shul or a coven or a masjid, I'll be a visitor. I have and will learn about other faiths, but Christianity is my home.

This 52-week journey is allowing me to experience my faith in a new, real way. My knowledge of myself as a Christian is increasing. There is a certainty that comes when you know something belongs to you: it's yours; you can lean into it and relax in it. I believe it happens along the way, when you journey down the path of self definition. It happened to me as I figured out what it meant to be African, African-American, Black. It happened to me in my professional life. It happened to me as I joined organizations and moved from being a newbie to an old-head.

It's apparently happening now in my spiritual life.

MID-DAY MEDITATION
ZEN BUDDHIST TEMPLE

4:00 p.m. service, Chicago, Illinois

After Mass and a little breakfast, I drove from downtown to the North Side of Chicago, where I met my friend Darnell for mid-day meditation at the Buddhist temple. When we walked into the temple, we took our shoes off and headed upstairs to the worship space. It was a sunny day, and the windows were open. Throughout the service I basked in the sun and literally heard birds sing.

In the front of the temple, there were mats, but Darnell and I sat in chairs. I waited for the service to start, focusing my intentions on being respectful of this place of worship as a visitor. My realization after the morning Mass that Christianity was my spiritual home put me in a frame of mind that allowed me to just enjoy the experience of being in the temple, without demanding much else.

Generally, during my 52-week journey, if there was a group reading, chant, prayer, or song, I would only participate if I felt like I could do so without being untrue to myself. I didn't call on any deities I'd just met that day, and didn't declare anyone to be the sovereign anything unless I understood and believed in what I was saying. This was a good, comfortable guideline and principle for me to follow. I find a great deal of freedom in *not* pretending to be what I'm not. I'm *not* Catholic, I'm *not* Buddhist, but I respect their traditions and I was honored to be allowed to be present as worship occurred.

On this day, I didn't really feel comfortable chanting anything that required me to ask something of Buddha (I don't really know Buddha like that), but anything that sounded like a universal truth from my world view, I chanted away.

The whole service was dedicated to meditation. As the teacher began to give us instructions about the meditation for the day, I thought of my father, who had been the first person to expose me to the practice of meditation. He meditated himself, and knowing that we both had the same kind of mind—always contemplating something, always analyzing, and thinking, and ruminating—he encouraged me to take up meditation in a serious and committed fashion.

In general, I'm convinced that I'll find peace in meditation. I really enjoy meditating. In fact, I delight in it. So why don't I do it? Why don't I just allow myself to commit to a regular practice?

Good questions.

No answers.

For all that I know about meditation, I'm always happy when I learn something new. On this day, as the teacher gave us the instructions for the meditation, she asked us to count backwards from 36 as a way to transition into a meditative state, concentrate and count outgoing breaths. Although the number 36 appeared to be a bit arbitrary, I complied, and was pleasantly surprised that it was indeed helpful.

36, 35, 34 . . . .

I thought: "Try that 36 trick later."

There were other instructions before meditation started. The teacher told us that when meditating, we shouldn't love or hate the thoughts that cross our mind, that we should just accept them and move on. She told us to "be without thinking, just completely be." To stop constant conceptualizing. To let the mind rest in its natural state. It takes time to trust the process. It seems deceptively simple.

We were reminded that, "the true nature of our mind is clear light," and that we shouldn't think of failure, just of execution; that there was no way to fail in the practice; that we should just learn not to resist what comes up in meditation, or in life.

The image of a tree in a hurricane was used—in a stormy situation, the trees that break are those that don't bend. The teacher urged us to learn to bend in the storm. In life, we should say yes, accept whatever comes, see that it is there, and bend if necessary.

Sound advice.

She shared thoughts about meditation and what it helps us do—keep our minds clear, our bodies stronger, and our reactions free. All who had gathered there on that sunny Sunday afternoon began to meditate together.

After we meditated for a bit, I heard a bell. It sounded like my text message indicator. My eyes flew open in terror that I had not remembered to silence my iPhone. It was, in fact, the bell they used to signify the end of the meditation. Thus, my emergence from the meditation was not exactly a gentle one.

After the meditation and the message from the teacher that day, there was an informative question and answer session. A group of young women from a nearby college had come to experience the service that day. I sat back and listened, learning from their questions.

The teacher shared that there were many schools of Buddhism. She noted the differences between Buddhist traditions that originated in India and the Tao influences that came from China.

She spoke to us of the "six perfections": generosity, ethics, patience, enthusiastic perseverance, concentration, and wisdom, and their places in Buddhist practice. She shared that Buddha was free from suffering, and discussed how the practice of compassion is important in Buddhism. When one of the students asked about one of the statues in the temple, she shared that the "statue was a role model."

During her discussions, she shared the significance of the lotus flower, explaining that lotuses—although they grow in muddy water—emerge with brilliance and beauty as they float above the water.

She assured us that, "we all struggle with ignorance," but we should, "be a light unto ourselves," while reaching for, "enlightenment for all beings, not just for ourselves, separately." I found myself feeling quite happy that I had the opportunity to participate in my worship double-header this Sunday.

We ended the afternoon by chanting together—speaking words from a chant that originated in Maur, India:

> Ocean mind.
> Mind is peace, love, and happiness.
> And so it is.

*   *   *

Today was a powerful reminder that meditation is easy, and difficult, and wonderful, and worth it. I look forward to any worship service—and any day in my life—where I am able to make space for quiet contemplation.

Week 22
It Takes a Village
Urban Village Church

10:30 a.m. service, Chicago, Illinois

The Spertus Jewish Center is an architecturally dazzling, glass encased building on the south end of Chicago's Michigan Avenue. For quite some time, I'd wanted to visit it because it was visually striking. I found it wonderfully ironic that my first visit there was for a Christian church service: The Urban Village Church, a Methodist church in Chicago.

Although my friend Jackie invited me, I had very low expectations. She had seen an ad for the church while riding to work on the train, and thought it might make a nice addition to my 52-week journey. It was apparent from their marketing strategy that they were a different kind of church. She was right, and they were different.

We made a plan to attend church and have brunch afterward. I was thrilled that I could leave my house and walk the few blocks to the Spertus Jewish Center for the service.

As I approached the auditorium where the service was to take place, I saw tradeshow-like standing signs with the name of the church on them and a catchy tagline:

Bold, Inclusive, and Relevant.

It was, apparently, a brand new church. As the jeans-wearing, bike helmet-carrying pastor began the service, he shared a little about the short, but intriguing, history of Urban Village. He answered the main question that I had as I contemplated the creation of a new church in a

city with many places of worship in it already. The church was started
when there was a realization that there were many new condos popping
up in Chicago's newly hip South Loop neighborhood, but not enough
new churches.

Fascinating. And true.

The first song the praise team chose to sing was one of my favorite South
African worship songs, learned at my home church. Often during this
journey, I would find that a song spoke to me and reassured me that I
was in exactly the right place of worship on that day. The song was,
"We Are Marching in the Light of God." We sang it in Zulu and in
English. The lyrics went like this:

> Siyahamba ekukanyen' kwenkos'
> Siyahamba ekukanyen' kwenkos'
> Siyahamba, siyahamba, oh!
> Siyahamba ekukanyen' kwenkos'

> We are marching in the light of God.
> We are marching in the light of God.
> We are marching, marching, oh!
> We are marching in the light of God.[31]

I was immediately excited and receptive after we sang this song. It
was especially relevant since I was preparing to head to South Africa
in the coming week for the World Cup—the first one on the African
continent, and my first trip to an African country other than Nigeria.
It felt like a sendoff and a blessing.

The next song was one that I also learned at my home church. The
lyrics:

> Woke up this mornin' with my mind
> Stayin' on Jesus
> Woke up this mornin' with my mind
> Stayin' on Jesus
> Halelu-Halelu-Halelu-jah[32]

The singing of familiar songs put me quickly at ease, and I found myself thinking about the impact of music on the worship experience and how much the musical experience at my home church meant to me.

Music had been a great part of my healing journey, as well.

At this point, it had been months since my father and grandmother had passed away, and months since my relationship ended. Often, there were still mornings when I woke up crying—missing my father, thinking about my grandmother, and missing my ex and just being sad in general.

This morning had been one of those mornings. When I woke up, I decided that I wanted to hear some music that sounded like I felt. I found myself listening to REM, "Everybody Cries," and bawling into my laptop as YouTube blared on. But I remembered the lesson from my various worship experiences, and the place that great music had in some of them, and decided to see if I could change my mood. I searched for some gospel songs that I knew would make me feel better. And it worked! After thirty minutes of songs, I felt uplifted and ready for the day. I marveled that I had not tried this before.

The songs I listened to were:

- "Sometimes You Have to Encourage Yourself" (sung by Donald Lawrence)
- "Thou Art a Shield for Me" (sung by Byron Cage; this was a favorite of mine based on Psalm 3)
- "His Eye is on the Sparrow" (sung by Lauryn Hill, from the Sister Act Soundtrack)
- "It is Well With My Soul" (sung by Wintley Phipps)

Then I branched out and found some secular music to raise my general level of optimism:

- "I'm the Greatest" (sung by R. Kelley)
- "One Day" (sung by Akon with Matisyahu)
- "Yes We Can" (sung by Will.I.Am)

The last selection, which was a song from the 2008 presidential election, made me think again of my father, but within a happy context. My father and I shared a love and enthusiasm for the exciting candidacy of our now first Black president, Barack Obama. Throughout the election of 2008, we would share stories of volunteering—me travelling to different places to campaign, and him doing the same—participating in phone banks, hosting college-age volunteers in the basement of my parents' house, and hosting events where he would invite neighbors to watch debates, providing "cookies and Coca-Cola" to those who showed up.

The crowning glory of this passion we shared was that we were able to both be in Washington, D.C. for the inauguration. By this time, it was beginning to be apparent to me that he was not moving as fast as he once had, and that was a foreshadowing of things to come. But I was glad that he was able to see President Obama be sworn in, especially because of the work we both did as volunteers for the campaign.

I always believed Barack Obama would be our 44th president—even when no one else did. But the tears that came at 10:00 p.m. Central time, November 4, 2008, when they announced that he actually won— Wow. I don't know where they came from, but I'm glad I was finally able to let go and cry them. I had obviously been holding them for a long time.

A memory of hope. Songs of hope.

By the time I was done with my little musical pep rally, I was up and going for a run. My best me had been awakened and I was able to jump-start my day so it didn't end up being sad.

I thought of this as I listened to the music at Urban Village that morning. I had an overwhelming feeling of home in the church, which was unexpected but delightful.

Then it was time for the passing of the peace.

This is a very common portion of many different worship traditions, acknowledging your neighbor instead of worshipping in silence and anonymity. As the pastor introduced this part of the service, he spent quite some time talking about how awkward this can be.

Maybe a little too much time? Or maybe, because I'd spent so many weeks doing a whole lot of worshipping with strangers-who-became-friends, I didn't really think that meeting new people had to be awkward.

He won me back over as he stated that, for those who found this weird, they should, "Imagine the hand you touch is the hand of God."

I liked that.

After the passing of the peace, it was time for meditation.

Any time there is meditation, I'm happy.

It was a neat meditation—the pastor called it a "gift of silence," which I found to be a delightful description. Seldom do we allow ourselves to receive or appreciate such a gift.

Our focus for the meditation was, the pastor explained, a chant from the islander community in Scotland. The words were:

Maranatha, Maranatha, Come Lord Jesus, come.

The contemplative chant set the tone for the rest of the service.

We also were invited to recite the Lord's Prayer. The instructions were that we should, "say the Lord's Prayer in whatever way we were comfortable saying it." The result was not really a recitation in unison, but rather everyone saying it under their breath in slightly different ways, at the same time.

At this point, my realization was this: churches that are more standard in their liturgy or worship traditions serve as a foundation. There wouldn't be churches to invite you to "bring your tradition" and embrace it, if most hadn't had a less loosey-goosey experience at some point.

I may not have even known the Lord's Prayer if I hadn't been raised within some tradition that thought it important that I should learn it. Perhaps, you can't create your own hybrid type of worship service, unless there are pieces and parts of traditional worship services that people bring to the table.

Perhaps.

I just wondered if it would be extremely difficult to start believing in God as an adult if you hadn't had some training or exposure as a child, even if it was in a tradition that you would ultimately reject.

The pastor delivered a very hip, very now sermon, complete with references to Facebook and Twitter. It had a global vibe— he mentioned various ministries all over the world, invoking the scripture, Acts 1:7-8 (NIV):

> He said to them: "It is not for you to know the times or dates the Father has set by his own authority. But you will receive power when the Holy Spirit comes on you; and you will be my witnesses in Jerusalem, and in all Judea and Samaria, and to the ends of the earth.

Be a witness . . . to the ends of the earth . . . .

In his sermon, he reminded us that we are called by God to go beyond our comfort zone to give voice to the voiceless. It was clear that there was a vision of this ministry to have impact above and beyond this auditorium in the South Loop of Chicago.

He provided a perspective on the directive to "Go Green."

He asked that, after the service, we all look at the tags on our clothing and write down where our clothing was made. He encouraged us to think of what we buy and how it was made.

I contemplated this as he challenged us: "Is the shirt you are wearing made by someone who is being yelled at? Who is being abused, or working their fingers to the bone to support their family? If so, what kind of energy is in that fabric?"

I never thought of it quite like that—that I might want to make sure I have the best energy in the things around me. It was a new spin on a reason to consider buying things that are fair trade. We are all interconnected, all of us in the world.

As we took a decidedly organic version of communion, which incorporated chunks of sourdough bread instead of garden-variety communion wafers, the song we sang was called "Oyahea Hallelu," by Rickie Byars-Beckwith:

Oyaheya

I am listening to the music
of the Wholly Holy Spirit
Oh what a song God is singing
I will listen all day long
I will listen all day long
Oyaheya oyaheya oyaheya hallelujah
Oyaheya oyaheya oyaheya hallelu oyaheya hallelu[33]

The service ended with us singing Bob Marley's "One Love," and I had a single, solitary thought.

I'll be back.

* * *

As the service at Urban Village ended, I thought back to earlier, when I was sad. I was pleased that I was feeling better. Isn't that one of the purposes of church? Of worship? To help you connect with the Spirit, remember who you are, and feel better? I thanked God for the peace that I felt.

I found myself getting excited about this church and what it would mean to be a part of it. I never thought of this journey as a "shopping expedition" for a new church or a new faith. I figured I would just attend the services that called to me and see what was revealed to me. It was very cool to think that I might be able to join in a new effort to worship the Lord, in a new place, in a new way.

At this point in my journey, I was really still processing my time at my home church, Trinity. My home church did a great deal to help me become comfortable with my African blood, history, and culture. It was my cultural and spiritual foundation as I became a real, live adult. I'll always feel at home at Trinity. But is it my future?

This remains to be seen.

WEEK 23
SEEK ME WITH YOUR WHOLE HEART
APOSTOLIC CHURCH OF GOD

9:10 a.m. service, Chicago, Illinois

There are several well known African-American churches in Chicago. My home church, Trinity, is one of them. Another one, Apostolic Church of God, is where I found myself this week.

A friend from college, Sharisse, suggested that we attend the 9:10 a.m. service. She knew the woman who was preaching that morning. She and I had been trying to get together for weeks. It seemed like the perfect opportunity to visit a new church with an old friend. I'd planned to visit Apostolic several times and was unable to do so for various reasons. I was happy to finally find myself in a pew.

I must say, I didn't and don't understand why the service started at 9:10 a.m. Initially, I thought it might be a reference to some Biblical verse that was from chapter 9, verse 10. This theory comes from the answer I received when I asked why my home church had prayer service on Wednesday evening at 7:14 p.m. I was directed to 2 Chronicles 7:14 (NIV):

> If my people who are called by my name, will humble themselves and pray and seek my face and turn from their wicked ways, then I will hear from heaven, and will forgive their sin and will heal their land.

That made sense. But 9:10 a.m.? Not so much. And when I asked someone at the church, I was told, "That's the way it's always been."

Fair enough.

From the beginning, the service felt like home. The African-American worship experience is one that I became comfortable with from the time I attended what was called simply "Black Church" at Stanford University in Palo Alto. The rhythm and cadence of a Black church service is familiar to me—starting with contemplation and music, moving through the collection and communion, and then to prayer, the sermon, the altar call, and the benediction.

As the service began, the leader of the praise team reminded us that, "There's nothing like singing Hallelujah!"

Having gone to many churches where there was media involved—lyrics to songs being projected up on huge screens behind the pulpit, or PowerPoint slides being shared for the congregation's reference—I found it refreshing to note that there was nothing like this here. On the stage was simply a group of singers with microphones.

Many Black churches simply have a high volume of sound during their services. There's no real way to explain the shouting, testifying, and signifying in any other way. This church was no different. The volume rose quickly.

I remember talking to my father about a visit to an African-American church in our neighborhood. "It was LOUD," he said, "Really, really loud." This made me laugh at the time. He was incredulous that the volume was really necessary. It was new to him, but having gone to many Black churches, I know the loud preaching style. I don't necessarily feel pressed when I have people screaming at me in a church.

As this journey continued, I found myself drawn to quieter, more contemplative services. I wondered if this was a transition in my worship style. I still appreciated a loud Black church service, but my soul was fed in a different way when the volume of the service wasn't so high. I wondered what that meant for what I might choose after this journey is over. I may be done with loud church . . . or maybe my spirit just needed more silent contemplation and meditation as I rode through this healing portion of my life and into whatever is coming next.

We'll see.

I looked around the sanctuary and saw Black families—men, women, and children. Every time my eyes landed on an older Black man, I thought of my father. This is something that happens a great deal these days. As I walk through life, I see older Black men and think of my pops. Especially if it is clear to me that they are African. Sometimes a tear comes to my eye. I say a quick prayer for each of them—hoping that they have friends and family that love, comfort, appreciate, and celebrate them.

The service moved right along at an impressive clip, which was notable because often, when I was looking for shorter services, I didn't assume I'd find one in an African-American church. Black church services are sometimes lengthy.

During the announcements, I had a moment of levity when a couple stood up and announced they were getting married. They gave the time and location for the service and the reception. When they said, "All are welcome," I thought, "Well, heck, I should jot down the details for the nuptials, they seem like nice people and they just invited me to their wedding!"

From all the applause and celebration, it was clear that the church community must know these two well. There are several ways that people choose to pass time to get through this life. Becoming a part of a community that means enough to you that you would invite everyone at the church to your wedding is certainly one way to do it!

Throughout my 52 Weeks of Worship, many asked me what means I was using to capture my experiences. Generally, at the beginning of the service, I would grab the bulletin, like any other worshipper, and I used that bulletin to take notes. I didn't want to be disruptive by taking pictures in the sanctuary—or even more disruptive trying to capture video of some sort. I did want to experience each service as much as I could, rather than focusing primarily on documenting it.

As I flipped through the bulletin looking for a place to write, I saw mention of a scripture that took me back and made me smile. The scripture was Matthew 16:24-26 (KJV):

> Then said Jesus unto his disciples, If any man will come after me, let him deny himself, and take up his cross, and follow me.

> For whosoever will save his life shall lose it: and whosoever will lose his life for my sake shall find it.

> For what is a man profited, if he shall gain the whole world, and lose his own soul? or what shall a man give in exchange for his soul?

Remember yearbook quotes? Some people chose lines from their favorite movies, and some (like myself) chose sappy but somewhat inspirational quotes. My senior quote in my yearbook was:

> You can't see the sunshine until after the rain
> And you can't feel the joy until you weathered the pain.
> For life is a mixture of laughter and tears
> That brings joy and laughter to all of your years.

Even the adult me, who still likes inspirational quotes, finds this to be somewhat corny. It was even less impactful because the yearbook committee only published the first couplet of the quote.

However, a classmate, Angela, chose a quote that has come back to me, repeatedly, over the years. It was a portion of the scripture in the bulletin, Matthew 16:26 (KJV):

> For what is a man profited if he shall gain the whole world and lose his own soul?

I remember reading this as a teenager and thinking two things. First, that it was weird that Angela would choose a Bible verse as her senior quote, instead of something witty and hip (and ultimately forgettable). Second, "What did that verse mean?"

At the time, I didn't understand what it meant, but now I do. You have to decide what is important to you. Understand that everything has a price. What price is too high? If you decide you want it all, will it be worth it if you have to sell your soul to get it?

Another biblical story that I didn't understand in high school was the story in Exodus where Pharaoh did not want to free the Israelites from years of slavery. A well-known phrase from that story has Moses telling Pharaoh several times, "Let my people go." Each time, Pharaoh comes close to letting the Israelites go, but then he changes his mind.

The phrase I found challenging in this story comes every time Pharaoh decides to free the Israelites: "God hardened his heart." Then Pharaoh changes his mind and decides he can't do it.

What is this weird dance between God, Pharaoh, and Moses, the teenaged me wondered. How did it happen that someone wanted to do the right thing, but then God hardened his heart so he didn't do it, then terrible things happen to him and his people over and over again?

Ten plagues: water turning to blood, frogs, gnats, flies, diseases on livestock, boils, hail, locusts, darkness. Then the death of everyone's firstborn.

Why didn't Pharaoh choose to do the right thing? Why did he let his people suffer so much pain? What was this "hardening of the heart," and was it really worth it? Why did God cause it?

It wasn't until I lived a little that I saw I had much in common with Pharaoh. Sometimes I too refuse to do what I need to do until there are present-day plagues that appear in my life.

Sometimes it's not easy to do what you are supposed to do.

The older women in the congregation were passing Ziploc bags of hard candy and mints through the pews during the service. A woman approached the microphone to sing a solo during offering time. Before she started, she shared that she had been going through a rough time in her life. She had experienced the death of a loved one, which of course made my ears perk up. She shared that she had been praying on a particular piece of scripture, Joshua 1:5 (NIV):

> No one will be able to stand against you all the days of your life. As I was with Moses, so I will be with you; I will never leave you nor forsake you."

All I could think was, "Wow."

What an impact that verse had on me. She spoke of being in a rough time in life, but trusting that you were not alone, and a feeling of gratitude washed over me.

She then sang a song with equally impactful lyrics. The name of the song was "In the Waiting," and the first lines of the song caught my attention:

> Pain
> The gift nobody longs for, still it comes
> And somehow leaves us stronger
> When it's gone away[34]

The remainder of the song's lyrics were equally powerful. After the song, it was sermon time. The speaker for the day was Sister Tea Poseris.

The content of her sermon was ironic, given the way I had been spending my worship time this year.

She spoke about how people were abandoning religion to focus on spirituality. She mentioned an acronym: Spiritual, But Not Religious (SBNR), and expressed her opinion that this was not a preferable way to live, that choosing a "have it your way" or "do it your way" brand of worship would only lead to confusion, and that the one true way was to choose Jesus.

Now, I'm a Christian, and was sitting in a Christian church. This sermon didn't surprise me.

However, given my current journey, it seemed that she was telling me that I was wasting my time. Others had shared their concern with me at the beginning of this journey. When I told a friend about my journey, she asked, "Why would you do that? That's shackin' "—referencing a commitment-phobic approach to spirituality, where you try a bit of this and a bit of that, but never make a decision about what you believe.

Both the speaker and my friend thought that perhaps I was looking for God in all the wrong places. I disagree. I was looking for and finding God everywhere.

She completed her sermon by encouraging us with a Bible verse from Jeremiah 29:13 (NIV):

> You will seek me and find me when you seek me with all your heart.

Seek me with your whole heart. I feel very confident God knows that is exactly what I'm doing.

* * *

My grandmother used to say, "If you lose something, and you don't look everywhere for it, you are really not trying to find it." After this service, I recommitted to searching for God everywhere. Why would I limit my journey and only look in certain places?

When the speaker said, "Jesus can't be side by side with Buddha . . . you must decide," I was skeptical. I'm not sure I'm willing to limit God that way. I believe that a God who can put a connection to Jesus in my heart can certainly speak to someone else through Buddha, or through anyone else, for that matter. That may be naïve or noncommittal, but that is what my heart currently tells me.

WEEK 24
DON'T PLAY WITH FIRE
MOUNTAIN OF FIRE AND MIRACLES

All morning service, Surelere, Lagos, Nigeria

Never had I been to Africa more than once in a year. Never had I been to any other country in Africa besides Nigeria, where my parents were born and raised, and where the majority of my extended family resides.

Until this year—a year of firsts in many regards.

This year, for the first time, the World Cup was to be held on the African continent. I felt that I had to be there—for myself and for my father, who was a soccer fan and a true African man.

It was also the wedding of my cousin, Enimien. I had to be there.

The wedding took place at Holy Cross Cathedral, right in the middle of Lagos, Nigeria. There was a full Mass at the wedding. I thought about counting it in my official count of places of worship for this year, but decided against it because I spent most of my time focusing on family and the festivities rather than the worship experience.

After the wedding, I just had one task to complete before leaving for South Africa for my World Cup adventure—to find another church to attend. You might think that by this point, I wouldn't have to negotiate with myself to get myself to a place of worship.

You might think.

Just like any sinner or saint, I still found reasons to maybe not show up at a place of worship, to maybe take a weekend off. I did want to go to one of Nigeria's well-known gigantic, Pentecostal churches. I had asked one aunt to take me to her church, but then I didn't connect with her at the wedding. And I just didn't feel like being a burden to the aunt and uncle who were hosting me, and would have to arrange transportation for me. I decided that it might be okay if I didn't go to another service in Nigeria.

Excuses, excuses.

Later that day, a cousin and his wife stopped by my aunt and uncle's house. As we were talking, I asked if I could go with them to church the next day. They agreed, and I figured I was all set.

Or not.

The next morning, it was raining.

Hard.

If you have seen the roads in Lagos, you will understand why the rain became an issue.

My cousin sent me a text message in the morning letting me know that the streets by his home were flooded. They would be unable to pick me up. Things in Nigeria are sometimes just a little more difficult than your average day in Chicago.

Fair enough, I thought, maybe it's a sign. I just won't go to church.

Yes, I still had thoughts like that—even halfway through this process.

My Uncle George, who was dressed and ready to go to his church, saw me loitering around the house and asked me what I was doing. "Aren't you going to church with Tosin?" he asked.

"They can't get here to pick me up because of the rain," I explained.

"Do you want to come with me?" he asked.

Well, I considered that as well, but seeing as I'd already been to his church in April, I didn't feel like I could or should attend his church a second time. There were many other places of worship in Lagos that I could visit.

I tried to explain this to him. I told him that I'd planned to go to church with two other aunts, but I hadn't connected with them, and blah, blah blah, I rambled, not making much sense.

He laughed (in a "What the heck is wrong with this one?" kind of way), said okay, and called my aunt. When he hung up with her, he told me that she was coming to get me to take me to her church. Then he left to go to his church.

Uncle George gets things done.

I thanked him, went upstairs to get ready, and when I came back down, my cousin's friend Jasper, who is from Sweden, was waiting in the foyer of the house.

"I heard you were going to church, so I thought I might join you," he said.

Now, I knew that we were going to a church that might not be the type of church that he expected. I think he expected to go to my Uncle George's church, which was a comparatively mellow Anglican church. Instead, we were headed to the Mountain of Fire and Miracles Ministries. The website for their international headquarters describes the church as:

> ". . . a full gospel ministry devoted to the Revival of Apostolic Signs, Holy Ghost fireworks, and the unlimited demonstration of the power of God to deliver to the uttermost."[35]

Holy Ghost fireworks?

The website for the Chicago-based branch of the same church describes the Mountain of Fire and Miracles Ministries as "the Domain of total deliverance and Heaven Shaking Prayers."[36]

Heaven Shaking Prayers?

I was not sure that Jasper was ready for Holy Ghost fireworks and Heaven Shaking Prayers, but what was I gonna say? No, you can't go?

Although African blood runs through my veins, I'm well aware that it doesn't take a rocket scientist to look at me and tell that I'm American. It may seem odd, but I'm clear that I appear to be American, and when I open my mouth, all doubt is removed.

But at least, I'm Black.

I like to think when I throw on some African attire and keep my mouth shut, I have a chance of not drawing attention to myself.

No chance of that, I thought, when I'm rolling with my cousin's friend.

I knew we were headed to a church that housed thousands of individuals in an enormous area, covered by tents. I was prepared for an overwhelming and unforgettable experience.

Even with my advanced knowledge of what we were in for, I was still amazed by what I saw when we arrived.

I saw thousands of worshippers in colorful African attire, praying loudly and fervently. The frenetic group energy electrified the massive tent, as the pastor's voice blared over loudspeakers. There was a sea of plastic chairs as far as the eye could see, but no one was sitting down. Everyone was on their feet, praising and worshipping. It didn't take long to realize this was serious business. These were believers.

The worship space was enormous. It was as if a little town all decided to come together to pray at the same time in the same place.

Because we were late, we had to walk to a different part of the site to find seats.

We walked. And walked. And walked. And people watched us as we walked.

I wanted to take pictures of this amazing gathering of people, but I had to remind myself of two things:

1) Blending was important, and

2) This was, in fact, a place of worship. A giant place of worship, but a place of worship nevertheless. Respect was due.

Jasper, however, had no such issues to deal with. He didn't hold back from whipping out his camera and taking pictures openly.

People started gesturing toward us, obviously trying to get Mr. Camerama to stop with the photo shoot, but he didn't seem to be fazed.

Pretending that everything was okay, I just kept walking behind my aunt. I said a few prayers myself that no one became more active in their opposition to their place of worship being turned into a tourist attraction.

We finally found a place to sit, and my aunt told me that we had missed most of the service, which had started at 7:00 a.m. By this point, it was about 11:00 a.m.

I figured, correctly, that there was still plenty of time for me to get a sense for how the service was going to go. We were there for about two more hours.

It was loud, but not in the same kind of loud that I experienced in African-American churches.

The loud here came from the multitude of people energetically repeating prayers and affirmations, in unison.

The congregation spoke the prayers and affirmations in English, but also in Yoruba, a Nigerian language.

People held pictures of their loved ones as they prayed. Hands were outstretched to the heavens. Tears rolled down some people's faces. People were shaking and swaying. The energy in the place put to shame anything I'd experienced as a child when my family went to visit Ernest Angley, a well-known televangelist.

I once served as a security guard at an *NSync concert (yes . . . long story). There, I saw teenage girls screaming and crying with frenetic energy. The level of energy here was close to what I was feeling on that day as I watched young girls swoon at the sight of that beloved boy band.

But these folks still had that experience beat. By a long shot. These people. Were. Not. Playing. Around.

Here, the pastor or prayer leader would share a piece of scripture or a phrase, then everyone would repeat it with energetic hand gestures and head motions, like their lives depended on it.

The pastor would say something like, "My enemies, hear the word of the Lord. Where you have knocked me down shall be my point of breakthrough. Say Amen seven times."

The response was rapid fire. Thousands said Amen in unison, seven times, shaking their heads and making rapid hand gestures.

Amen! Amen! Amen! Amen! Amen! Amen! Amen!

There were prayers hailing the coming of breakthroughs, and endless mentions about "my star," which I didn't really understand.

The call: "Every yoke upon my star, break."

The response: Break! Break! Break! Break! Break! Break! Break!

The call: "Powers of witchcraft over my star, die in the name of Jesus."

Witchcraft?

The response: Die! Die! Die! Die! Die! Die! Die!

Die?

There were also many references to fire, which I guessed made sense, as we were at the Mountain of Fire and Miracles Ministries.

"My days of greatness start by FIRE."

FIRE! FIRE! FIRE! FIRE! FIRE! FIRE! FIRE!

These worshippers were not just about phoning it in. There was no way that these people could pray these prayers unless there was a deep belief and conviction regarding what they needed to do about what was going on in the world.

When the pastor said, "It is these prayers that affect the lives of Nigerians all over the world," who was I to really debate that?

When life is hard, are these types of energetic prayers required? When I see people praying like this, I realize how little I might really be doing with my sometimes lazy, half-asleep praying.

When I told my mother about the church experience, she said, "It's just affirmations, brought to a level the people can understand."

I don't know. It was not just Jack Handey's Deep Thoughts, or "I'm good enough, I'm strong enough, and darn it people like me." This was hard core.

Say what you want, but I was reminded in the week following this church visit that this type of corporate religion was nothing to play with.

Following my general guidelines not to participate in any manner of worship with which I didn't feel comfortable, I didn't participate fully in the prayers and affirmations. I did pick one or two that seemed a little less extreme, and let's just say that there was one that didn't fit that description.

Towards the end of the service, the pastor presented the following prayer to the congregation:

"Evil monitoring power assigned against my star, receive blindness."

"Receive blindness?" I thought. What does that even mean? I even got a kick out of thinking about which "evil monitoring powers" should be the focus of this scary energy. Anyone who has ever been through a breakup may understand what I was considering!

I chose not to repeat this prayer . . . until I was in South Africa with my cousins. I was telling them about my experience at the church, and one cousin, who isn't particularly religious, found this affirmation to be . . . funny.

As we talked about the nefarious ways we could use this affirmation (especially since we were watching World Cup Soccer and trying to help our favorite teams win), we ended up laughing hysterically and screaming "Receive blindness!" when the opposing team stole the ball, or approached the goal. We meant no harm, but were just being silly and taking the prayer out of context into a different realm of comedy and sportsmanship.

Hey, I never said I was perfect.

Now, you can call me crazy if you want, but the next day after our laughapalooza, I experienced my very first eye infection ever.

No joke.

Both of my eyes started out itching, then they started to ooze a white pus-like substance (I know, gross). By the time the evening came, my eyes were completely swollen shut.

I couldn't see clearly for two days.

All I thought about the whole time was the service at the Mountain of Fire and Miracles Ministry. Two words rang in my memory.

Receive blindness.

I know better. I know the power of prayer. I believe in the power of prayer. I know that what is happening in these churches isn't something to play with. I have always feared the presence of pure evil. I can't even watch scary movies because I have a real and solid knowledge that pure evil exists. Perhaps the knowledge of that type of evil, and the need to combat it, is what motivates these prayers.

I prayed in the only way I know how, and asked for forgiveness. When my sight came back, I breathed a sigh of relief, and sent up a thank you.

My cousins said that my eye infection was probably unrelated to our joke-fest, but we agreed that we probably should laugh about something else from now on.

Good idea, I thought.

*   *   *

A simple lesson from this week: don't play with fire. You might get burned.

WEEK 25
THE BEAUTIFUL GAME
OUR LADY OF THE CEDARS,
MARONITE CATHOLIC CHURCH

9:30 a.m. Mass, Fathers Day, Woodmead, Johannesburg, South Africa

It was freezing in South Africa! One thing I have learned, as a southern girl, with African blood, who has lived in the Windy City for half of her life, is that if you don't respect the cold, you'll be miserable.

I was told that it would be cold in South Africa.

"Define cold," I said.

The forecast predicted temperatures around forty degrees Fahrenheit. I scoffed, packed a jacket, and kept it moving.

I'm basically from Chicago, I reasoned. Forty degrees isn't that cold.

Well, we didn't see the forties the whole time I was in Johannesburg. It was more like the twenties, and there was just one little space heater in our stylish condo. There was no central heating. In an attempt to stay warm, we tried to bundle up, but mostly we froze.

I wished I had my Chi-style coat.

My trip to South Africa was wonderful and freezing, and crazy and freezing, chock-full of soccer, and expensive and memorable and freezing. I spent my time shuttling between cheapo activities with my cousins and muckety-muck events with my uncles, all the while haggling for rands with taxi drivers who would quote one price to me and then another to my African-born cousins.

We travelled from Soweto to Sandton. All the while, I thanked God that I had the ability and the desire to travel.

Travelling for me is like therapy.

It's in my blood. My parents both left their home country and travelled from Africa to Europe to America looking for opportunity and adventure all the way. Their blood runs through my veins. Years prior, I had written in my journal that "I was concerned that I wouldn't be satisfied by living in just one city."

I was born in New York City, raised in Atlanta, went to college in California, lived in Connecticut for a few years, and currently live in Chicago. My parents are from West Africa, and I have lived in Germany and Japan. I have friends and family all over the world. The word "home" means many things to me. I love learning about different people and different cultures, and rarely feel uncomfortable in a situation. All my life, I have had to be a bridge and have gotten pretty good at it!

After my father passed away, I knew I would spend as much time as I could on a plane as part of my healing process. I think the time you spend between here and there on a plane is some of the most peaceful time in the world. Trips to the African continent from Chicago give you plenty of that time.

I remember asking my father once if he had ever been to a country in Africa besides Nigeria. He told me no.

I wished that he could be with me on this South African journey. He would have loved it. I broke down into tears when the Nigerian national anthem began to play before the Nigeria versus Greece game in Bloemfontein.

I knew he was with me, and I knew he had a front row seat to the game.

I bought a white hat that said Nigeria on it in green. After the game, I wondered what I would do with it. In the past, whenever I travelled somewhere, I would buy my father a hat from that location. Whenever I was in a country other than the U.S., I would buy him a soccer jersey, since Nigerian soccer jerseys were not easy to find in the U.S., a country that is not at all soccer crazy.

What would I do with all this World Cup gear if I couldn't give it to my pops?

I still have that Nigeria hat, shoved in a drawer in my bedroom.

Things, it appeared, were different, never to be the same again.

The experience was overwhelming. I called my ex, knowing he and his son would love the vuvuzelas that were becoming the signature World Cup souvenir. I bought a few, in my heart knowing that he would likely never see them.

Those vuvuzelas are still in my closet.

When it came time to determine where I would worship in Johannesburg, the process of finding the church was complicated. I'd researched a few churches when I was in the States, but none really spoke to me. When we were in Soweto, we did visit the famous Regina Mundi church, which is the city's largest church. It played a critical part in the student uprisings in 1976.

That day ended up being such an impactful and emotional day—we visited Nelson Mandela's house in Soweto, and the memorial for Hector Pietersen, who became a symbol of the 1976 Soweto uprising. He was killed at the age of thirteen when police opened fire on protesting students.[37]

After my day in Soweto, I realized that I would need to find a church elsewhere. Logistically speaking, Soweto was far from where we were staying, and would cost quite a bit to get there by taxi.

I decided to just hop in a cab and ask the driver to suggest a church for me, and go wherever the universe should send me.

This was maybe not the best plan.

My cab driver told me I should come with him to his church, as they were having a twenty-four hour worship and prayer service. It had started the night before, he shared, but there was probably still nine hours left, if I was interested.

Politely, I declined. I was not up for a worship service that lasted all day and night. I told him to take me to one of the churches that I'd found while researching online. It was in Woodmead, an area not far from where we were staying in Sandton.

The consultation continued, however. Since I'd told the cab driver that I wanted to go to any church, he pointed out all the churches that we saw along the way, and tried to pull over to each of them.

I finally had to be very clear and tell him to please take me to the Maronite Catholic Church only.

Please.

When we finally arrived at the church, I was late for service. This made me sad because I'd missed a good part of the ritual and liturgy at the beginning of the service, which I generally enjoyed.

There were flags of different countries in the church everywhere because it was World Cup time. It was clear that there was love for the beautiful game, even in the church. There were people wearing Brazil jerseys everywhere. The Brazil versus Ivory Coast game was later that night. I was excited that I would be able to attend. It was nice to see that people still thought it was important to praise the Lord before the soccer match.

I'm sure there were many prayers for victory going up to the heavens.

Even though I missed some of the initial call and response, I was there for the reading, in unison, of the Nicene Creed. I love participating in call and response of almost any kind. Call and response soothes me; it makes me feel part of the body of worshippers. Praying in unison often makes a group of strangers become one.

We spoke together:

> I believe in one God, the Father Almighty, Maker of heaven and earth, and of all things visible and invisible.

> And in one Lord Jesus Christ, the only-begotten Son of God, begotten of the Father before all worlds; God of God, Light of Light, very God of very God; begotten, not made, being of one substance with the Father, by whom all things were made . . . . [38]

Some prayers in Lebanese followed the recitation of the creed. I marveled how, through my random selection of churches in South Africa, I'd hit a Lebanese Catholic Church—a cultural bonanza!

There was a song, "Kyrie Eleison," which reminded me of my childhood friend, Nicole. We spent countless hours making signs saying "If you can dream it, you can do it," preparing for cheerleading tryouts, and eating beignets at Huey's (a now-closed Atlanta restaurant). Nicole moved to San Francisco when we were in high school. She sent me a football program from my dream college, Stanford, which I later attended. We also both felt very strongly about the eighties version of the song by Mister Mister:[39]

> "Kyrie eleison down the road that I must travel . . ."

Once again, this journey brought up old precious memories. I hadn't thought about Nicole in quite some time, and made a mental note to reach out to her.

The service focused on the value of community within worship. We participated in call and response with the pastor, and read prayers together. Once the sermon began, the pastor reminded us that, "Everyone has a responsibility to his people, and to all people," and "there is no contradiction between loving your people, and loving all people."

A relevant and useful message to the country, South Africa, who was hosting visitors from various countries for one of the most watched sporting events in the world—the World Cup.

As wonderful as the service was, the most memorable portion of my experience for the day was yet to come.

After the service was over, not wanting this worship experience to end just yet, I wandered around the church grounds. I found a remembrance garden behind the church. Ivy vines curled around the gate surrounding the garden; a cobbled path led to the garden entrance. It was well tended, and had pictures of deceased church members hanging in different locations around the grounds. Immediately the tears came.

Today was Father's Day—the first Father's Day without my father.

I'd tried up until that point to put on a brave face, but the synchronicity of me wandering into a remembrance garden on this special day for fathers was undeniable.

A woman saw me, and she stopped me to ask if I had someone commemorated there. I told her no, but that it was my first Father's Day without my father. She told me that her husband had passed away the year before. It was a first for her too. She told me that they were both members of this church for many years, and showed me the section of the garden dedicated to him. We talked about how it felt to lose someone you loved. She told me it was also her birthday. She introduced me to her children, and talked to me about how this church was one unified church, not just Lebanese, not just Catholic, but a place for all people to come and share in God's love. We hugged, and immediately connected.

* * *

This journey just keeps blessing me. The kindness of strangers is real, and overwhelming, and wonderful. A new friend in a remembrance garden in South Africa reminded me that my challenges are not mine alone. We shared a "first" together. We remembered our lost loved ones together. And in sharing, we helped each other.

My experience in South Africa reminded me of one simple truth: there *is* healing for your spirit.

Week 26
Get up and Eat
Fourth Presbyterian Church

4:00 p.m. service, Chicago, Illinois

Due to my movement from "I can't believe this is Africa" cold in Johannesburg to "This is more like it" hot Lagos on my way home, paired with a couple of extremely long plane flights, guess what I was when I returned to Chicago?

Sick.

Because of this, I certainly was not up for an early morning service, nor was I up for a loud, afternoon gospel-o-rama.

A little research revealed the perfect solution.

On Michigan Avenue, in the heart of the Magnificent Mile, and surrounded by marvelous shopping, is a church that commands your attention. The Fourth Presbyterian Church. I'd walked by it several times, but never entered. Today was the day I would visit.

They had a 4:00 p.m. Jazz service with communion. As soon as I entered, I knew I'd made the right choice. A jazz quartet at the front of the sanctuary played softly. It was sweet, and peaceful, and fed my spirit from the moment that I entered the church.

The service had an interfaith flavor as evidenced by the invitation that, "All were welcome to take communion."

151

After having visited churches of other faiths where I'd decided not to take communion for various reasons, it was nice to participate, and thank God for safe travels from Chicago to Lagos, to Johannesburg, and back.

As the congregants lined up for communion, we recited a memorable Prayer of Confession:

Almighty God,
We confess that we have broken covenant with you
And accused you of forgetting us.
Our lives do not praise you; our actions deny you;
And our work is carried out without reference to your will.
Forgive us for not trusting you to care for our every need.
Free us from the shackles of fear and a sense of failure
that keep us from stepping bravely into your future.
Turn us toward you for strength
To be instruments of your purpose.
Hear now our silent prayers . . .

After communion was completed, came the sermon. The pastor read the scripture for the day, 1 Kings 19:4-8 (NIV):

I have had enough, LORD," he said. "Take my life; I am no better than my ancestors." Then he lay down under the bush and fell asleep.

All at once an angel touched him and said, "Get up and eat." He looked around, and there by his head was some bread baked over hot coals, and a jar of water. He ate and drank and then lay down again.

The angel of the LORD came back a second time and touched him and said, "Get up and eat, for the journey is too much for you." So he got up and ate and drank. Strengthened by that food, he traveled forty days and forty nights until he reached Horeb, the mountain of God.

The name of the sermon was, "All we need for the journey." The pastor spoke of a God who wants to visit us, who wants to make sure we have what we need for our journey, whatever that journey may be, and even if we didn't think we were worthy of taking time for ourselves.

Get up and eat—for the journey is too much for you.

The pastor reminded us that sometimes, "Before we can take the next step, we need physical and mental strength." She also acknowledged that, "You may have many doubts, but never doubt that the God that has called you will support you and provide you with all you need."

She referenced being "stuck in a cave," and how sometimes we get into situations that we believe we can't get ourselves out of. But that isn't the end of the story, she shared. God is continually inviting us, beckoning us to embrace life. God has hope for us, even when we don't have hope for ourselves. God provides for us.

Thank goodness.

During the offertory, a soloist sang a quiet and soothing song named "For the fruit of all creation." The lyrics began:

For the fruit of all creation, thanks be to God.
Gifts bestowed on every nation, thanks be to God.[40]

The Prayers of the People followed the offering. Along my journey, I have always appreciated community prayer from the body of the faithful. Often in services during Prayers of the People, members of the congregation sit in silence, and people are invited to share what is on their hearts.

In this service, Prayers of the People started with prayers by the worship leader focused on world events. There were prayers for peace in the world, prayers for world leaders, and prayers for healing for community and world tragedies. Then, members of the congregation spoke their concerns aloud, while everyone listened. When this section was over, then the congregation prayed as a whole over these concerns.

Once again, on this day, I was blessed by those who shared their struggles aloud by asking for prayers. There were many mentions of people with cancer, which was the illness that my father had. Many people were suffering.

In suffering together, we are never alone.

What a gift.

*   *   *

Whatever your journey, make sure that you take the time to prepare for it. Whatever your challenge, you have what you need to meet it. When you are tired, rest. When you need sustenance, eat. When you feel alone, know that you are never alone. We are never forgotten. With soft jazz playing in the background, I was reminded of these lessons.

Get up and eat—for the journey is too much for you.

WEEK 27
OM. PEACE. AMEN
ANANDA CHURCH OF SELF REALIZATION

9:00 a.m. meditation, 10:00 a.m. service, Palo Alto, California

I have a deep, abiding love for my college alma mater, Stanford University. As a young girl, I remember my mother's friend, Aunt Narvie, talking about Stanford. She was from Oakland. As she told my mother about Stanford, all I heard was "excellent university" and "California." California was far away. That is what I wanted. The Bassey girls, being raised by Nigerian "tiger parents," were on lockdown. I figured the only way to gain a little independence was to do the best I could in school and try to convince Stanford's admissions committee, all the way in California, that I would be an asset to their freshman class of 1993.

It worked. Stanford challenged me academically. I had many great experiences, and made wonderful friends. At Stanford, I joined my beloved sorority, Delta Sigma Theta Sorority, Inc. This weekend, I travelled back to the Bay Area to attend the wedding of one of my sorority sisters.

I decided to fly out a day early so I could spend time in Palo Alto, visit a new spa, and have brunch at the world-famous Hobee's, with its delicious coffee cake. I spent a few hours just wandering around "The Farm," as we affectionately call the Stanford campus. I strolled by each of the dorms in which I'd lived, walked through the Quad and White Plaza, the site of many Friday "chillouts," a lunch time ritual sponsored by the African-American community at Stanford, and stopped by the bookstore to get some new gear.

A special part of campus was Memorial Church, or MemChu, as we affectionately call it. Because of the 1989 Loma Prieta quake, it was closed during most of my undergraduate career, so I'd been unable to enjoy it. However, it is central to the campus' overwhelming beauty. I looked forward to attending a service there as part of my 52 Weeks of Worship.

Online, I found that the sermon topic for the weekend would be, "Finding God through Literature." For some reason, that didn't move me. I'm interested in literature, and obviously interested in finding God, but when I saw the title, I thought it sounded like a lecture, and concluded that, "Maybe I needed to go somewhere else this week."

So I did. This had been a rough week for me, and I looked forward to a worship experience that was new and different, but that helped me along my personal journey. Boy did I find it in the Ananda Church of Self Realization.

I arrived at the church just before 9:00 a.m. for the meditation and was sad that I missed the first part of the service—the Fire Ceremony. It's described in Ananda's literature as:

> A simple version of an ancient Vedic Ritual. Fire symbolizes the transforming power of divine grace. Purified butter (ghee) poured into the fire symbolizes the pure aspiration of the heart. Rice symbolizes seeds of karma burned up in the fire of self-offering. Mantras are ancient Sanskrit prayers led by Swami Kriyananda (via recording).[41]

The meditation that followed The Fire Ceremony started with a purification ceremony. Each of us received a piece of paper on which we wrote a prayer. We then approached the altar, kneeling in front of the light bearers. The light bearer in front of me was kind. Her energy was peaceful. She also helped direct me because after I knelt, I had no idea what to do. We stayed there—for just a little too long—me kneeling, and she facing me, until I opened one eye as if to say, "Um, what now?"

She smiled and instructed me to say the phrase, "I seek purification by the grace of God." She then prayed for me, touched my heart chakra, and then sent me to burn my paper, asking me to accept God's grace in my life. Her prayer was one of freedom and mercy. Before she began, she told me: "This is a prayer to free you from whatever may obstruct the natural flow of grace in your life."

Oh, how much I needed this.

I prayed to be free from fear—fear of lack, a scarcity of love, and fear that it was too late for me to find true love. I could tell that the fear of life passing me by was affecting me. I don't know when I became fearful, but this purification ceremony helped me, in that moment, to face this fear head on.

After the purification ceremony, there were forty-five minutes of silent meditation, which I needed and enjoyed. I did find myself falling asleep within the meditation, but the process of falling asleep intrigued me. At times, I would nod off. I would recognize this, and then pull myself back up to focus on the meditation again. In some ways, that is how my life had become—falling, recognizing, and pulling myself back up. It was a process, but I was certain it was a process that would help me to gain peace, perspective, and solace.

The sermon followed the meditation. Before the sermon began, a woman with a harp accompaniment sang the Beatitudes.

It was the anniversary of the first Ananda community in 1968. Many people had chosen to celebrate at Ananda Village in Nevada City, California, so there were not that many people at the Palo Alto location. Nevertheless, for me, it was special.

The same peaceful light bearer who had helped me during the purification ceremony assumed her role as minister. She shared that she was a Yogi who was raised as a Jew.

Well, you know I loved that.

Spiritual journeys inspire me. Evidence of the interconnectedness of all spiritual pursuits intrigues me.

She spoke about why we aren't happy when we aren't fulfilled. "We are born into this world with the inner certainty that fulfillment is possible," she said.

She talked about reincarnation, not in the sense of one full life following another, but about reincarnation within the span of one life, how we keep trying, tweaking something about ourselves, and then trying again.

We learn by and through experience.

She shared, "One of the realities of life is the search for love . . . God wants us to experience infinite joy. The question for us is: will we receive it?"

"I'm trying," I thought.

Appropriately enough, the minister shared stories of people over the years who asked what to do so that they could find love, a life partner, a mate.

She talked about what she tells those who say, "I have all this to give and no one to give it to."

Well, she had my attention.

Her advice: "Imagine how you would express yourself if you found a partner. Well, express yourself that way now."

The thought was that in acting in the way you would if you had a partner, you would not only figure out who you are and what you needed, but it would also help you to search for and find that feeling of unbroken connection to someone else.

She spoke of attunement; that all of spiritual practice is an effort to seek attunement with the divine. She encouraged us to bring our attention back to God when we wander away from that singular focus.

She said that life is a process of attuning yourself, continually, and that when you wander off, come back. When you are attuned, you'll be at peace. You'll find joy.

"And who doesn't want joy?" I thought.

The last half of the sermon held special interest because the minister talked about divine understanding, and Divine Mother.

She shared that, "Divine Mother has, vibrating in the universe, everything your heart desires." She encouraged us to say to ourselves, "I have that right now," and to believe it. Surrender preconceptions. Tell Divine Mother, "I know you are there." Surrender any contracts standing in the way of you receiving your good.

I know this sounds very much like, "The Law of Attraction," but the mention of contracts reminded me of a conversation that I had with my cousin, Anehita years ago. She asked me if I prayed about my "eternal state of singledom."

Usually, whenever this topic came up with family, I made a joke and changed the subject quickly, because it isn't my favorite topic. But this particular cousin—who has the nickname, mi prima favorita (Spanish for, "my favorite cousin")—has privileges others do not have because we have a special connection. She loves me from a very deep place in her heart; I love her the same way. I know her intentions are pure.

She asked me something that made me sigh heavily. She prefaced it by saying, "I know this is going to sound crazy, and I hate to even say it, but if you have tried everything . . ."

Well, I didn't know if I'd tried everything (maybe I just fall for the wrong types of guys?), but I was curious to hear what she had to say.

She said, "Maybe someone has put some sort of contract (read: hex) on you, preventing you from getting married."

Since I have lived around and in a West African culture that speaks freely about things like "juju" or "otherworldly spiritual practices," I didn't think this was as weird as others might.

Let's just say, I haven't started praying to combat witchcraft, contracts on my life, or agreements made by (who?) others to prevent me from having a relationship that ends in marriage. But it made me think when Anehita said it, and I contemplated it again when this Jewish Yogi in Palo Alto, California mentioned it.

Towards the end of the service, there was a prayer. We ended the prayer with the words, "OM. Peace. Amen."

*   *   *

In a memorable portion of the Ananda service, we said, in unison: "By sensitivity to others' reality, I keep myself in readiness to perceive truth, no matter what garb it wears."

"That's 52 Weeks of Worship in a nutshell," I thought. I felt blessed to experience truth in so many different ways throughout my journey.

WEEK 28
POPSICLES AND PRAISE
MISSIO DEI CHURCH

6:00 p.m. service, Bucktown, Chicago, Illinois

I found the churches that I visited in all different ways. Sometimes it was an invitation, and sometimes I found my next spot because of a targeted web search. Sometimes, I would drive by a place, see a sign, pull over, write down the name of the location, and add it to the list.

One day, when I was driving around the city with Mr. Friend Zone, I saw an eye-catching sign in front of a store in Chicago's hip Bucktown neighborhood. He, being used to me talking about my journey, didn't find it odd that I pulled over. I asked him to please write down the name of the church for me.

Mr. Friend Zone was really becoming my friend.

Awww.

On the following Sunday afternoon, grief-induced sadness prevented me from getting up early. I found myself driving to Bucktown in the afternoon to worship at Missio Dei Church.

The church (and everyone there) was very hip.

I wouldn't list "hip" as the number one adjective to describe me, but that's okay. When I entered the church, it was abundantly clear that I was a visitor, but not in a bad exclusive way. Given that I'd stood out in several different places of worship in several different ways since January, I was actually quite comfortable.

The church was a unique space with a mural of Jesus painted on the wall and ornate stained glass windows. There were cool vintage pews. The service was extremely casual. The pastor was wearing a t-shirt, shorts, and flip-flops.

As people arrived for service, Sting was playing.

Well if I could listen to Michael Jackson with the Scientologists, I could certainly listen to a little "Free, free, set them free," with these folks.

It was extremely hot inside the church. There was no central air in this one hundred-year-old church building. Some volunteers started handing out hand fans for all of the congregants. They also handed out popsicles.

Mine was apple. I would have preferred strawberry, but I tried not to be ungrateful as I removed the wrapping and enjoyed this soothing, icy perk.

As the service started, a rock band started to play. Nobody here had a problem rocking out for Jesus, apparently.

After the initial medley ended, we had five minutes to meet our neighbors. The woman next to me introduced herself. Her name was Jeanna.

Jeanna had a strawberry popsicle. What would Jesus do? I thought. Probably focus on what she was saying and not on the fact that I would have liked to trade popsicles.

Jeanna was very friendly and told me that she was headed to Haiti for a four-week mission.

Very cool, Jeanna.

Not only was the church active in the Chicago community, it was active globally.

Worked for me.

After the five minute meet-and-greet, a vuvuzela sounded (seriously!) and it was time for announcements. As part of the announcements, they mentioned that there would be a water baptism in an upcoming week. I found it curious to hear such a traditional announcement in such a non-traditional setting, but it made me think. When I was baptized, it was not a water baptism.

As the man giving the announcements said that Jesus commanded that we have a water baptism, I thought, "Maybe I should get one."

Then I remembered that all of us were eating popsicles as the announcements continued, and I figured I shouldn't make any religious decisions at that very moment.

The pastor held his popsicle while he preached. It was melting. I figured the best I could do was pay attention to the message before there was a popsicle incident.

As the pastor shared the sermon, I heard some familiar themes:

- Act with resolve. Commit to doing what the Lord wants, versus what you want.
- Act with restraint—do what God says and don't ask him why.
- Hold back self will and submit to God.
- Trust God. Have Faith.
- Pray.
- Seek the Lord.
- Be Humble.
- Look to God for guidance.

At this point, I had been to many places of worship, and I was hearing similar messages. Still, I struggled.

I still missed my ex.

I still missed my father.

I had other personal challenges, and was not allowing myself to move on in many areas of my life. I was in an emotional soup.

I tried to invite God into the healing process.

I tried to let the gifts of every week touch me, soak in, bless me:

- To focus on God as love
- To humble myself
- To remember that maybe there are some things that I can't do, but God can do

When the pastor mentioned that, "God sometimes brings us low so we learn," I thought about an alternate view that I read in the book, *The Shack*. There, one of the manifestations of God says to one of the main characters as they are trying to make sense of the tragedy that has befallen his young daughter:

> . . . just because I work incredible good out of unspeakable tragedies doesn't mean I orchestrate the tragedies. Don't ever assume that my using something means I caused it or that I needed it to accomplish my purposes. That will only lead you to false notions about me. Grace doesn't depend on suffering to exist, but where there is suffering you will find grace in many facets and colors.[42]

Whether God creates bad situations to teach us lessons, or God just uses the situations that already exist to accomplish his purposes is a theological conundrum. In both situations, it sometimes takes longer than we want before we feel better. The challenge is, will we stay patient and humble until the tide turns?

Then the pastor referred to 2 Samuel 6:14 (NIV), and told us what David did when God finally exalted him:

> Wearing a linen ephod, David was dancing before the LORD with all his might.

Well, nobody in the church was wearing a linen ephod, but we were invited to dance anyway—to dance before the Lord because that is joy. The pastor reminded us that David didn't care what anyone else thought, and we shouldn't either.

The "Back in Black" Jesus band started playing, and everyone around me started to dance.

And far be it from me to be the only one not dancing.

Because when we do finally get a breakthrough, we *should* dance. We should celebrate.

I danced along with the rest of the congregation until the music ended.

After the sermon, we sang, people prayed, and it was time for communion and offering.

Let's just say, in the many months of my journey so far, this was my favorite communion and offering.

The pastor instructed us that we could partake in the body and the blood of Jesus, and drop a little something in the offering box.

In no particular order.

There was music and people were praying. People began moving toward the communion table.

When they were ready.

I looked around, and when I was ready, I followed some of the people to the side of the church, picked up my cracker and juice, left a little something in the offering plate, returned to my pew and gave myself communion.

*　　*　　*

So, between the popsicles, and the preaching that reminded me that I was still struggling with some heavy stuff, I have to say this service was fun. When life gets a little heavy, there's nothing wrong with having a little fun. Missio Dei was different than any church service I had ever experienced, but everything from the music to the dancing to the communion was organic and peaceful, and I enjoyed it.

WEEK 29
TAKING TIME OUT ON A TUESDAY
SHAMBHALA MEDITATION CENTER

7:00 p.m. meditation, Rogers Park, Chicago, Illinois

Monday had not been the best Monday for me. Mr. Friend Zone and I had a big fight. I was overly emotional, and I ended up driving around for hours contemplating the state of my life.

I was in dire need of some peace of mind. I decided to do some research to see where I could find it.

I typed "Tuesday Chicago meditation" in my search engine because I knew I really needed some quiet time. Lo and behold, I found a Tuesday night meditation at the Shambhala Center of Chicago.

Thank goodness.

The center was located in Rogers Park, on the North Side of Chicago. On my drive there, I retraced my past—driving up Lakeshore Drive, past my first Chicago apartment on Sheridan Road, along the route I took to Northwestern University, which is what brought me to Chicago in the first place. I rarely get up there anymore, but it's always a delightful drive up memory lane.

When I arrived at the address, I found a lovely little house. I was sure I had driven past it a thousand times, but had never thought to stop. I buzzed the door, and entered a place full of many different kinds of people, all there for the Tuesday meditation. I must have looked new, because a helpful woman approached me. She asked me if it was my first time, and I said yes. She took me on a tour of the different meditation rooms, which all just looked peaceful, especially given my current state of emotional mess.

The woman took me upstairs after asking if I needed an initial introduction in meditation. I was thinking, "Well, I basically know what to do," but when we went upstairs, in the first moments of explanation, I learned something new. There are many different types of meditation—this I knew. What I didn't know was that in the type practiced at this location, Tibetan meditation, you meditate with your eyes open. The idea is you want to be able to be master of your thoughts and your responses in the real world, where you have to live with your eyes open, so why meditate with your eyes closed?

Brilliant, intriguing, and very challenging.

My new tour guide also mentioned that meditation isn't just for relaxation (i.e., meditate until you fall asleep). It is also for learning to be a warrior—learning to be able to deal with anything that comes your way.

"Well, yeah, I'll take some of that." I thought.

After the intro, I went downstairs to join the group. The eyes open thing was challenging, but the first sitting meditation went okay.

Then we moved to walking meditation. We were just walking in circles. The point was to just focus on breathing and putting one foot in front of the other.

Now if that isn't a tool for walking through grief toward healing, what is?

The walking meditation calmed me down and helped me to clear my head. When we were done walking, I already felt like my perspective on my problems had improved.

We did a last set of sitting meditation, and I was lazy about it. I decided to just close my eyes and, of course, I fell asleep.

I guess I needed some rest.

Then came refreshments. The meet-and-greet portion of this evening was slightly awkward. I didn't really know anyone. I was feeling sufficiently self-absorbed with my own emotional concerns that I didn't have much energy to make an effort to meet my fellow attendees. I spoke for a little while to a cool young lady with a tattoo on her back. She was a neuroscientist, who was studying the effects of meditation on the brain. Based on what she already knew, she felt that meditation was something we all should do, that it's just good for your brain.

Bonus.

The evening up until this point had been just what the doctor ordered.

Then it got better.

We went back to the meditation room, sat in a circle, and read a chapter together from a book called, *Shambhala: The Sacred Path of the Warrior,* by Chögyam Trungpa. Everyone read, and—one paragraph at a time—we shared in the wisdom that is summarized in the book's description:

> There is a basic human wisdom that can help solve the world's problems. It doesn't belong to any one culture or region or religious tradition—though it can be found in many of them throughout history. It's what Chögyam Trungpa called the sacred path of the warrior. The sacred warrior conquers the world not through violence or aggression, but through gentleness, courage, and self-knowledge. The warrior discovers the basic goodness of human life and radiates that goodness out into the world for the peace and sanity of others. That's what the Shambhala teachings are all about, and this is the book that has been presenting them to a wide and appreciative audience for more than twenty years."[43]

After we were done reading the passage as a group, a discussion began. We talked about how meditation gives you the tools to just face life, whatever it gives you, and to never "be amazed by life," whether it presents you with someone giving you a million bucks or threatening to kill you.

Don't be amazed.

What a great life mantra.

We talked about learning to be a warrior, and how to be fearless.

Who doesn't want to be fearless?

We talked about how to "ride life" like a jockey rides a horse but doesn't fall off.

We talked about how the universe, or God, or whatever you want to call it, will call up situations and people that will challenge you in just the way you need to be challenged in order for you to grow in just the way that you need to grow.

A memorable quote summarized this: "If you need to be humbled, the universe will push you down; if you need to be bolder, the earth will push you up."

My first thought was, "Fantastic!"

Then, "Oh, there it is, the discussion about humility again."

It wasn't surprising that the theme of humility kept coming up in these various places of worship. But given that I'd been to a church service the prior Sunday where humility was a central theme, and then I heard it again on this Tuesday evening, I found myself really thinking, "Is it possible that I'm too full of myself?" Am I telling myself that I'm merely very self aware and self reflective when I should be seeing that I'm overly self absorbed and self centered?

Perhaps.

And is that the cause of the majority of my pain?

It isn't something that I liked to think about often, but when it came up repeatedly on a weekly basis, it was a little difficult to avoid pondering it.

As I turned these thoughts over in my head, one woman shared an experience in her life where she "received a message" from the universe. She shared that the death of a family member had moved her to change her career, and then—two years to the day, within the hour of her family member's death—she received a job in her new career.

This opened the discussion further. Everyone started talking about people who had passed away. Two women had lost their husbands on that very day years ago. One woman had recently lost her mother after a long illness. One woman lost her brother the day after she received a message while meditating that she should forgive him.

It made me think about how much it affected me that almost a year had gone by since my father passed away. I still thought my life was a mess.

And I really wished it wasn't.

Even with all these worship experiences, and all these reminders that everything is going to be okay, I was still not really okay.

I remembered a story my mother shared about an individual she knew who was always talking about spirituality and meditation, who was always reading a book about angels, or miracles, or healing. Apparently, this person was still a mess, full of anger and hate. My mother didn't understand how someone who soaked in all of that uplifting stuff could still be stuck in mess.

Well, I get it.

Sometimes you need a constant flow of positivity just to maintain equilibrium. Sometimes life is just that hard.

Even after weeks of my journey had passed, I still felt that life was difficult.

I shared this with the group. They listened and we all supported each other.

They encouraged me to be kind to myself. This isn't something I'm good at—I realize that I'm my own worst critic.

I'm working on it.

*   *   *

Once again, I was able to lean on the kindness of strangers, which is just what I needed. It was clear that I was meant to be in that place at that time. I was reminded that someone else is going through my same struggle, at every moment. I was also reminded that meditation is good, helpful, and important.

And the best part: I was reminded that all I have to do is keep living, and everything will be what it is meant to be.

WEEK 30
NO PRE-CONCEPTIONS
HARVEY CHURCH OF CHRIST

10:45 a.m. service, Harvey, Illinois

Before this day, I had only had three experiences with the Church of Christ:

1) A good friend joined the Church of Christ when she was in college, then her parents freaked out when they decided it was a cult. They planned an intervention and dragged her away from the church.

2) Years ago, while grocery shopping, someone from the Church of Christ approached me in the frozen foods aisle. They struck up conversation with me, asked me if I had a church home, and invited me to worship with them. Politely, I declined.

3) My ex had family members who belonged to the Church of Christ, and, although I had my apprehensions, I went to church with them. I never felt any undue pressure when I visited their congregation. Everyone was extremely friendly. I kept wondering when and if I would get the hard sell, but I never did.

On this day, however, I agreed to join my friend Cobbie and head to Harvey, a suburb just south of Chicago, to visit the Harvey Church of Christ. More than once, I had heard that the Church of Christ was a cult-like denomination that I should avoid. I went with as few preconceived notions as I could.

At this point, I was free about entering into different places of worship with an open heart and good intentions. I knew that nothing could really happen to me that was harmful, bad, or irreversible.

173

I was free.

And it was nice.

When we entered the older church building and everyone was friendly, I was friendly in return. People said hello, and my friend, who had invited me to join him for service, introduced me to different people.

The majority of the congregation was African-American, so there was no chocolate chip experience for me this Sunday. I stood out not because of my race, but because this appeared to be a church where people knew people.

And that was okay.

The service started with a hymn, "God is Real," which was sung *a cappella* by a soloist. It had been a few weeks since I'd visited an African-American congregation. It was nice to settle into the familiar feeling of home that I always experience when I go to a "Black church."

I loved seeing all kinds of people coming to church to be fed. I generally meshed well into the congregation. But today, although I went with a friend, I still felt alone.

My friend was one of my few remaining male friends. At this point in my life, I was seriously considering whether it served me to have male friends at all. This discussion I had with myself reflected my general weariness about always being the cool, smart girl, who made great friend material but was rarely chosen to be the girlfriend or the wife.

My ex had chosen me. I trusted that he had cared about me and believed I would be someone who was significant in his life. But that was over now.

Although it was nice to be in the presence of attractive, smart, charismatic men, if they saw me as "just a great friend," sometimes it was hard to see what benefit that really held for me at this point in my life.

It was a real issue I was grappling with. And I was not the only one grappling with an issue on this day.

At the beginning of the service, almost everyone stood up, and then sat down after the singing was over. Those who remained standing had prayer requests.

I love community prayer from the body of the faithful, and today, there were a few people who needed some prayer support from the community:

- One woman said she needed to make some decisions in her life and asked for prayer.
- One man shared that he had been fighting with a friend and asked to be forgiven—in front of the church.
- One woman shared that she had been away from the house of the Lord, and was glad to be back.
- One man shared that he was struggling with feelings of anger, and wanted to overcome them so that he could regain custody of his children.

The opening prayer incorporated these concerns. It was a wonderful way to let everyone know that what concerned each member concerned the entire congregation. Throughout the prayer, the congregation shouted "Amens," and "Hallelujahs" as they rallied around those who had asked for help.

It was at this service that the minister shared a verse that really communicated the heart and soul of this journey: Matthew 6:33 (KJV):

> But seek ye first the kingdom of God, and his righteousness; and all these things shall be added unto you.

"Why am I doing this," I thought? As this verse stated, I wanted to *intentionally seek God's face*, rather than deal with some sort of automatic spirituality or automatic Christianity.

175

Thanks to this journey, worship services feel like a place where I can rest. Wherever I'm present among a body of worshippers, I feel at home.

The music at this service brought me home, too. Every song was sung *a cappella*, no choir, no instruments. There was one musician in the back of the choir with a microphone. He was providing the bass to accompany the soloists.

I wondered why there were no instruments. A pamphlet in a packet of materials given to visitors explained:

> In the days of the apostles, mechanical instruments of music in connection with singing were not used in the worship of the church. Then, all worshippers sang psalms, hymns, spiritual songs, and made melody in their *hearts* unto the Lord.[44] Vocal music was the only kind used. Instrumental music in Christian worship was not practiced until centuries later, after the church had been corrupted by error. We, of the church of Christ, sing the praises of God but do not use mechanical instruments of music in Christian worship since the Lord left them out of his church, and the New Testament nowhere authorizes their use.[45]

We sang one song repeatedly. It was called "Let it Rise," by Holland Davis; a portion of the lyrics were:

> Let the spirit of the Lord, rise among us,
> Let the spirit of the Lord, rise among us,
> Oh oh oh, let it rise.[46]

As we sang, I felt forgiveness washing over me. As I thought about several friends and issues that I'd been worrying about, I felt a forgiving energy and healing. I considered this a blessing, even as I knew I would need to keep focusing on forgiveness for it to stick.

It made me think about what you really need to worship. What elements of church feed you? Even without a big choir and an elaborate "music ministry," the songs in this service were able to reach all of us in the congregation.

The sermon began.

"You can't afford to fight against God" was the message.

I found this humorous, because the previous evening, as I sat drinking milkshakes with Cobbie, I'd told him, "I don't think there's anything wrong with struggling or wrestling with God." As we talked, he invited me to visit his church, and I felt like this sermon was a direct response to our conversation.

I really do think God is big enough to deal with whatever fight I have. If I have questions or concerns, or am pondering contradictions, then why can't I share that with God?

I think God can handle it.

The minister shared that there is no need to fear that which is allied with you—that someone on your side can't hurt you, and God was on our side.

He also talked about working with God, and with the body of Christ. He pointed out—correctly, I thought—that when a group of people has a common enemy or a common goal, they come together. But when people are safe, comfortable, and not facing a challenge, we don't generally come together effectively.

The lesson, I thought, is this: I should try to take solace in the fact that all of this strife helps me grow.

The minister challenged us to think about how we are showing our love for the Lord. He asked some key questions:

1) Are you giving the Lord something?
2) Are you talking to the Lord every day?

3) Are you willing to repent? Change your mind? Change your life? Resolve to do better?

Good questions.

The minister reminded us that the Word of God is going to stand forever. This made me think: what is the value of my word? Does it stand? For how long? How many times have I promised that I would change different parts of my life? Improve my fitness? Walk away from my ex and toward a new life? Be a woman of my word?

Failure is always around.

But God is good.

*   *   *

The service ended with a memorable benediction, and a valuable take-away: "Think only on things that make you happy. And if you must think on things that make you sad, think of them as blessings."

I meditated on these words during the upcoming week as my journey continued.

Week 31
Shabbat Shalom
Beth Shalom B'nai Zaken Ethiopian Hebrew Congregation (House of Peace for the Children of the Ancient Ethiopian Hebrews)

10:30 a.m. Shabbat services, Marquette Park, Chicago, Illinois

My 52-week journey was more than halfway over before I attended my first Shabbat service of the year.

Weeks before, I had Googled the terms "Hebrew Israelites," knowing that there was a community of Black Jews in Chicago with whom I wanted to worship. What I found was the Beth Shalom B'nai Zaken Ethiopian Hebrew Congregation—the House of Peace for the Children of the Ancient Ethiopian Hebrews. Their temple is located in the Marquette Park neighborhood in Chicago, where Dr. Martin Luther King led a series of protest marches against housing segregation in the late '60s.[47]

On this Saturday morning, I drove to this historic section of Chicago.

Driving down Kedzie Ave., I picked up clues about the neighborhood. While there are many types of people in Chicago, it is a city of neighborhoods and, arguably, one of the most segregated cities in America. Often, you can tell who lives in a section of town by just looking around. As I drove to the synagogue, I saw evidence of a Spanish-speaking neighborhood via Spanish store signs and Mexican people. I wondered when the neighborhood would change, assuming incorrectly that a community of Ethiopian Jews would exist in a primarily African or African-American neighborhood.

I parked across from the synagogue. The web page stated that service started at 10:30 in the morning. It was a few minutes past that already. I was hurrying. I thought I was late, but the cultural "fluidity of time" was in effect here at this place of worship. Service didn't start until the turn of the eleven o'clock hour.

As I walked in, I was greeted repeatedly with the phrase, "Shabbat Shalom." I asked the man at the door if I needed to cover my head. He mentioned that it was customary. I learned an important lesson at that moment: when worshipping in an unfamiliar situation, it's smart to bring something to cover your head, just in case.

I was given a head covering and appreciated that they were able to accommodate me. I was also given two holy books, which I carried with me. I assumed one was a Torah, but was not immediately sure what the other one was. In a moment, I would find out.

In the temple, men were on one side, women on the other side. I noted also that there were Mexican as well as Black people, which was a surprise to me.

I realized at that moment that I knew even less about the existence of a Spanish-speaking Jewish community than I did about the existence of Jews of African descent. My ignorance made me chuckle as I thought of the comments made by our 43rd president of the United States, George W. Bush, who famously asked the Brazilian president, Henrique Caroso, "Do you have Blacks, too?" Luckily, his African-American Secretary of State, Condoleeza Rice, rescued him by educating him about the existence of Black people in Brazil.

I made a mental note to educate myself. Later, I would do some research about the existence of Jews from Spanish-speaking countries, and learned about the communities of Jews that exist in Argentina, Brazil, and Mexico, to name a few.

Throughout the service, translation headphones were available. There was a man in front who was translating everything to Spanish.

From Hebrew to English for some, and to Spanish for others.

Fascinating.

The opening Psalm was Psalm 150 (NIV). I'd heard it often during services at my home church, Trinity.

> Praise the LORD.
> Praise God in his sanctuary;
> praise him in his mighty heavens.
> Praise him for his acts of power;
> praise him for his surpassing greatness.
>
> Praise him with the sounding of the trumpet,
> praise him with the harp and lyre,
> praise him with tambourine and dancing,
> praise him with the strings and flute,
> praise him with the clash of cymbals,
> praise him with resounding cymbals.
>
> Let everything that has breath praise the LORD.
> Praise the LORD.

The opening prayer was sung in Hebrew. Although I didn't understand a word, my ears took profound pleasure in the sounds. There is something special, I think, about prayers spoken or sung in a language that I don't speak. Because I don't understand the words, I have the freedom to just feel the songs. Sometimes, that is even more impactful.

I must have looked like I was enjoying the music. A woman behind me tapped me on the shoulder and asked me if I spoke Hebrew.

"Um, no," I replied.

She introduced herself as the wife of one of the leaders of the community. I told her I was worshipping there for the first time. She welcomed me, but then left me to worship in peace.

Another woman, however, who was sitting in front of me, decided that she would be my tour guide throughout the day.

As the opening worship song continued, she turned and whispered to me, giving me the rundown of how things would go: "This book has the songs in it," she said. "This book is the Torah, and this is the Haftorah." She pointed out the scripture for the day, and the pages that we would be reading throughout the service.

"Shabbat Shalom," she said, and she kissed me three times—first on my left cheek, then my right, then my left again, telling me that this was the custom.

She checked in with me frequently throughout the service, pointing out the places where the service jumped from page to page, and giving me little pointers about what was going on. I did appreciate her help, although it might have been more natural for me to attempt to feel the rhythm of the service based on my best guess at how to read the Hebrew that was in front of me.

After all, although the Hebrew was written using characters, there was also the transliteration where it was written phonetically. I was able to read along and soon I was flipping pages along with the others in the congregation. I was keeping up, and I drew some pride from that.

Having spent some time in college studying Japanese, another character-based language, I delighted in the remembrance that although it was difficult to read a character-based language, it was something I had experience doing. Hebrew read like Japanese, from right to left.

The day was just full of new discovery.

In some ways, this time with the Hebrew Israelites served as a training of sorts for the times to come when I would go to a more traditional synagogue, temple, or shul[48]. I knew every service would be different, but at least anticipated that I would now know a little about what I was doing next time I was visiting a Jewish worship community.

182

Before this time, my only experience in a Jewish worship community was at the Bat Mitzvah of my childhood friend, Leslie. My parents thought it was plenty fine to have me go to the service, but not the party. I was there, one of the only young people who was not related to Leslie. Although I was sad that I would miss the party where most of my peers would celebrate with Leslie, I remember enjoying hearing her participate in that rite of passage, with the reading of the Torah and all the other elements of the service.

As the Shabbat service continued, the mixture of cultures intrigued me. There was still a great deal of call and response, something that is prevalent in African-American Christian worship traditions. As the rabbi was talking, a woman behind me testified. "Amen!" she would call out. "Preach!" she would say when he imparted some wisdom that would touch her spirit and sensibility.

I wanted to ask her about her spiritual journey. What was her spiritual background? What lessons had she learned throughout her life that led her to embrace the Jewish culture and worship tradition? Whenever I heard her testifying, she told me that in her past she had occupied a pew where there was some Jesus going on.

As the rabbi spoke, and as we read through the service, familiar sections of Scripture jumped out at me. Psalm 15, Psalm 30, Psalm 135, Psalm 92. Sections of 1 Chronicles. More Psalms. Verses from Isaiah. They reminded me that my frame of reference was Judeo-Christian—even if I'd spent more time on the Christian side of the fence.

The rabbi reminded us of the importance of, meaning of, and purpose of Shabbat. "It is one day out of seven to focus only on God," he said. He reminded us that, "Every Shabbat, you should experience the Torah at a deeper level," and that prayers should elevate you to a higher level.

He reminded us that we had a few responsibilities as people of God:

1) When you wake up, you should thank God.
2) Before you eat, you should thank God.

3) You should keep the Sabbath holy.
4) You should love the Lord with all your heart, soul, and mind.

At times, the structure of the Torah confused me. It seemed to be different than my memories of the structure of other religious texts I'd read. The service pointed us to a verse in Deuteronomy. I flipped around looking for Deuteronomy 34, but couldn't find it. A little later, we were directed to a verse in II Kings, and I couldn't find that verse either.

Between the help from my self-appointed guide to Shabbat service, and my attempts at context related searching through both texts, I was not doing too badly. All in all, I enjoyed following along during the service, and the reading of the Torah.

Some services just read their holy texts. In contemplating the fact that the reading and re-reading of familiar service elements was, in fact, most of the worship service, I found myself pondering this thought: Did the earliest founders of these worship traditions ask themselves, "The scripture is here, what is the need for a sermon?"

Is interpretation necessary in order for people to understand religious concepts and teachings? Or is it just an opportunity to create a little religious entertainment for the people to enjoy?

I also wondered why some portions of the Torah were sung rather than spoken.

"There must be a reason there," I thought.

The central prayer of the Jewish prayer book, the Siddur, begins with the phrase:

"Shema Yisrael, Adonai eloheinu, Adonai echad," which means:

"Hear O Israel, the Lord is our God, the Lord is One."

This I found to be an alluring call to worship. Later, I learned that this statement refers to the covenant that Abraham made with God to set the Jewish people apart from other people at the time. It highlights the Jewish belief that there is only one God, not many.

Also striking were the following words that I heard repeatedly:

"Baruch Atah Adonai . . ." which means:

"Blessed are you, Lord . . ."

A portion of the scripture talked about blessings. The rabbi reminded us that the choice is ours—we can choose to be blessed or not. He stated that it is a blessing if you listen and follow the word of God and a curse if you don't, and that a curse isn't a superstitious idea, it's when we don't take advantage of what God is offering.

The rabbi reminded us that we are responsible for our actions, and that God didn't determine if someone would be righteous or wicked. It was our choice, and we had free will to be one or the other.

During the service, members of the community went through the process of walking with the Torah to the front of the temple, and reading from it. I watched as four strong Black men read from the scroll (the Torah) in Hebrew. I didn't understand anything they were reading, but it really touched my spirit. It provided different images of Blackness. Members of the African-American community are many different things, many of which you never see if you just watch the news or experience popular media.

It was a long service. It started with the Siddur, then the Torah, then there was singing. We sang a familiar gospel song, "Marching to Zion," which was one of my favorites. Then, apparently, it was time for a sermon by an upstanding member of the worship community.

By this time, I had already been there for quite some time. I contemplated the fact that part of the meaning of the Sabbath was that the faithful should spend the entire Saturday here at the temple.

I hunkered down for the next portion of my worship experience.

The sermon was part Judaism, part self determination. It included familiar "let's take care of our community" themes reminiscent of every sermon that I'd heard over my many years in my home church. The speaker was talking about Booker T. Washington and Tuskegee!

Honestly, up until this sermonic portion of the service, it had felt as though I was having a different worship experience than any I had previously. Once the sermon started, I found myself in a very familiar place, sliding into the universality of the Black worship experience. I was wearing a head covering and holding a Torah, but I could have been at any Black church, or community event that I'd attended throughout my life. The intersection between faith and works is a common theme in any church community of color. It isn't enough to talk about God's love. It's our obligation to help those who are less fortunate than we are. After all, God helps those who help themselves.

I have to confess that even though I was soaking in different worship traditions, I was not immune to thoughts that were less than holy. This sermon went on endlessly. It was the longest worship service I'd attended in months. A service this long required pre-planning (I needed to eat a good hearty breakfast before dashing out the door, and maybe even stash snacks in my purse), a prior knowledge that the service is going to be long, and a different spiritual focus. I started listening to my stomach rumble and thinking about how I could be spending time with friends or running weekend errands.

I asked myself, "Is a four-hour service necessary? Or is a thirty-minute service sufficient?"

I know these are not the most spiritually developed thoughts. But, I have to say, when I looked at the rabbi, he too looked a little exhausted during this long and sometimes rambling sermon. At one point, I swear I saw him napping.

Okay, maybe he was praying . . .

Maybe he was praying that this lovely man of God would wrap up what was becoming an "everything but the kitchen sink" sermon. This made me ask myself if an imperfect (too long) sermon was an appropriate way to show your faith?

There was (at least) one part of his sermon that caused me to pause. Although he spoke of the importance of diversity in Judaism, he encouraged the congregation to learn what it meant to be Jewish. He stated, "No longer can you call yourself Israel without realizing what Israel really means."

This was met with applause, which was not strange, but the next thing he said, I found curious. He said, "Aren't we glad to be Israel—not part of the deaf, dumb, and blind filling up the churches tomorrow?"

"Why was that necessary?" I thought? "Why does each person have to be right(er) than the next?" He brought the service back to a more inclusive note by stating that spirituality is found in constantly focusing on God's presence among us by seeking truth, performing mitzvot for Jews and Non-Jews alike, and telling us to always seek God's favor, but the comment about the Saturday worshippers versus the Sunday worshippers did stick out in my mind.

Toward the end of the service, when an offering was taken, I wondered, "Is there generally tithing in a synagogue, or is this a remnant of the Black church experience?"

More questions.

At the end of the service, we sang *all the verses* of the Black National Anthem, Lift Every Voice and Sing! I was reminded again that this was no ordinary synagogue. We even did the "Harambee!" movement at the end, with the Black power fist raised as we sang "true to thy native land." I wondered which native land they were referring to—Israel? The African continent?

Overall, it was a fascinating experience and definitely something new. It was nice to spend a few hours just praising God. And although I see the value in the idea of keeping the whole Sabbath, when they asked me if I would join them to eat, all I could think was, "Dude, I'm done! I've been here for hours!"

*   *   *

The feelings I felt after this service were similar to the feelings I felt after my experience at Saviours' Day. Mostly, I was glad I had further expanded my horizons beyond Christian worship experiences.

For me, this was a special kind of Jewish service. The mixture of community, culture, and religion made it especially memorable. I enjoyed it, and as I drove home, I thought about how I looked forward to visiting other synagogues, shuls, and temples to see what was different and what was the same.

Week 32
Creating a Safe Space
New Life Community Church of Hope

11:00 a.m. service, LaPorte, Indiana

After the long service with the Hebrew Israelites the previous Saturday, I found myself at an online service that Sunday, at my home church. It was just nice to have a virtual drive by the old country, and recuperate from the longest worship service I'd been a part of since the beginning of the journey. I do maintain that online services and services on TV and radio count, although they were not the primary focus of my 52-week journey.

On this day, I was rejuvenated, and ready to make a ninety-minute drive to a church that my friend Jackie had told me about. The last time she suggested a spot, The Urban Village, it ended up being a great experience. I was excited about the experience to come.

Jackie picked me up and we headed to LaPorte, Indiana, a small town in Northwest Indiana. All we really knew was that we were going to a "Gay-affirming Christian Pentecostal ministry in LaPorte, Indiana," and I was extremely curious to know what the service would be like.

This part of Indiana was unfamiliar to me. We arrived early and found the small church building. Inside the church, a Bible Study was in progress. Rather than interrupting, we chose to wait until the actual service started before we entered.

I'd called ahead to let them know that we were coming, and to make sure that they were okay with visitors. This is something that I generally did—just to make sure that I wasn't disrupting the flow of their usual service.

When we entered the church at service time, it was clear who we were—two chocolate chips from Chicago. The congregation was a varied group, including some younger men and elderly women. I counted fifteen people, including Jackie, myself, the two pastors, and seven members of the choir.

A woman with snow-white hair handed Jackie and I visitor's cards and told us to fill them out. At this point, I had an impressive collection of visitor's cards. I can't say it was my first priority to fill it out. I placed it on the chair next to me and waited for the service to start.

Rows of chairs were neatly lined up in the small but inviting sanctuary building. There was a box of tissues on every seat. It took me back to the one time in my life when I tried therapy. Shortly before a milestone birthday, my relationship with my ex hit a rocky patch. A good friend suggested that I talk to her therapist. I made an appointment and hoped for the best.

The therapist was kind and fun to talk to. There was nothing wrong with having an impartial ear to listen to me as I tried to work through the issues I was dealing with at that time. Unfortunately, the whole setup didn't really work for me. There was too much "you're smart, you'll figure it out," and not enough concrete help in coming up with solutions.

One thing I do remember was that she had endless supplies of tissues in her office, just as in this church.

"It's one of the tax-deductible items in my business," the therapist told me. "I can buy as many boxes of tissues as I want, and I can write it off."

I remember thinking how brilliant that was. She was able to have tissues at the ready for those patients who found themselves crying the tears that would inevitably come with their attempts to work through their issues, share their pain, and march bravely through their lives.

It seemed to me that the boxes of Kleenex at this church in LaPorte, Indiana might be serving a similar purpose.

In some way, my 52 Weeks of Worship was my own brand of therapy—going through the process of re-booting my spiritual foundation in the hopes of dealing with things in my life that had been especially painful in the previous year.

As the opening hymn, "We Come to Praise Him," began, I smiled at what was a very familiar song from my home church experience. I contemplated the silent dignity that comes in meeting people where they are. If you had to choose the most liberal or progressive areas of the United States, Northwest Indiana wouldn't probably come to mind. No matter, the church here was providing a safe space where God's love could be shared with those who might otherwise be hesitant to come to church. A place where they could praise God, however they were able to conceive of God, in a place that felt like home.

It seems like everyone deserves that at the very least, don't they?

The elderly lady who had met us at the door interrupted my musings. It seemed to be especially important for her to get our visitor cards. I picked it up and filled it out, respecting her need to do her job thoroughly, and chuckling a bit, as well.

She was serious.

She also had another job, apparently: master tambourine player. As the pastor played at the front of the room and the praise and worship songs continued, she diligently shook her tambourine to the beat of the music. Her dedication was noteworthy.

During one of the songs, she left her chair, and started walking around the room, shaking her tambourine, and leading some sort of praise-victory-Conga line-type march around the sanctuary. Others in the congregation followed her around the room praising God and shouting Hallelujah.

I'm not going to lie, I found all of this humorous. My friend and I tried to suppress our laughter—not at the group, but just at the fact that we were two chocolate chips from Chicago sitting in an Indiana congregation while everyone else was circling us in the praise-victory-Conga line around the room.

Prior to this service, I'd contemplated what a "Gay-friendly" Pentecostal church would feel like. The music provided the key for the answer to my questions. Not only were the songs familiar, but the way they were played was familiar, as well.

Anyone who has been to a Black church has experienced the extended-remix gospel song, where the song just goes on and on and on. With it, there is an escalation of emotion from the congregation, complete with loud Hallelujahs, praising the Lord, and even someone "catching the Holy Ghost" or "getting happy"—which might look like dancing, or someone running around the church, or falling down on the ground.

Because the congregation here was relatively small, there wasn't as much of the drama of people catching the Holy Spirit, but some of the songs went on and on and on, in the style that you might find at a Spirit-filled church, as they are sometimes called. I learned later that the pastor was from Georgia, where I grew up. He spent many years in Southern Baptist churches before he came out. When I found that out, it all made sense.

As the pastor began to speak, he reminded us that we need to be ourselves, that God made us for a purpose. He encouraged us to FROG (Fully Rely on God), and invoked a popular verse from the New Testament, John 15:18(NCV):

If the world hates you, remember that it hated me first.

The theme of persecution came up often during the sermon, which made sense, seeing as we were in a congregation of people who probably see a great deal of persecution and discrimination in their lives.

As a person of color, I understand this first hand. I understand the challenge of being yourself when that means that you'll face discrimination. I understand the challenge of figuring out of how not be silent when you see persecution in your community.

The pastor, who incorporated Jackie and I into his sermon, drove this point home. He kept calling us "the sisters from Chicago." As he discussed the struggle for personal and civil rights, he referenced Martin Luther King. I have thought often about the similarities and differences between the African-American Civil Rights Movement and the struggles for equality currently being waged by the LGBT community. Apparently, this pastor saw more similarities than differences.

The pastor also had no problem emphasizing that we are all God's children. Saying that "God has only children, no grandchildren," he pointed out that "God has more sheep than white Caucasian heterosexuals."

Agreed.

The pastor went on to share his belief that most people are frantically searching for pleasure, possessions, and power. He emphasized that God's peace is worth more than all the possessions in the world, and that it was important to say no to things that didn't serve us and learn to have a relationship with God.

The pastor then discussed five different ways to live an effective life:

1) **Relax, chill out, and be yourself.** Refuse to be someone else. Choose to be you.
2) **Accept responsibility for your own life and your own situation.** Don't say it's not my fault. Do something about it. Decide to change. People who take responsibility for their lives lead effective lives. When you take something negative

out of your life, put something positive in it. Make no excuses. Circumstances do affect you, but you don't have to stay there. No one can ruin your life except you.

3) **Write your story**. But know that you can't end the story with, "Woe is me." The story ends with victory. You can't blame others for the state of your life. You can't live someone else's personal commitment, you have to commit yourself.

4) **You have to have some values.** Establish a value system for your own life. Ask yourself: What is worth dying for in my life? What is worth being uncomfortable for? You are as close to God as you want to be.

5) **You have to have vision.** Vision is a matter of faith, and waiting is one of the greatest tests of faith. Waiting creates character and integrity. It is important to remember that God's delays are not his denials. Never take your eyes off the goal, and understand that maturity is knowing the difference between "No" and "Not yet." Renew your vision to overcome discouragement.

Words of wisdom, and more food for thought.

Later, after the service, my friend and I talked to the pastor about his experience running a "Gay-friendly" church in this part of the Midwest. He mentioned that the reception from the community was mixed, but mostly challenging. Because of this, he noted that some people were afraid to come to the church, because that would identify them as a member of the LGBT community. He spoke to many gay people in the community and invited them to come to the church. Some of those who wanted to come would tell him that they were comfortable going to gay bars, but they didn't feel safe coming to the church. They were afraid of the backlash they would receive if anyone saw them coming in or out of the church house.

Although the concept of this church being a "safe space" for people to worship was the goal, not everyone saw this church as being that space.

*   *   *

The final lesson from the service was that, even though those who have the courage to live according to their truth are often persecuted, none of us should be afraid to go out into the world and be ourselves.

Overall, I was happy that Jackie and I made the trip to LaPorte, Indiana. After several months of this journey, I still had to coax myself sometimes to keep my commitment to find myself in someone's place of worship every week. But every time, I did, I was blessed by the old friends who accompanied me and the new friends I made along the way.

WEEK 33
REMEMBERING
SAINT X CHURCH

7:00 p.m. Mass, Lincoln Park, Chicago, Illinois

August is likely going to be a difficult month for the rest of my life. August was the month in which my father was born, and the month in which he died. I was preparing to make a trip with my family to spread my father's ashes in the Pacific Ocean to commemorate the one-year anniversary of his passing.

This was my last Sunday before that trip. On my way to Lincoln Park, where I would be worshipping on this day, I drove through many Chicago neighborhoods. This made me think about my Chicago journey. After I graduated from college, I contemplated two serious options: moving to Japan to teach English, or coming to Evanston, a suburb of Chicago, to begin a master's program in Computer Science. My mother voted for Japan, my father for Chicago.

That's how I ended up in the Windy City. My father was heavy on my mind this day, and I was well aware that my spirit needed a boost. I considered attending many different places, and ended up at Saint X Church.

Saint X wasn't really the name of the church.

The church bore the same name as my ex (and I suppose he deserves some level of anonymity in the telling of this story). Worshipping at Saint X Church had a multi-layered purpose.

I found myself wishing that I could speak to my ex, that I could lean on him as I prepared to honor my father's passing by spreading his ashes—just as I wished I could have leaned on him a year prior when my father passed away.

Neither wish was granted.

While my father's life was ending, so was my relationship. Having done my best to support my ex when his mother had passed away in 2008, I wanted his support as I said goodbye to my father.

On the day that my father passed away, I called my ex to let him know. He told me he would come to Atlanta to the funeral, and I needed him to do that.

But he didn't come.

The morning of my father's funeral, I was expecting a phone call from my ex letting me know he had arrived in Atlanta. Instead, I received a voicemail letting me know he was not coming. Suffice it to say, my spirit was crushed by his choice not to show up. I focused my energy on my family and on preparing to give a eulogy at my father's funeral, but I felt so, so alone.

But it wasn't that simple. Although my ex had not shown up for the funeral, he had been there intermittently for me throughout the very difficult year when my father's illness was getting worse.

In April of 2009, my family and I travelled with my father to a cancer treatment center for more intensive therapy. Since my career allows me the flexibility of setting up a virtual office wherever my laptop is, I travelled with my mother and father to provide moral and tactical support. The course of treatment was three weeks; I planned to stay for one week to help my parents get settled, then my ex (who was still my boyfriend at the time) would fly with me to Mexico for some much needed R&R.

Well, it became quite clear after a week that I couldn't leave my parents. I told my ex this, gave him the out of travelling to Mexico by himself, and will always remember what he said to me: "No, I don't want to go if you aren't there. Can I come to stay with you? I want to be there for you and your family."

So he came. And it was no kind of vacation for him, for us, but he was there. I was exhausted, falling asleep at dinner tables and while watching the NBA finals with him. He listened to me talk about the complexities of watching a parent die. He understood, because he had been there before.

He wanted to see my father. They had met once, years before, just after we started dating. The man he saw this time was a very different man, much thinner, more frail, and without energy for or interest in pleasantries.

Nevertheless, my dad and my ex spent some time together. I'll never forget the brief conversation they had. As my dad sat across from my ex, few words were exchanged. My ex said, "Dr. Bassey, I just wanted to let you know that your daughter has meant a lot to me. She has had a great impact on my life."

My father, with a tired smile, replied, "Well, that makes two of us."

And with that, he was done. He returned to his room, leaving me sitting with my ex, processing the exchange. Tears filled my eyes.

My ex was the only boyfriend that I'd ever brought to meet my father. I hadn't dated much, and never had anyone in my life that was important enough to introduce to my parents. But my ex and I had talked about marriage and family. I believed in those conversations. I believed that the two men who I loved most in the world at that time should know each other. So, they met.

Now they were both gone. And I was faced with the knowledge that my father may never know my husband—whoever he might be. And that was heavy on my heart.

I relived all those feelings as I approached Saint X Church for Mass.

Despite all that we had been through, I knew that I needed to take my ex with me in my heart to San Diego for the remembrance and ash scattering. Although he was not with me at my father's funeral, and our relationship was decidedly over, he was the one person whose presence could always make me feel like everything was going to be okay, even when there was plenty of evidence to the contrary. I missed that, craved that, to the point where I was still, months into our breakup, constantly, creatively trying to get it back. Suffice it to say that just because I was on a spiritual journey didn't mean that I'd worked out the kinks about how to always trust God, and how to always choose behavior that I wouldn't regret later, especially when it came to my ex.

What can I say? I'm still a work in progress.

How heavy regret can be. How hard it can be to walk away. How hard it can be to forgive. How hard it can be to forget.

For the past few weeks, I'd been bracing myself for an emotional week, and was a little concerned that even being in a place with my ex's name on it would be too much to handle.

It turned out that this was right where I needed to be.

My father loved the Catholic Church, and the Catholic service. He used to tell us all the time about how he used to be a choir boy, and how the Catholic Church really saved him when he was in medical school in Germany all alone. My father, a pharmacist from Lagos, Nigeria, took the opportunity to move to Germany and attend medical school. He, being brilliant and confident, took the plunge. After he arrived there, however, he experienced what many students do: a lack of funds, a little homesickness, and the challenge of completing a difficult course of study. Adding to his challenge was the fact that he didn't speak German when he arrived on German soil. He learned German and medicine at the same time.

He didn't view this as an obstacle.

Along the way, he did receive some help. As children, my sisters and I often heard about a woman named Christiana, a woman who apparently spent a good amount of energy making sure that my father was okay. Christiana was part of a Catholic family who realized that my father's family was a pillar in the Catholic Church in Nigeria. When they met my father, and he shared his struggles, they responded with support. Why, she asked, should he starve alone? She made sure that she and the church provided him with support that came in handy as he battled through medical school. He graduated at the top of his class.

My father accepted help in his early years that he would give out again and again throughout his life.

I remember when I was a self-absorbed teenager, and Christiana visited us in Atlanta. I didn't know who she was, nor was I particularly concerned. I remember my father being very upset that my sisters and I didn't act more interested in this woman who just seemed to be an old friend of my father's.

Years later, I tried to redeem myself. As a consultant living in Munich, Germany, I made the trip to see my father's university, The University of Bonn. I visited Christiana and her family. More mature, I was able to see her, speak to her in my not-so-impressive German, and thank her for taking care of my father years before.

I thought of all this as I sat in Mass.

I allowed myself to feel the intertwined grief from my father's death and the loss of my relationship.

Like my father, I also learned to love Catholic mass: the liturgy and the ritual, although I still hadn't mastered it all. Sometimes I didn't know what to say when during the mass, when to sit or stand and why. Sometimes I got it right and sometimes I didn't. In addition, in my efforts not to be a hypocrite, there were certain gestures I didn't make, mostly because I didn't know the depth of their meaning, and I wondered if others noticed that I didn't make the sign of the cross, or kneel next to the pew before sitting down. Catholic churches had become an awkward yet familiar worship experience.

The church was gorgeous. Absolutely breathtaking. I was soaking in the delight, the privilege, and the wonder of being able to just sit in a glorious place and feel God.

Fittingly enough, the homily addressed parent-child relationships and discipline. As the priest spoke, I thought about my relationship with my father and how it had evolved. It changed over the years from me being a young girl who was a little bit afraid of an autocratic father, to me being a woman who felt she understood her father's heart.

I thought about the discipline that might come in handy if I was ever able to truly forgive and forget my ex and move on.

Important things to consider.

Because I'm not Catholic, I never took communion at Catholic Masses. On this evening, a woman next to me also didn't take communion. She seemed to know all the different Catholic movements and responses. I decided in my mind that she was raised Catholic and came back for a visit to a familiar place, but still didn't feel the need to participate in the very serious matter of communion. It put me at ease, since often I was the one person in the pew that people had to climb over because I wasn't moving toward the communion plate. It made me remember: God is all of ours, no matter our denomination.

During the communion song, I cried. I missed my father. I was tired of not being able to get over my ex.

I wept heaving, body-wracking tears.

My neighbor asked me if I was okay. I was not.

I was touched that she asked.

The gift of the kindness of strangers.

*   *   *

At the beginning of Mass, I felt alone. But I knew by the end of the service that I was not. God used my neighbor to remind me. I took that knowledge with me as I prepared to join my family to honor the memory of my father on the anniversary of his death.

At the end of the Mass, the priest spoke the following benediction: "The Mass has ended. Go in Peace. Love and Serve the Lord."

Amen.

WEEK 34
MONKS, MEDITATION, AND ME
ISKCON, THE HARE KRISHNA TEMPLE

5:30 a.m. Japa Meditation, San Diego, California

I'd travelled to San Diego to join my mother and my sisters for the scattering of my father's ashes in the Pacific Ocean, and the memorial, which took place on August 24, the first anniversary of his passing.

It was now the morning of August 25, and it appeared that I'd survived.

Physically.

But emotionally, I was drained.

The day before the memorial, I'd taken a walk by the ocean to try to settle my emotions. On the way back, I chose to walk through the city streets to return to the hotel where I was staying with my family. To my surprise and delight, on my route home I saw a Hare Krishna Temple, and knew immediately that there was a reason why I'd chosen the route I did to walk back.

I entered the temple, asked when they had services, and was given a listing of what I thought were service times. I was planning to fly back home in the afternoon the next day. I made a decision to attend a 5:30 a.m. meditation at the temple.

Yes, 5:30 a.m. God help us!

On this very early Wednesday morning, I drove to the temple in the darkness thinking it was slightly odd for meditation to start so early, but looking forward to it. Several times, I drove past the temple and had to turn around because I didn't see anything to indicate that the temple was even open. Finally, I drove back, located it and parked.

It looked exceptionally quiet.

I was a little apprehensive, but I figured, "I'm here. I might as well go inside."

I exited my car, walked over, opened the door to the temple, and peeked my head in.

Inside I saw monks in flowing orange and white floor-length robes holding prayer beads in their hands and wearing them around their necks. Some were preparing for their day by performing their morning tasks. Many more were meditating—sitting and walking around the temple. A continuous, low buzz filled the temple as the monks spoke and chanted ancient and powerful mantras.

Quickly someone spotted me and came over to help me. I probably looked confused and out of place.

I was feeling both.

The monk who was so kind as to approach me brought a smile to my face when he told me that I was welcome to stay and participate in the meditation, but he warned me that everyone might be preoccupied with their morning tasks. "We are not unfriendly," he explained, "we are monks and this is when we meditate to get ready for the day."

Well, that would explain the 5:30 a.m. start time, I thought.

And the fact that everyone else there besides me was a monk.

Assuring him that I was honored to be in the temple and would happily meditate in a corner where I would bother the least number of people, I followed his direction as he gestured toward the section of the temple where I was to sit: "Women sit over there," he said. I realized I still had my shoes on. I went out to take them off, then moved to the section where I would meditate. Some kind monks brought me prayer beads, which looked much like a rosary, and demonstrated how to use them, praying bead by bead.

They brought over a small stool—so the beads wouldn't touch the ground—and a small package that contained some sort of sweets and some literature, then I was ready.

The founder-acarya of the International Society for Krishna Consciousness, Swami Prabhupada, sat on a decorated altar in the corner of the temple opposite from where I sat. He meditated with a laser focus, eyes open, not moving a muscle for hours.

He may have blinked, but I didn't see it.

His calm was amazing. It felt like he was in such a state of pure meditation that it was humbling.

I tried to be unobtrusive, but I wondered if the Swami and the other monks were curious about the unfamiliar girl in the corner.

Probably they had better things to do.

I tried my best not to spend too much time gawking at the monks. There was meditating to do! I had the beads, and the initial mediation instructions I was given. I contemplated the Hare Krishna mantra on which I was to meditate.

I had no idea what it meant.

Later, I did some research to find out. This is what I learned:

> . . . the word "hara" is a form of addressing the energy of the Lord. Both "Krishna" and "Rama" are forms of directly addressing the Lord and they mean "The highest pleasure." Hara is the supreme pleasure potency of the Lord. This Potency,

addressed as Hare, helps us in reaching the supreme personality of God head.

> . . . the three words—namely hare, Krishna, and rama—are the transcendental seeds of the maha-mantra and the chanting is the spiritual call for the Lord and his internal energy, hara, for giving protection to the conditioned souls. The chanting is exactly like genuine crying by the child for his mother. Mother hara helps in achieving the grace of the supreme father hari, or krsna, and he reveals himself to such sincere devotees.[49]

My initial attempts at saying the Hare Krishna mantra felt disingenuous. I tried silent meditation, first with my eyes closed, as I'd learned in the Buddhist temples I'd visited earlier in the year, and then with my eyes open, just focusing on my breath, as I'd learned from the Shambhala Center. Then I did about forty-five minutes of passage meditation, which I had learned the previous fall at a Passage Meditation seminar. Then, finally, I completed one round of beads, saying the Hare Krishna mantra.

I felt like hours had gone by. Somehow, the monks who had been meditating before me were still meditating, and the Swami still hadn't blinked an eye.

I later learned that the goal is to do sixteen rounds of prayer beads. Wow. I felt like sixteen rounds would have taken me all day. Later, I learned more about the practice:

> . . . japa is a spiritual discipline involving the meditative repetition of a mantra. Repetitions are counted using a string of beads known as japa mala. The number of beads in the japa mala is generally 108, which has great significance. It is not uncommon for people to wear japa beads around their neck, although some practitioners prefer to carry them in a bead bag to keep them clean.

> . . . when one chants the mantra 108 times, starting at one end of the mala to the other (excluding the large bead bearing thread),

that is called one round. The goal is to achieve a discipline of 16 rounds a day, to make steady progress on the road to Samadhi, complete spiritual absorption. If one cannot immediately do 16 rounds daily, there is no harm, but one should vow to chant a fixed amount daily if one truly wants to experience the inner fulfillment and self-realization afforded by this time-tested method of the yoga science.[50]

After about an hour of meditation, I was fidgeting and moving. I couldn't sit cross legged anymore. My legs were tingling uncomfortably.

Patience has never been my strong suit. When I was doing the Japa meditation, I was constantly checking to see how close I was to completing the round, rather than staying in the moment, focusing on the current bead.

I'm sure the monks continued to meditate after I finally decided, after several hours, to leave. I left with a profound feeling that I would never forget this experience.

*   *   *

When the journey of my life is done, I'll be able to tell the story of the morning I spent meditating with monks at a Hare Krishna temple.

My father would have loved it.

I was able to complete the week of mourning and remembrance with a memorable meditation experience. I was honored and humbled that the monks allowed me to share their meditative space.

WEEK 35
WOULD YOU LIKE TO SEE A CHAPLAIN?
NORTHWESTERN MEMORIAL
HOSPITAL, EMERGENCY ROOM

Early Morning, Chicago, Illinois

Would you like to see a chaplain?

The question startled me.

I expected to be poked and prodded in a teaching hospital—different nurses putting in IVs and taking my blood pressure, while physicians and residents alike asked me a plethora of questions. I put up with the madness because, as it happened, I thought of friends and family who were medical students and residents. I respected the process they went through to learn how to practice medicine.

But never had I been asked if I wanted to see a chaplain.

In my mind, hospital chaplains were for people who were dying, to be comforted by the presence of God in the face of impending death.

Chaplains were not for me. Not today.

The last time I'd contemplated the presence of clergy in a hospital had been almost a year before to the day, as my father lay dying in his hospital room. I walked the halls to take a break from the bedside vigil, and on that walk, I saw a chapel. I walked in crying, and I prayed, "God, please help my father."

Help at that point meant any number of things. I didn't like to see my father in pain, but I didn't want him to die. I didn't know what to pray.

And today was August 29, my father's birthday. The year before, I was delivering his eulogy at his funeral in a church filled with family and friends.

And, today, I was in the emergency room.

And my physician was asking *me* if *I* wanted to see a chaplain.

Hospitals were like home for my father. A physician for so long, he walked the halls of hospitals in Germany and in New York City as he trained, and in Atlanta as he practiced for over thirty years as a nephrologist. He helped countless individuals with issues of kidney disease and hypertension—chronic diseases that required my father to be the face of continued hope for those with serious diagnoses that required years of dialysis treatment. He never complained; he loved being a doctor and the hospital was where he practiced his beloved craft. He knew what to do and how to be of service. He was, as one colleague stated after he died, a doctor's doctor.

Hospitals for my father were like airports are for me. Having worked as a consultant for the majority of my career, I became a road warrior. I know just how to pack so I can get through security the fastest. I know how to stride with purpose at the right speed through the airport to get to the gate not too early and not too late. And I know how to get just the right amount of frequent flier miles so I can board first, get in the fast lines, sit in the front of the plane, or in the exit rows so I can travel comfortably, exit quickly, and be about my business. I collected frequent flier miles like a champion, gifting them to friends and family so we could all have free flights and upgrades, and all the perks that come to frequent travelers.

For years, I was the weekly traveler: out on Monday morning and back on Friday night, with just a short weekend rest before I did it again. At the height of my corporate travel, I used to fly from Chicago to London or Munich for work, every month back and forth; and sometimes for a weekend meeting or "team building exercise" with my colleagues.

But my life as a road warrior betrayed me. Not long after my European travel ended, I experienced some strange symptoms. Out of nowhere, I noticed that I was so short of breath that a brief jog left me winded. As a recreational runner and former marathoner, this was odd. I knew I was not in the best shape of my life, but I was not in the worst shape either. I was young—still in my twenties—and with no history of health issues.

Walking across a parking lot one day left me so winded that I was terrified something was horribly wrong with me. I ended up going to get a massage—maybe I was stressed, I thought. Lying on the massage table, I had a panic attack because I couldn't relax. I was feeling even worse. I left the spa and went straight to the hospital. After a number of tests, my doctor told me that I had to be hospitalized. I had a pulmonary embolism—a blood clot in my lung. And those can kill you.

People get blood clots for various reasons, but one of the well-known reasons is due to excessive travel.

As I spent the next few days in the hospital, my father talked to me and my physicians, and calmed everyone down. No need to worry, he explained, yes, this was serious, but here's what was going on, and, most importantly: everything would be okay.

The cure: a few months of blood thinners and an admonition to be mindful, to watch for the recurrence of symptoms. Once you have a blood clot, you are at risk of having another.

Years went by before I had another one.

For my thirty-fifth birthday I took a short trip to Rio De Janeiro, Brazil to visit a friend, Naomi, who was living there at the time. We went to Samba school, and visited Sugar Mountain and Corcovado. We walked on the beaches at Ipanema and Copacabana. We danced all night in

Lapa. On our last day together, we shopped at a street festival, ate at a churrascaria, and I came home.

A short time later, I ended up in the emergency room with yet another blood clot—this time in my leg.

My father was there with me that time as well. He drove me to the emergency room, and waited with me for hours. It was the Christmas season and the hospital was packed. He assured me that everything would be okay, and explained to the physicians at the hospital that there was no reason for me to stay in the emergency room over night, that I was a "compliant patient," and that he knew what to do to make sure that I was okay. I felt like everything would be fine, because he was the best doctor I knew. He said everything would be fine, and I believed him.

This time—although I'd ignored it—I knew exactly when my condition returned. One night, I'd been driving around Chicago, restless, upset, and still grieving. After coming home, after long and passionate prayers, I collapsed into a fitful sleep on my living room couch. When I woke up, I felt a familiar feeling in my right calf—like someone had kicked me in the leg with a steel-toed boot . . . or like I'd been working out vigorously.

Neither had happened.

What had happened, just a few weeks before, was a long distance trip: Chicago to Atlanta to Lagos, Nigeria for my cousin's wedding, then to Johannesburg, South Africa for the World Cup. During this time, there was a road trip of several hours to Bloemfontein, South Africa to watch Nigeria play Greece. Back to Lagos, then to Atlanta and then to Chicago. Countless hours of sedentary travel—one of the things that can cause blood clots.

After this trip, it didn't take long for the symptoms to reappear.

I didn't want to face the truth, so I ignored it. I made and missed an appointment with my primary care physician who knew my history. I half-heartedly visited an urgent care center, instead of the hospital, to have them do an ultrasound. The inept individual who completed the test told me, "No, you don't have any blood clots."

I knew she was wrong, but I didn't want to believe that I had to face this challenge again. "Why me?" I thought. To this day, no tests have revealed why I'm susceptible to blood clots. When she told me that the pain I was feeling was probably muscular, I nodded, smiled, and left. When I walked home from that appointment, I could feel my breathing was not normal. But I shook it off.

In the coming weeks, I flew to California and back for a girlfriend's wedding. I drove to Cincinnati to see one of my best girlfriends and her family. Five hours in the car both ways. More risky travel.

And just the week prior, the symptoms were so pronounced that I had to wear heels in the house to relieve the pressure in both of my calves, and I had to focus on inhaling and exhaling. Nevertheless, I flew to California and back to commemorate the one-year anniversary of my father's death. A four-hour flight each way. My shortness of breath as I walked on the beach the day before the ceremony and my inability to sit still when I was meditating with the Hare Krishnas were not just because I was out of shape, or because I needed more practice in sitting still. It was because the blood in my legs and my lungs was fighting to circulate, being hampered by multiple clots. When I returned to Chicago, I couldn't ignore the truth anymore.

I ended up going to the ER early on that Sunday morning, August 29. From previous experiences, I knew the patterns of the ER. Early morning, the ER is often emptier. I wanted to get in and out of there. I was a compliant patient. I knew the drill, and I figured this would be like the other times.

Except my father was not there to tell me everything would be okay.

The irony of me being in a hospital on my father's birthday was not lost on me. In fact, in retrospect, maybe I was waiting for his birthday so he could, in some small way, accompany me on this mission. I felt his presence as I approached the hospital doors. I felt my heart racing as I entered the building. The last time I'd been in a hospital was the day he died. The check-in process was quick, but as I was escorted to my room in the ER, I saw people in pain, and people dying, and tears came to my eyes.

Tears of remembrance.

After all the tests, my physician told what I already knew: I had multiple blood clots in my legs and in my lungs. She looked at me and asked me if I knew how serious that was. Of course, I did. I'd been here before.

But never without my father.

That is when she asked me if I wanted to see the chaplain.

Believe it or not, I thought of my 52 Weeks of Worship journey, and thought, "Well, I don't know what happens with a hospital chaplain, and that might be a memorable worship experience." So I said yes.

She went away to fulfill my request and while she was gone, my sister arrived. My sister is also a physician. We had a bit of church there together, me in my emergency room gown and she assuring me that everything would be okay, as my father, the first Dr. Bassey, had done before. My worship experience on this day would be one that included two sisters, both who knew the seriousness of the situation, praying together—calling on the Divine to receive guidance. We asked for healing in the face of a scary medical challenge.

When my ER doctor returned, she told me she wanted me to be admitted. I told her that wouldn't be necessary. I knew what I needed to do to be okay. Although the idea of rest in the hospital appealed to me, I knew I couldn't stay in a hospital bed, thinking about my father and the promises I'd made to him about how I would take better care of myself.

Broken promises.

My sister, the other Dr. Bassey, helped me to navigate the necessary discussions that allowed me to check out of the emergency room, instead of being admitted for what might have been a week-long stay, where they would monitor me until my situation was a little less life threatening. I had to sign paperwork that said I knew I was leaving against doctor's orders. They must have thought I was nuts.

I never did get to meet that hospital chaplain.

*　　*　　*

When I returned home, I spent some time thinking about the fact that life and death are flip sides of one coin. When you're grieving, sometimes you wonder why you're still alive. On the roughest days, you might even consider if it would just be easier if you weren't.

But, as I sat in that hospital room, contemplating the life-threatening situation that I was in, and the comparatively simple actions I needed to take in order to make sure I never found myself in that situation again, I thought of my father. He lived a full life, and I know he would want the same for me.

I wasn't ready to see a chaplain who would pray with me as if the end was near.

I still had too much living to do.

WEEK 36
TORAH AND HAFTORAH
KAM ISRAEL ISAIAH

10:30 a.m. Shabbat Service, Hyde Park, Chicago, Illinois

Since childhood, I'd never been a big fan of Halloween. It detracted from a much more important day (in my opinion): my birthday, which is the day after Halloween. As a child, I was focused on waiting for my birthday to come, while everyone was worrying about costumes and candy (which I couldn't eat anyway, thanks to my mother's vigilance about health and nutrition).

As I grew up, I never really got into the costume thing, but on one occasion, when my best friend invited me to a Halloween party for adults, I accepted. The party was held at a large, luxurious home. The owners were wealthy lawyers who had downsized from an enormous estate in the suburbs to an enormous house in Hyde Park, a well-known neighborhood on the South Side of Chicago.

The house was down the street from then Senator Barack Obama—back before there were roadblocks that would prevent you from driving right up to that house and parking in front of it. I remember the host of the party mentioning that likely someone would "take a plate" down to the Obama's house so that they could participate in the Halloween festivities.

Even then, I found that humorously impressive.

Times had changed. When researching my place of worship for the weekend, I saw the following warning on the synagogue's website:[51]

Now that our famous neighbor, President Barack Obama, and his family have moved to Washington, D.C., there are still a few security precautions around the synagogue.

Vehicular access is still limited to Greenwood Avenue at 50th Street, but cars are generally allowed through without impediment, although an officer may stop you to ask for your destination. Pedestrians may enter through 50th & Greenwood or Hyde Park Blvd.

As before, please be prepared to show a photo ID at all times. When the family is home, you may be required to open the trunk or hood of your car to check for explosive devices.

As I drove to Hyde Park on this Saturday, I was excited that this journey was bringing me out of my house to enjoy the cool, sunny day. I wondered what I would have to do to get to KAM Israel Isaiah, where I would be spending the Sabbath.

I was able to drive into the parking lot for the synagogue with little fanfare, although I could see the roadblocks that would have prevented me from driving any further.

Early for the service, I wandered around inside for a while, reading the plaques and the announcements on the walls, and waiting for service time. Every week during my journey, I took a picture of the place I where was worshipping. When I walked outside to do that, I was directly in front of the President's house. There was a car parked out front, and I felt extremely self-conscious as I tried to position myself to get a good picture of the synagogue with my iPhone without looking like I was slyly trying to take a picture of the President's house. Because I hurried to take the picture, of all the pictures of all the places where I worshipped, the picture of the synagogue is the least impressive.

When I walked back into the synagogue, I ran into the rabbi. She introduced herself. I told her I was visiting and asked her what the rules were: did I need to cover my head? Was it okay for me to participate? She was extremely welcoming and put me at ease, letting me know that there was nothing special that I needed to do, and that she would be in shortly to start the service.

As I headed toward the sanctuary, I greeted everyone by saying, "Shabbat Shalom," remembering my experience at Beth Shalom B'nai Zaken Ethiopian Hebrew Congregation, and being grateful that I had that experience to help scaffold me as I walked into another experience with Judaism.

Copies of the Torah, song books, yarmulkes, and prayer shawls were available at the door. I heeded the rabbi's assurance that I needed nothing special—no head covering or anything. I entered and sat down.

I was one of a small group who was there for service. The men and the rabbis wore yarmulkes, but, unlike my last experience, the women didn't cover their heads. As my 52-week journey progressed, I was learning about the different communities within communities of worship, for example:

> In North America today, the four main branches of Judaism are Orthodox, Conservative, Reform, and Reconstructionist. Within these denominations themselves, however, there is a great degree of variation in practice and observance.[52]

So much to learn, and so many different ways to worship.

This service started with praise. I felt comfortable, following along with the service, and contemplating the wisdom the rabbi was sharing.

In the message for the day, she encouraged us to, "Make our lives be one link in a chain of goodness." In the Torah portion of the service, she focused on the fact that we should know that things are not too hard for us to do. Turning to God isn't too hard; changing our ways isn't too hard. She explained that whatever we needed to become the people we were called to be was in us already—we may need to relearn it, or to fire it up, but it was still in us.

During the service, we did what was called a Mourner's Kaddish.

The Kaddish is a prayer that praises God and expresses a yearning for the establishment of God's kingdom on earth. The emotional reactions inspired by the Kaddish come from the circumstances in which it is said: it is recited at funerals and by mourners, and sons are required to say Kaddish for eleven months after the death of a parent.

The word Kaddish means sanctification, and the prayer is a sanctification of God's name . . . . It is customary for all the mourners in the congregation to recite Kaddish in unison . . . . The Mourner's Kaddish is recited for eleven months from the day of the death and also on the yahrzeit (anniversary of a death). A person may say Kaddish not only for parents, but also for a child, brother, or in-law.[53]

I found this to be quite appropriate, given that I'd just celebrated the one year anniversary of my father's death.

*   *   *

Coming away with the encouragement that, "Things are not too hard for us to do," gave me the fuel I needed to continue my journey.

My time at KAM Israel Isaiah was a gentle and inspiring experience, which left me looking forward to more experiences with different types of Judaism.

Week 37
Unsure
Seventeenth Church of Christ, Scientist

10:30 a.m. service, Chicago, Illinois

On this September weekend, my cousin, Nefe visited me from the United Kingdom. I asked her if she would like to join me for church, told her about my journey, and gave her four options for places we could visit. She said she would like to join me, and because neither of us could decide where to go, we ended up writing four options on small pieces of paper and placing them in a bag so she could do a blind choosing.

The winner: The Seventeenth Church of Christ, Scientist.

The Seventeenth Church of Christ, Scientist, is housed in a well-known and very distinctive building at the corner of Wabash and Wacker in Chicago that most would recognize as a landmark in Chicago's downtown Loop area. The building takes up the whole block, and it has a large, round exterior that makes it look somewhat like a space ship. The name of the church is displayed prominently on the building. I'd walked by and driven past that building a million times. I looked forward to experiencing a worship service within its walls.

I had extremely high expectations. Unfortunately, out of all the services I attended during the whole year, this one was most underwhelming— maybe because my cousin was with me and I wanted to have a good experience with her, I don't know.

Many worship traditions I experienced had a structured service, but this one appeared to take structure to another level. The content and the energy of the service left me feeling like there was more structure than spirit.

Apparently, every Christian Science church has the same service each Sunday. They read from the given readings, some of which were from the Bible and others from the text of a book by Mary Baker Eddy, the founder of Christian Science.

There was no interpretation, no sermon. Maybe there was no interpretation because they felt we had all we needed to understand God's word? I was unsure.

There was some singing.

And that was it.

Usually, when I visit a place of worship, I feel spirit immediately. Here, that didn't happen for me. It felt very sterile. It was difficult for me to connect with the service. Only a few members sat in the green plush chairs in the auditorium-shaped sanctuary. I wondered more about the few who attended the service—were they regulars? How did they feel? Why did they choose this church? Did they feel the same way I did?

During the service, The Lord's Prayer was read in call and response fashion, excruciatingly slowly. It was contemplative to the point that it felt like slow motion. Why?

As the service continued, I started to get sleepy and fidgety. I'm inspired by intelligence, but I don't think I want to reduce my experience of God to something scientific only. That is what this service felt like to me.

* * *

I did not come away from this service with a strong sense of the beliefs of The Seventeenth Church of Christ, Scientist. I did not feel that my spirit would be fed by this style of worship. But that was okay!

Sometimes, when you visit a place of worship, you will be completely confused. Sometimes only partially. But sometimes, you will make a complete connection. Each experience teaches you something about yourself.

Although this worship experience was a bit baffling to me, I left contemplating the wisdom of two wise teachers, whose words were prominently displayed at the front of the sanctuary. They said:

And ye shall know the truth and the truth shall make you free.

—Jesus

Divine Love always has met and always will meet every human need.

—Mary Baker Eddy

WEEK 38
ATONEMENT
TEMPLE SHOLOM

8:15 p.m. Kol Nidre service, Chicago, Illinois

It was Yom Kippur, Year 5771. I wanted to experience some portion of the holiday, so I Googled around to find a temple to attend. Not knowing anything about this Jewish Day of Atonement, I vacillated between different places of worship. Ultimately, I chose to attend the Yom Kippur evening service—Kol Nidre—at the Temple Sholom on the North Side of Chicago, a temple in the Reform Judaism tradition.

But, what is a day of atonement?

The only real experience I had with the concept of a "Day of Atonement" was the Million Man March, years before. A million or so African-American men descended on the Mall in Washington, D.C. to ask for forgiveness and to pledge to do better. Research revealed the following to be the focus of the Jewish holiday:

> Yom Kippur (the Day of Atonement) is one of two Jewish High Holy Days. The first High Holy Day is Rosh Hashanah (the Jewish New Year). Yom Kippur falls ten days after Rosh Hashanah on the 10th of Tishrei, which is a Hebrew month that correlates with September–October on the secular calendar. The purpose of Yom Kippur is to bring about reconciliation between people and between individuals and God. According to Jewish tradition, it is also the day when God decides the fate of each human being.[54]

When I told a friend that I was attending this service, she asked me what I thought the Christian version of a Day of Atonement was. "It seems like many religions have them," she said. We thought about it and talked about it. We could only come up with the season of Lent as a similar, but not exactly the same, time of reflection and atonement.

So much still to learn.

As I sped up Lake Shore Drive, the announcer on the radio warned of horrendous traffic backups on Chicago's lakefront expressway, reminding me that Dave Matthews was performing that night in Wrigleyville. This, of course, was right where the temple was located. How's that for good planning?

Repeatedly, I circled the block around the synagogue, realizing that getting inside might be more difficult than I initially thought. There was the normal lack of North Side Chicago parking to contend with, combined with a high holiday and a rock concert.

I said a quick prayer: "God, I really want to go to this service. Please help me find some parking."

The first time around the block, I tried to park in the synagogue parking lot. A traffic guard told me that it was reserved for disabled congregants. I travelled through the neighborhood, searching for a parking space that was not located next to a "Tow Zone" sign. Finally, I found myself driving by the synagogue parking lot again. This time, the traffic guard waved me into the lot. As we were getting closer to service time, I guess he figured there was room for more attendees to park in the lot than they had initially anticipated.

The temple was large and imposing from the outside. Amazingly enough, I'd driven past it frequently on Lake Shore Drive and never noticed it. It felt good that I was seeing it for the first time.

On the stairs of the temple, there was a table set up for selling tickets. I remembered my experience in the Beth Shalom B'nai Zaken Ethiopian Hebrew Congregation. I had wondered if it was customary for there to be a collection taken up in a synagogue as I'd experienced in various Christian services. Well, here was my partial answer. The ticket for the High Holiday cost me $100. I'm not sure if I paid more or less because I was not a member of the synagogue. I also realized that not only was this a sacred day in the Jewish faith, it was likely one of the days where a good portion of the operating income for the synagogue was raised.

I'd called other synagogues and temples and they told me that if I was unable to pay they wouldn't turn me away, which was comforting. In the end, though, I figured I might as well contribute to the cause since I was able. I bought the ticket. This afforded me admission to all of the weekend services, even though I only planned to attend one service for the weekend.

The inside of the temple was as exquisite as the outside. There were brilliant stained glass windows all over the sanctuary and several rows of chairs. The place was packed.

It was clear that this was a day when the entire community came out for the service.

I grabbed the Torah and The New Union Prayer book and chose a seat. Soon, I was following along with the service, and enjoying the readings just as much as I had in my previous visits to Jewish worship services.

During the service, I saw a family making their way to their seats and realized that one of the family members, Robert, was a friend of mine from high school. As he walked by my seat, I called out his name, and he walked toward me. He looked at me, puzzled, gave me a hug, and said, "What are you doing here?"

He wasn't being inhospitable, he was just confused. I simply replied, "It's a long story, I'll tell you later," then I smiled to myself as he walked away.

Later, when we talked, he said, "I thought you had converted—you looked like you knew what you were saying and doing."

True, I felt comfortable following along with the service. There was a great deal of reading—both in English and in Hebrew—and as I followed along, I contemplated the differences between worship experiences. It seemed to me that Christian (non-Catholic) churches have the most improvising as part of the service—the sermons, primarily. Many other faiths seem to keep the message consistent by using prayer books, where sections are read and re-read from week to week. I wondered why that was, how that had evolved historically, and what I thought was better.

Surprisingly, this service had something in common with the Catholic churches I'd visited—there was a great deal of sitting and standing.

At one point during the service, I found myself fiddling with the cross that I always wear around my neck. All at once, I had a realization: I'm wearing a cross in a Jewish temple. My next thought was: That's okay.

I wasn't conducting this journey to pretend that I was something I wasn't. Although, every week, I did try to blend, it was mostly so I wouldn't disrupt the worship experience of the congregants.

I wasn't making any bones about who I was and why I was there. I thought, "Christians on respectful journeys are included in the 'All are Welcome' message that most places of worship espouse, right?"

At Temple Sholom, the emphasis on community was clear. During the service, members of the community came forward to share how temple had impacted their lives and the lives of their friends and families.

The rabbi built upon these testimonials when he began to speak. He based his sermon on the questions: Why are we here? What do we seek? What do we find?

He talked about how the synagogue was a gathering of sinners who needed God, and that the synagogue was meant to serve as a house of prayer, a house of study, and a house of assembly.

He defined a synagogue as an ideal place for Jewish worship, and a place where heritage can be preserved.

He shared that Judaism is based on community, and emphasized the importance of relationships. He spoke about tolerance of other religions, and the importance of religious freedom.

He spoke of the "armor of faith and fortitude," stating that is what our ancestors put on to get through all of the different trials they faced.

As a Black woman listening to this service, it was hard not to see parallels to my home church, Trinity, which definitely served as a place for worship, a place for community, and a place where heritage could be preserved. Many Sundays, I sat in those pews and listened to stories of the faith and fortitude that had inspired members of my community to move through the challenges that they had faced as Africans and the descendants of Africans.

*   *   *

As I sat and listened to the rabbi, I noted the fact that places of worship were places where community, culture, history, and celebration were intertwined—where we are encouraged to remember those before us, as we utilize their wisdom to manage the lives that we are living today.

Overall, I enjoyed the experience. When the rabbi, during his benediction, said, "May the one who blessed our fathers and mothers bless our entire congregation," all I could say was: Amen.

WHICH WITCHES?
MABON (WICCA) FESTIVAL, THE AUTUMN
EQUINOX, SKY FIRE SONG COVEN

6:00 p.m., McHenry Illinois

In the week after my Hare Krishna experience, I felt a shift in the way I approached this journey. The year was moving along quickly. It was increasingly important for me to diversify the types of worship experiences I was having before my 52-week journey ended.

Although I'd done some things that may have been outside of the average person's comfort zone, I really had not had many experiences yet where I felt anxious. There was my experience visiting the Mormons, which was challenging, and my time with the Hare Krishnas, which was outside of my normal realm of interaction, but neither made me overly uncomfortable, in retrospect.

I felt challenged to do something that made me stretch—to visit a place where I had to trust that everything was going to be okay, even though I didn't know anything about that worship tradition.

After taking a look at the list of worship experiences I'd compiled, I opened a search engine window and typed:

Wiccan religion.

I was ready to learn about Wicca.

I found several very informative websites. One site in particular included a number of contact numbers for Wiccan priests in the Chicagoland area. Unfortunately, many of the contacts led me to disconnected phone numbers, but when I called one number, I connected. I left a message with a high priestess, letting her know that I would like to learn more about Wiccan traditions and perhaps attend a service or a ceremony or something.

Then I waited.

About a week later, I received a message from an individual named Craig, who said he was calling on behalf of his high priestess. He said that he was calling to respond to my message, and was available to talk to me about Wicca, which he also called The Craft.

When I returned his call, we had a very long, informative discussion. Amusingly enough, he had more questions for me than I had for him. All I wanted to know was, "Is there a service I can attend, and where is it?"

He told me what to look out for and what I should run from if I experienced it. Apparently, a great many people are creating provocative experiences in the name of Wicca. He discussed the following:

1. If you talk to people who you think are Wiccans, and they say they worship Satan, run. True Wiccans are not Satan worshippers; they do not worship the devil.
2. If someone tells you that you have to participate in an orgy, or any other sort of sexual rite, to be a Wiccan, run. There are no mandatory sex rites that are part of Wiccan festivals.
3. If you are told that you have to wear certain gothic-type clothing in order to be a Wiccan or participate in a Wiccan ceremony, run. Wicca is a religion, not a fashion statement.
4. If you are told that it is mandatory that you drink large amounts of alcohol or use certain drugs or other substances, run. That's not true.

The list went on and we talked for a long time. He asked me many questions about who I was, and what my interest truly was. He told me about Wicca, about the different traditions and communities that practiced different versions of The Craft. At the end of our chat, I felt pretty comfortable with our interaction.

Along the way, he explained to me that Wicca was an earth-based religion, and that The Craft sees divinity as being female and male—in the form of Mother Earth and Sky Father. He told me there were eight festivals per year, and the next one was a Harvest Festival. If I wanted to experience a Wiccan ceremony, he would ask his high priestess if it was okay if I could visit his coven.

He also mentioned that, after the Harvest festival, there were only two more festivals left in the year: Christmas (called Yule), when I wouldn't be around, and Halloween (called Samhain), which I probably wouldn't be allowed to attend. When I asked why, he mentioned they called that time of year "crazy season," because they received countless requests from people who wanted to "hang out with witches for Halloween." The general feeling was that those were not the kind of people they wanted to attract to one of their sacred festivals.

That made perfect sense to me. Who wants their sacred spaces to be turned into a sideshow?

It appeared that Mabon, the Harvest festival for the Autumnal Equinox, was the one that I would aim to attend. I let him know I was interested, and he told me he would check with the high priestess and get back to me. In the meantime, he gave me some names of websites, books, and people to talk with to learn more about The Craft. I knew I wouldn't be embarking upon an in-depth study of Wicca, but thought I should talk to at least one other person before I decided to visit Craig and his coven.

He directed me to another well-known individual in the community, and I talked with him, as well. Our conversation was a little more formal—he, too, was interested to know my motivation for wanting to attend a festival. He said he would be happy to invite me to his coven, but that he would be more comfortable doing so after I'd completed a multi-week course of study about Wiccan religions. It was an "intro course" that he taught—and he could teach it at his home or in a public location, whatever made me most comfortable. He mentioned that if I went without knowing anything about the festivals and the components of a gathering, I might be confused and wanting to ask questions. He wanted to make sure that I did not disrupt the energy of a sacred ritual.

I completely respected his perspective, but was not sure I was up for a multi-week course in Wiccan traditions. When Craig called me back to let me know he had received the go-ahead from his high priestess for me to come and visit, I accepted the invitation.

Remembering how I felt when I went to the Sunday Scientology service, I asked if I could bring a friend with me. I let him know we were two Black women, and asked if there would be any resistance to our presence at the ritual. He said there was no problem there, and I told my friend Jackie (who had told me she wouldn't allow me to go by myself) that we were on.

It was an uneasy agreement. As the day and time approached, Jackie and I confirmed and reconfirmed with each other that we would go:

"You still want to go?" she would say.

"Yeah, do you?" I would reply.

"Well, only if you want to go."

The fear of the unknown is real.

The anxiety was not just that we would be experiencing Wicca, a worship tradition some see as witchcraft at best. It was also that the coven would meet in a living room in McHenry, Illinois, a county about an hour and a half away from our homes in Chicago's Cook County. I had never worshipped in someone's living room, and felt apprehensive about going to a stranger's home for any reason.

Let alone to hang out with some Wiccans.

On the day of the festival, we left the city late. We then took a route that led us through road construction, which further delayed us. The conversation in the car centered on whether the Universe was telling us that we shouldn't, in fact, go to McHenry, Illinois, to experience an evening with the Wiccans.

Craig had told us that the gather time was 4:00 p.m., and the ritual would start at 5:00 p.m. We were also told that the ritual may start according to "Pagan time," which apparently was the same as the relaxed attitude to time that Africans and African-Americans laugh about when an event that is supposed to start at one time may not start until much later.

But on the day of the ritual, we were just leaving downtown Chicago at 5:00 p.m., and realizing that a little self-sabotage (read: fear) was probably the reason, I decided to be courteous and call our hosts and let them know we were late. We didn't want to hold them up.

Jackie and I agreed that—whatever their response was—we would take it as the final "communication from the Universe" about whether this experience was to be.

When I called, I asked for Craig and told him the situation. He, in a hearty and welcoming tone, said, "No worries, we're just arriving and we're waiting for you. We won't start without you."

I let him know it might be a good hour before we showed up. That didn't seem to deter him.

We entered the highway heading to McHenry, and put any doubts and fears aside.

When we arrived at the house, we sat in the car, outside of a perfectly normal-looking house in a perfectly normal-looking suburban neighborhood.

We checked in with each other.

"If either of us feels uncomfortable," we agreed, "we will just leave, no questions asked and no regrets."

We also agreed we wouldn't eat anything or do anything that would make either of us uncomfortable. We had been told that after the ritual, there would be a potluck. I had brought a bottle of wine to contribute, but we weren't planning to stay long.

Of all the worship traditions I'd experienced so far, this was the most apprehensive I'd felt.

Realizing that we couldn't sit in the car forever, and that we were already extremely late, I said, "Let's say a prayer and go in."

Jackie agreed, we held hands, and I prayed a simple prayer:

> Lord, we know there is no place where you are not present. We are entering this home with an open heart and good intentions, and desire only to see your face in a new way, with new people. Keep us safe, and we will give you all the glory. Amen.

As we opened our eyes, Jackie said, "That was a good prayer."

I smiled. We walked to the house and rang the doorbell.

Almost immediately after we walked in, I felt fine. There were six or seven people in the priestess' living room, and they were, in fact, waiting for us.

After all the build up from the initial phone call and research, all the way to the prayer we had just said in the car, the actual ritual was perfectly comfortable and I learned as much from this worship experience as any other. I asked them if they wanted us to sit to the side, remembering the conversation that I had with the other Wiccan priest, and wanting to be respectful. They gave us a program of sorts, explained briefly what would happen, and said they thought it would be fine if we participated.

I gulped, as that was not what I'd expected. I made eye contact with Jackie, she seemed fine. I decided everything would be okay.

And it was.

The first step in the ritual was the purification of the space. Because the ritual took place in a living room, the first thing that had to be done was to turn the living room into a sacred area. This was done with different combinations of water, incense, candles, and other representatives of the four elements: earth, air, water, and fire.

At different times during the evening, the sign of the pentagram was made. This made me slightly uncomfortable. Later, I was told that the five-pointed star was not, in fact, a Satanic symbol. Rather, it was a symbol used by many Wiccans and Pagans. Each of the points of the star represented the elements of earth, air, fire, water, and the Spirit of Self.

Early in the ritual, I heard someone mention the Wiccan Rede, which is the rule governing Wiccan behavior:

An ye harm no one, do what ye will.[55]

This translates roughly to: "Do no harm to anyone."

"Well, that sounds reasonable," I thought.

I found that I was experiencing the ritual, but—as in the case with my Scientology visit—at every turn, I was asking myself, "Are you okay, does that feel okay?"

The answer was always yes.

Then I had a moment that brought tears to my eyes.

During the ritual, after a prayer, these words were spoken: "So Mote It Be."

My eyes flew open and a feeling of calm and well-being washed over me.

Why? As a child, when we said grace over our food, my family and I recited a prayer:

> May the blessings of God
> Be granted unto this food
> So that we may magnetize the divine vibrations of our hands
> And well fulfill the needs of our bodies.

At the end of the prayer, we said the words, "So Mote It Be."

My parents, at various times in their lives, studied in various mystical traditions. The ending to this prayer, "So Mote It Be," came from one of those mystical traditions. It means, "And So It Is."

In hearing those words, I thought immediately of my father, who seemed to be saying to me once again, "There is nothing here in this living room to fear. There is nothing you are experiencing here that I didn't experience myself. You are safe. I am with you, and God is with you."

From that moment on, I felt completely at home in that living room with that coven in McHenry, Illinois. We completed the ritual and joined the group for food, drink, and conversation afterwards—breaking our "no-eating" pact that had been born of fear. I marveled at this journey and how far I'd come.

*   *   *

Approaching any unfamiliar situation with an open heart and good intentions is a good first step. Taking friends along is sometimes not a bad idea. Experiencing this new way of worship with my friend Jackie, who was so supportive throughout all aspects of my 52-week journey, made this week even more memorable.

This week, I was reminded that just because a lot of people tell you something is weird, doesn't mean it is. I was also reminded of my father's spiritual journey, and that gave me comfort.

Becoming a member of the Wiccan community is not in my future. But I appreciated the opportunity that the members of the Sky Fire Coven gave me to step out of my comfort zone, join their celebration, and learn something new.

An Evening Chant, "Kirtan"
as a Spiritual Pathway
Lake Street Church

5:00 p.m., Evanston, Illinois

By the time this day rolled around, I was in the last stage of a "Spiritual triple header." I'd spent Friday night with Jews, and Saturday night with Wiccans. What else would I do besides spend Sunday afternoon at a Kirtan?

What's a Kirtan you ask?

> Kirtan is a form of devotional chanting whose roots go back over 500 years to India. It is a form of Bhakti Yoga (yoga of devotion) and has the power to open the heart. The singing is accompanied by musical instruments and rhythmic drumming and the audience is encouraged to participate by chanting, clapping and dancing.[56]

Today's Kirtan took place in a parlor in the back of the Lake Street Church in Evanston, a church committed to exposing their congregants to many different ways of worship. I attended with my friend Ebony, who had expressed interest in experiencing a new way of worship with me. Once inside, the smell of incense directed us to the location where we would experience the Kirtan.

During the Kirtan, there was education and explanation about the process and tradition, as well as the actual chanting. The leader of the Kirtan sat on the floor with a guitar. Next to her, someone played a sitar. On her other side was a person playing another unique-looking instrument: a harmonium.

Our Kirtan leader first led us in a chant to create a sacred space, which made me remember the first thing that my Wiccan friends had done before their ritual started. She told us that the Kirtan was a place for us to sing as loudly as we wanted, quoting Russell Paul, a South Indian Christian, who said, "There is no instrument that will touch you as deeply as your own voice."

She spoke of Shakti, the divine feminine principle, and discussed heart-opening techniques, telling us that, "Life throws us things we don't want to open up our heart for." The more challenging, but more rewarding response, she encouraged us, was to stop saying no all the time, open our hearts anyway and let ourselves be transformed.

In the middle of her talking and explaining, she led us in a number of chants—the Hare Krishna mantra, the Sri Ma mantra, and the Hanuman mantra. Once we started chanting the Hare Krishna mantra, I was reminded of my time in San Diego and it made me smile. Because she explained each chant, she added a little more meaning to my Kirtan experience, as well as clarifying my previous visit to the Hare Krishna temple. I was thankful that I finally had a clue how I was supposed to chant when I was doing the Japa meditation a few weeks prior, where I'd just made it up as I went along.

She talked about Hanuman, the monkey god, told us about Sita, Ram, and the epic story of Ramayana. She identified Ganesh as the remover of obstacles, and explained that Hanuman, the humble devotee, loved Sita and Ram, and talked about the Hindu trinity of creation, preservation, and resolution. She mentioned Vishnu, the energy of peace, and Krishna being one incarnation representing love. As she described the Hindu gods and traditions related to the chants, I realized that I understood very little about the Hindu religion. I made a mental note that I had to make sure to visit a Hindu temple as part of my journey.

*   *   *

Throughout this experience, I had very little idea what our Kirtan leader was talking about. But something she said helped the whole evening make sense. She said, "Breathing together is transformative, even if the Sanskrit is not familiar."

I thought to myself, "She's right, worshipping together is transformative, even if the ritual isn't familiar."

In seeking healing, connection, and remembrance, I was really seeking transformation. In worshipping together with new friends and old ones, that transformation was taking place, one week at a time.

WEEK 39
A COMFORTABLE SILENCE
57TH STREET MEETING OF
FRIENDS, QUAKER HOUSE

10:30 a.m. service, Hyde Park, Chicago, Illinois

I had asked my Facebook friends where I should worship on this day, giving these options: a Hindu Temple, a meeting at the Quaker house, or a service at the Nation of Islam's Mosque Maryam. The vast majority voted for the Quakers. My sister, Idara, posted one comment: "The Quakers are *very* quiet."

I would find out later just what she meant.

I travelled to Hyde Park, a university community on the South Side of Chicago, for my experience with the Quakers. The church was on a tree-lined street with many churches on it. Although it invited me to stroll and consider all the different worship experiences that I could have that morning, today was Quaker time.

When I walked up to the building, I saw a sign that read, "57th Street Meeting of Friends, Quaker House." Above the door of the house was a sign that read "Torture is Wrong."

As I took in the architecture of the house, a woman approached the door, looked at me, and then gestured toward the door in a way that said, "Won't you come in?" So, I did.

When I walked in, I saw a room to the right with about ten people in it.

Ten quiet people.

My sister had not been joking.

I wasn't sure if the service had begun or not. I walked in and mirrored what the others were doing, which appeared to be nothing.

But they were doing what they would do for the majority of the service.

I wasn't sure how long we were to sit there, but I had enough time to silently ponder a few things:

First, I contemplated the need for loud worship versus contemplative worship. My home church was the opposite of this worship experience. It was loud and proud. This was silent and humble. Both had a place. Both appealed to different parts of my spirit.

Then I spent some time thinking about my past week. I had work (there is always plenty of that), I watched football, made new friends, contacted old . . . I was doing something almost all week. The lesson that this service had for this doer was that sometimes it is necessary to do *nothing*.

Absolutely nothing.

Doing nothing has never been my strong suit. This silent worship was challenging.

Then I napped (yeah, it was unintentional, but it happened), meditated, and daydreamed. I observed those in the room with me—there was a couple who appeared to be married, a Black woman, a middle-aged white man, and an older white man.

I tried to quiet my mind.

About the time that I felt I was settling into quiet contemplation, about an hour into the service, a gentleman with long, thick, wild grey hair, and a bushy grey beard stood up and made a loud, jarring comment:

There will come a time when all will be called to reckoning! At that time the establishment will be destroyed! All evil empires will be smashed. Finally, all good will prevail! People, be vigilant!

After speaking, he sat down, silent once again.

This outburst startled me, then almost made me laugh. It was the only comment during the whole worship time.

Apparently, this is how a Quaker service goes: you sit silently, doing nothing in particular. Then if you feel moved to speak, you stand up and share what is on your mind. It just happened that during this day, only one person felt moved to speak. Apparently he was thinking about smashing evil empires—but you can speak on whatever is in your heart.

As I contemplated whether I had something to blurt out, people started to move, hug, and shake hands. Someone, who appeared to be the leader, started talking. He asked if there were any joys or sorrows to share, but no one said anything. A few children came in and joined the married couple sitting on the other side of the room, then announcements commenced.

I learned later that there are many different Quaker groups. It is possible to be Jewish and Quaker, or Christian and Quaker. As part of the announcements, there was a meditation group announced. I asked the contact for that meditation if it was a Quaker meditation group. He explained that it was his Buddhist meditation group. He wanted to invite others to join.

After the service, food was provided. At this point I was able to see that this church was also a community. People took time to share, catch up, and break bread together.

*   *   *

I left that morning, having had a distinctive—and quiet—experience with a unique set of Friends.

Throughout my year of healing, I often found myself trying to figure out what to do to feel better. With the Quakers, I had a chance to contemplate the wisdom of just doing nothing.

WEEK 40
FAITH, CULTURE, AND THE IMPORTANCE OF LANGUAGE
INDO-PAK UNITED METHODIST CHURCH

5:00 p.m. service, Chicago, Illinois

With a few months left in my 52-week journey, I was actively seeking new and different worship experiences. This morning, I wanted to combine the familiar with the unfamiliar. I found a Christian church to attend—but one in which I knew I would be experiencing a new context, a new culture, a new community, and a new spin on being a chocolate chip.

I found a Methodist congregation on the North Side of Chicago, who described themselves in this way:

> Indo-Pak United Methodist Church of Chicago is a friendly community of Indian and Pakistani Christians, who come together for worship, Bible study, fellowship, and cultural celebrations for the purpose of growing in Christ and sharing the Gospel of Christ with others.[57]

I have always been curious about the different ways in which the same religion can present itself in different cultures. In my experience, Christianity in other cultures can present itself in a much more . . . enthusiastic manner.

I spent the summer before my senior year of college in Tokyo, Japan. I loved the culture, and my desire to see as much of the world as possible was really born that summer. I spent countless hours exploring Tokyo's streets and neighborhoods.

One day, I was approaching one of the main train stations in Tokyo—Shinjuku station. There were a number of Japanese Christians sharing the good news outside the station. Like many people: I don't really feel the need to stop and participate in an evangelical session when I'm just minding my business walking down the street. But this group was so enthusiastic, and it appeared that the majority of the people walking by were enthusiastically ignoring them. Since I generally took any chance that I could to practice my less-than-impressive Japanese, I decided to stop and talk to one of the men waving a Bible around.

"Konnichi wa," I said, starting with a basic greeting of, "Good afternoon."

As was my experience often that summer, in response to my Japanese, he greeted me in English. "Hi! How are you! Are you a Christian!??!"

"Hai," I said, nodding.

What happened next was startling and unexpected. This spirit-filled sharer of the good news reached over, gave me a bear hug, and said, "Then you are my sister!!!"

As I stood awkwardly in a hug that lasted a little too long, I thought, "How in the world did I get here?!"

I suppose he was right—given that we were both Christians, we were, in fact, family. But I was nineteen, and no poster child for Christian evangelism. I was, honestly, a little freaked out. When he released me from my holy hug, I spent some time talking to him, in Japanglish, about the group he was with, and how he came to be waving a Bible around in front of a train station in Tokyo.

This was my only previous experience with Asian Christianity.

Today, I surmised, would provide a different perspective.

I took the drive up to the Rogers Park neighborhood, where the church was located, within blocks of the historic Devon area where many Indian and Pakistani businesses are located.

As I entered the church, a few people looked at me as I sat down, wondering, no doubt, if I'd wandered into the wrong church building. Everyone else appeared to be of Asian descent.

As I began to read the bulletin, a gentleman began walking toward me. I felt very special as he asked my name and welcomed me to the church. He told me we were actually worshipping in the West Ridge Community United Methodist Church. He pastored both churches.

Apparently, the morning service is in English and the evening service was in Hindi/Urdu.

Well, it wasn't morning.

He warned me that I wouldn't understand most of the service, which just made me chuckle. He mentioned that certain portions of the service would be in English, and asked if I was okay with that? I told the pastor to preach as if I wasn't there, using no more English than usual. I would be fine.

Something is humbling, wonderful, and frightening about being in a situation where you don't understand anything being said. I highly recommend it to everyone. In my world travels, I have lived in Japan and in Germany, and travelled throughout Mexico. In those cases, I spoke (badly) Japanese, German, and Spanish, so at least I had a (very small) clue about how to make myself understood. But some of the most memorable experiences I've had included travelling in countries where I didn't understand a word, trying to figure out how to get around Luckily for me, much of the world speaks English, and many are proud enough of that fact that they delight in practicing with native speakers. In big cities, you're likely to have more luck communicating. But when you travel in the less-populated areas of any country, you can experience how challenging it can be to navigate when language barriers separate you from others.

I thought of my father—a young, confident African man who left his home in Southeastern Nigeria to go to Bonn, Germany, to attend medical school.

He didn't speak a word of German when he landed.

How do you even do that? How do you have the confidence to land in another country with little money, and no grasp of the language, and know that you'll be okay? How did he get to the campus from the airport, I wondered? How did he get his first apartment? How did he even begin to read a medical text when he was still learning the language?

For as long as I live, I'll always be in awe of my father for this feat of his. And yet, that's what you do when you're in a situation where you're trying to make your life better. Once, while living in Germany, I was talking with my friend Tracey, a first generation Trinidadian-American. She shared that her father was also a physician. As a young man, Tracey's father travelled from Trinidad to medical school in France to do what my father had done in Germany.

It is the stuff of immigrant lore, these great feats undertaken in the name of searching for opportunity and challenging yourself to be the best you can be.

Along the way, there are always questions, though, aren't there? As you move from your home culture to another culture, how are you going to preserve the culture that you know, as well as memories of your heart? How are you going to remember the land you left? How are you going to teach your children about who you were before you left home looking for opportunity and new experiences—especially since they're going to have their own land, their own experiences, and their own ideas of what is normal and familiar?

As I grew older and more thoughtful, I really tried to understand what it was like for my father, who left his beloved Nigeria, travelled through Germany, and landed in the United States of America, where he made his home, raised his children, lived his life, and ultimately died.

I spoke to my father several times when he was alive about how his life had not turned out as he had expected. Before we were here, when he dreamed of how his children would be, he didn't imagine that we would be hyphenated Americans—born and raised far from his home country, culturally African-American, and speaking only a few words of his mother tongue, Ibibio.

One of the most poignant memories I have from the end of my father's life was when I realized that his time with us was short. I called my cousins, Anthony and Phillip, who were studying at the time in the UK, and asked them to please just talk to my father. I wanted my father to hear some words in his beloved first language before he left this earth.

I was saddened that I couldn't be the one to have that conversation with him.

I thought about my upbringing. The beginning of my life was focused mostly on achievement, as is the case with many children of immigrants. Self-definition, culture, and social development came next. When attending college, I had my first opportunity to take the time then to learn what it truly meant to me to be a Black woman. It was not, however, until I was in graduate school—and due in large part to my time at my home church, Trinity—that I began asking myself what it meant to be the American-born child of an African. It was then that I started embracing my complex cultural heritage, and learning as much as I could about it.

I thought about this as I looked around at a number of worshippers at the Indo-Pak United Methodist Church, imagining that they had come from different countries, seeking the American dream. Perhaps this church was their chance to experience familiar cultural cues within a church context. I looked at the children, many of them young, and imagined that they were like me: first generation, hyphenated Americans. Perhaps they were slightly less concerned about the cultural immersion lessons that they were getting, and slightly more concerned about not appearing to be too different from their American-born peers.

But they were different. The fact that they sat with me, listening to a service in Hindi/Urdu and English meant that they were being groomed to be cultural bridges. Perhaps they had the experience, at home, of listening to their parents and family members speak in a combination of their mother tongue and English.

I remember hearing my father talk on the phone, in Ibibio sprinkled with English, mixed, like the sermon by Pastor Singh. I found it fascinating. It wasn't until I started studying other languages that I understood: sometimes, when you are referring to things uniquely English or American, there is no word for that thing in another language. I thought about all of these things as I clumsily followed along in a service where I understood very little of what was being said. Scriptural selections were projected in English but read in Hindi/Urdu. I watched others and listened for words that sounded familiar.

During prayer time, I bowed my head, with one eye open looking for clues that the prayer was over so I could raise my head again.

And when did I know that the prayer was over?

When I heard something that sounded like "Amen," and people stopped talking.

When the congregation said the Lord's Prayer, I had a feeling that it was being recited. I recognized the cadence, joined in, and miraculously ended when everyone else ended.

I also thought about these issues of being a hyphenated, first-generation American, and the importance of language, as the children approached the altar for story time.

Reminding me of the "Children's Hour" that had been a part of many church services at my home church, I watched as Pastor Singh shared, "a message for the children."

It was in English.

The topic for the message was, "I pass the baton to you."

One of the two scriptural references he used was Hebrews 12:1 (NIV):

> Therefore, since we are surrounded by such a great cloud of witnesses, let us throw off everything that hinders and the sin that so easily entangles. And let us run with perseverance the race marked out for us . . .

The other scriptural reference was 2 Timothy 1:14 (NIV):

> Guard the good deposit that was entrusted to you—guard it with the help of the Holy Spirit who lives in us.

He shared with the children what was expected of them:

- Defend your faith. Faith is important.
- Remember that you were not given a spirit of fear.
- Utilize the power of love, and the power of the divine.
- Look to your families and your own experiences to find great examples of people who persevered and overcame adversity through faith—there are witnesses and examples everywhere.
- When you are challenged, remember you are not alone.
- Draw strength from those who came before you—both within your family and outside your family.
- Remember that your faith is stronger than you think.

This, of course, was not just a message for the children, but a message for everyone sitting in that congregation. Given that it was the only part of the service I understood, I decided that it was no coincidence that the message included ideas for me to consider and keep close to my heart.

Have faith.

You are not alone.

Draw strength from family, friends, and the people around you.

As I contemplated these nuggets of wisdom, the time for sharing the joys and concerns of the congregation began. During this time, visitors were welcomed. In the middle of some other words I didn't understand, I heard Pastor Singh mention my name. This impressed me because I was unaware that he took note of it when we spoke before the service.

I didn't know what they said about me and why I might be visiting that day, but the pastor, and several others in the service, turned toward me, smiled, waved, and welcomed me.

I smiled and waved back.

*   *   *

In my ignorance (which I have no problem admitting when the occasion arises), I didn't realize how revolutionary it was to have one church in which both Indians and Pakistanis worshipped together. After service, I researched and learned a little about the cultural, political, and historical differences of and conflicts between the two South Asian ethnic groups.

It was memorable to be in a place where different ethnic groups came together in pursuit of worship and fellowship.

This week reminded me that my journey was about God, and community, and experience, and worship, and culture, and family, and love.

WEEK 41
HAPPY SABBATH
SHILOH SEVENTH DAY ADVENTIST CHURCH

11:00 a.m. service, Chicago, Illinois

Before I selected my place of worship for this week, I called my mother. She, a devout Christian, was nevertheless intrigued by this journey of mine. "Where to today?" she asked.

I told her that I'd planned to worship with the Jehovah's Witnesses on that Saturday morning, but when I called them, I found out that they didn't worship on Saturdays, as I'd thought. The nearest Kingdom Hall had a service on Wednesday. So, I found myself considering a visit to a Seventh-Day Adventist Church.

I started my pre-worship research. I called the Seventh-Day Adventist church in a nearby Chicago neighborhood. The person who answered the phone shared that it was some sort of children's day, and didn't sound too encouraging about me visiting. He seemed very insistent that I know that the regular choir was not singing and that the kids were leading the service. I would have been happy to experience whatever the church had to offer on that day, but I decided to pay attention to his lack of enthusiasm and look for another location.

Later, I found another church, Shiloh SDA, which was about ten miles away. I called and found out it was children's day there, too. However, the gentleman who answered the phone at this church was enthusiastic and welcoming. He told me the names of the kids programs were the Adventurers and the Pathfinders, and explained a little bit about each program.

251

At the time that we chatted, it was less than an hour before service.

"Come on down and join us," said the voice on the end of the phone. He asked where in the city I was currently located. When I told him, he said, probably looking at his watch, "If you hurry, you can make it!"

I got myself together, got in my car, and drove to the South Side of Chicago to spend a little time with the Seventh-Day Adventists.

As I sped down South Michigan Avenue on my way to the church, I enjoyed the brisk fall day. When I arrived, I sat in my car for a moment and admired the church's ornate stained-glass windows. It was clear that this was a community gathering place. There were adults talking outside the building, and kids playing. Everyone seemed to be meeting and greeting before the service.

Immediately, I felt like I was in the right place for this Saturday morning. I walked into the church building, grabbed a bulletin, and entered the sanctuary. Along the way, many greeted me, saying, "Happy Sabbath." I returned the greeting. As I took my seat, I began to take in the enormous sanctuary, which was neither full nor empty. Worshippers dotted the pews. White and grey patterned walls surrounded the sanctuary. A number of ornate lamps hung from a vaulted wood ceiling.

My eyes were drawn to the front of the sanctuary. Above the pulpit, surrounded by a stone frame and an outer panel made of bricks and wood, was a large, circular stained-glass window. The words "Laws of God" appeared at the top of the circle. Beneath those words, within tablet shaped borders were the Ten Commandments, five on each table. A multi-colored stained-glass beam of light shone from the top right of the circle to highlight the fourth commandment, preceded by the Roman numeral IV. Clearly written was the verse, Exodus 20:8-10 (KJV):

> Remember the Sabbath day. Six days shalt thou labor and do all thy work, but the seventh day is the Sabbath of the Lord Thy God . . .

252

At the beginning of the service, the pastor invited everyone to recite the church's affirmation of faith. I was still trying to identify unique characteristics of this Seventh-Day Adventist worship tradition. I thought the affirmation might give me a clue.

The affirmation, however, was a familiar verse, John 3:16 (KJV):

> For God so loved the world that he gave his only begotten Son, that whosoever believeth in him should not perish, but have everlasting life.

The prayer that followed this affirmation referred to God as "The Lord," and ended with the words, "In Jesus' name" and "Amen."

So far, the main difference I saw between this service, and other Christian services I experienced was the focus on worshipping on the Sabbath—as highlighted in the beautiful stained-glass reminder at the front of the sanctuary.

I felt a touch on my shoulder. A young lady asked, "Are you new here?" I was a little apprehensive, not for any reason that made sense. Maybe because I just assumed that today I would sit and worship alone? I had to check myself and remember that part of this whole process was connecting with others in new situations. When my new friend asked me to come join her and her friend a few pews back, I did. She told me that the service had many parts. The program began with children's presentations. My new friend had children in the program and pointed them out to me as they participated in these presentations, where the children recited scriptures and told stories and acted out little skits.

Then there was a children's pastor. He did puppet shows and presentations on faith. He shared that he was from Atlanta, where I grew up. His southern accent sounded like home. His presentation and puppet show was long.

As the seemingly endless presentation continued, the pastor didn't seem to be affected. I felt no sense of urgency from him. Clearly, he felt that what he was saying was important, and he was going to complete his entire presentation, no matter how long it was.

After three hours, I was trying to stay present and open to the messages that the children's pastor was sharing. I was a little frustrated, especially since I'd been sitting in the service for quite some time, but still didn't feel like I knew much more about the Seventh-Day Adventists.

At the three-hour mark of the service, there was a transition from entertaining the kids to talking to the adults. We viewed a video presentation called, "*The Importance of Prayer.*" When the video presentation ended, I was exhausted. He was still not done.

Just as I was accepting that I wouldn't really learn anything about the Seventh-Day Adventists or come away with a spiritual lesson, the children's pastor shared the main message: that you should pray without ceasing, and that even when a situation in your life exhausts you, you should still pray.

By this point, I was so tired and distracted that I almost missed the acronym for PRAYer given by the children's pastor:

Praise—offer thanks, gratitude
Repent—ask for forgiveness
Ask—ask for what we need
Yield—let God do the work

He reminded us that the prayers of a righteous man are very effective. He encouraged us not to "quietly pray from your heart" but rather to "speak our prayers out of our mouths."

By the end of the service, I was starving and dreaming of a post-Sabbath meal. I said goodbye to my new friends. They hugged me and told me to come back any time.

*   *   *

When this service ended, I left Shiloh knowing that I would have to attend another Seventh-Day Adventist church service, or do further research in order to learn more about the denomination, it's worship traditions, and what happened on a Sabbath on the days that the children were not leading.

This was frustrating, especially since I had spent such a long time in the service. Sometimes the length of time one spends in a place of worship may or may not be related to the size of the blessing received there.

But, I thought, as I left the sanctuary, I did get the one point about PRAYing. And sometimes, one point is enough.

WEEK 42
MEMORY LANE AND THE MOSQUE
MUHAMMAD MOSQUE NO. 2,
MOSQUE MARYAM, NATION OF
ISLAM CENTRAL REGIONAL HEADQUARTERS

1:00 p.m. service, Chicago, Illinois

Often during my journey, I thought about visiting places that I'd driven past a thousand times during my time in Chicago. One of those places was Mosque Maryam, the Nation of Islam (NOI) Central Regional Headquarters on Stony Island Road in Chicago.

Stony Island Road is a well-known thoroughfare on the South Side of Chicago. Prior to finding Stony Island, I'd found a convoluted way to get to my home church, Trinity, from my first Windy City apartment in the Edgewater neighborhood of Chicago's North Side. I would take Lake Shore Drive to Highway 55, then to the Dan Ryan Expressway, and exit on 95th Street. On one snowy Chicago winter morning, I contemplated why I just couldn't continue driving down Lake Shore Drive to South Shore Drive. I tried it . . . and it was an experience.

When Lake Shore Drive appeared to end by the Museum of Science and Industry, I didn't really know what to do. I followed the people in front of me, in the years before the GPS, and tried to figure out how to get where I wanted to go. I cobbled together a new route, which included a long road I'd never been on before, as well as some poorly plowed side streets that were more like ice skating rinks than roads. I finally arrived at church, late, frustrated, and a little irritated with myself that I knew so little about how to navigate around this new city that I'd just made my home.

The mystery of the long road I found myself on that winter morning was solved one day, a few months later, when I was driving my boyfriend at the time to his mother's house. I wasn't familiar with the South Side of Chicago, so he was directing me, and we ended up on Stony Island. I didn't know where I was, and didn't yet know where his mother lived, and he happened to be mostly asleep in my front seat as I was driving. I kept reminding him to let me know where I should go, and where I should turn. All he said from the time that we hit Stony Island to the time that we arrived at his mother's house was, "Follow the road!"

Follow the road!

I did, and eventually I learned how to get to his mother's house.

And I learned about Stony Island.

Even after we were no longer dating, I used Stony Island as a means of getting to my home church without having to get on the Dan Ryan Expressway. It was a nice alternative.

A Caucasian friend of mine from grad school once told me that she took Stony Island to get to the Skyway, which is a faster way to get to Indiana, where her boyfriend lived at the time. As she was explaining her process for making that trip, she shared that she locked her doors, said a prayer and sped down Stony Island until she reached the relative safety of the Skyway.

I found that to be a slightly racially tinged message. Yes, Stony Island is an urban thoroughfare. But I saw Stony Island as a place where I could view what was happening in a special part of the Black community. Stony Island provided the backdrop for one of the first Common Sense videos I ever saw. Moo and Oink, a famous grocery store, is located on Stony Island. BJs Market and Bakery—a favorite post-church soul food brunch spot was on Stony Island. In addition, Mosque Maryam—the mosque of the Honorable Minister Louis Farrakhan's Nation of Islam stands tall on 7351 S. Stony Island.

Today was the day for me to visit that Mosque. I woke up, put on some African attire, and headed to the South Side of Chicago.

When I arrived at Mosque Maryam, I was a little perplexed because the parking lot was empty. The website for the mosque stated that service started at 10:00 a.m., and I was right on time. I decided to do some further investigation. Standing near the door was an authoritative-looking man. He let me know that the service today would commemorate the fifteenth anniversary of the Million Man March. It would start at 1:00 p.m., and would include a broadcast by the Honorable Minister Louis Farrakhan.

"Today was the Holy Day of Atonement," he said. The broadcast would be from the NOI Annual Convention in Florida. The theme was, "Atonement, Reconciliation, and Responsibility," and the spirit of the Million Man March was being celebrated, he said.

As I walked back to my car, I contemplated the fact that it had been fifteen years since the Million Man March. I remembered that march vividly. It was an unforgettable event, especially for the Black community. All Black men were asked to come to Washington, D.C. for the march, which focused on atonement, self-determination, and strengthening the Black family. All Black women and children were asked to stay home in solidarity—to participate in a "Day of Absence" to complement the actions of the Black men headed for the nation's capital.

I'd just finished graduate school. I was in my first three weeks of training with the consulting company I would work for during the next six years. The training was an intense three weeks where we were sequestered in a suburban location outside the city of Chicago.

I had a decision to make. Could I, would I, miss a day of training? It would be a conspicuous absence and perhaps not a good idea from a professional perspective. But, how could I not stand in solidarity with my community?

In one of the most memorable adult decisions I'd made up until that point, I informed my instructor that I had to miss a day of the training. I was so nervous when I told him that I can't even remember the reason I gave. He didn't really seem concerned, and told me it would be okay.

I breathed a sigh of relief and watched the historic events unfold on television. I was glad that I had the courage to participate in my own little way.

I was only slightly mortified when, the next day, my instructor asked me, "Were you in Washington, D.C. yesterday?" I said something inarticulate. He let it go, and I was thankful for that.

In the following years, my sister and I drove to Philadelphia from Connecticut, where I was working at the time, and participated in the Million Woman March.

These powerful memories came flooding back as I stood in front of Mosque Maryam.

But, the fact of the matter was, I was at the mosque at 10:00 a.m., and the service was at 1:00 p.m. And I was dressed in African attire, which is normal for me, but I didn't really want to answer any questions or get strange looks that morning by strolling into a grocery store on Stony Island to run some errands. I contemplated where I could go (besides home) for a few hours to pass time until the service at 1:00 p.m.

There was only one answer.

Trinity.

At Trinity, no one bats an eye when you are wearing African attire. As a matter of fact, members of the church are encouraged to wear it, and when Reverend Wright preached, he would wear African attire regularly, as would the choir. The men would often wear the four pieces of the traditional male attire—the pants; the buba, or shirt; the agbada, a flowing robe worn over the buba; and a matching hat. Some would forgo the agbada for a more casual look. The women would wear their own four-piece ensemble, which included the buba or shirt; a "wrapper," or skirt; a gele, or hat; and a shawl. Another option would be the more casual one-piece bubu, which is what I had on that Sunday morning.

It was this comfort with African culture, clothing, and heritage that initially drew me to Trinity. I also appreciated the focus on community and Christianity, which was instructive to me as I contemplated issues related to identity and faith.

I figured correctly that I would be able to arrive at Trinity in time for the 11:00 a.m. service, and the praise and worship that preceded it. I would be able to hear the opening choir and prayers. I love gospel music, and the Trinity choir is one of the best.

On the drive from the mosque to Trinity, a mere ten minutes, I thought of my father. At the corner of Stony Island and 95th street, I saw a billboard advertising dialysis services. My father was a nephrologist and managed multiple dialysis clinics. Whenever I see mention of such services, I think of him.

He is everywhere, still, as I make my way through the world.

New flags flew on poles outside the church. They read, "Community, Culture, Christ." I thought, "That about says it, doesn't it?"

I entered the sanctuary, listened to the music, then left. I wanted to get back to the mosque by the time the doors opened at noon, in case it was packed. When I returned to the mosque, I found that it wasn't yet packed. It was still early.

I went in the mosque, then went through a security check. It was reminiscent of the experience I had at the United Center when I attended the Saviours' Day festivities.

After the security check, an usher led me to a seat at the front of the sanctuary. On the right side were all the women, and on the left side were all the men. Once again, like the experience I had at Saviours' Day, I felt the emphasis on my femininity—everyone called me Sister and Queen. I sat with the women.

The woman to the right of me knew the woman to the left of me. I sat quietly, leaning back so that they could greet each other and chit chat. During their conversation, one asked the other, "Is Muhammad here?" and then she laughed and said, "Oh right, everyone's name is Muhammad around here."

Hilarious.

I started talking with the women around me. The woman to the right of me said that she was married to a Muslim, but worshipped with the Hebrew Israelites on Saturday, and still went to church from time to time on Sunday. She said she was all about making sure she made it to heaven. She was covering all her bases.

Well, alrighty then!

She told me that she could see that I was a seeker. She advised me to keep looking until I found what I was looking for. I found that curious, because I gave her no indication of why I was there, or what I'd spent the last several months doing.

She told me that there was Jumu'ah (Islamic Prayer) Friday at 1:00 p.m. at a masjid in the Hyde Park neighborhood of Chicago. She also mentioned that there was another one at 90th and Stony Island, just down the road from where we were sitting. I wrote these things down, knowing that I would visit a masjid sometime soon. When I mentioned that I hadn't been to a non-NOI mosque yet, and was a little apprehensive about knowing what to do in a Muslim service, she assured me, "Just go with the flow," she said. "Follow those around you, and if you need to—go on the Internet and research how things go before you attend the prayer service. That way you won't feel lost."

Wise words from my multi-faceted friend!

Both my new friend and the woman in front of me had headscarves that said, "I love Jesus" on them. I smiled. What a diverse gathering of folks in this mosque today!

I began to think about how the Nation of Islam might serve as the "Gateway to Islam" for many. I wondered how many people had learned of Islam through the Nation, how many stayed with the Nation, and how many proceeded to a religious experience that connected them with their Muslim brothers and sisters outside of the Nation. These thoughts were similar to those I had about the Beth Shalom B'nai Zaken Ethiopian Hebrew Congregation, wondering what their relationship was with Jews around the United States and around the world.

Classical music played while we waited. My friend let me know that the Honorable Minister Louis Farrakhan liked classical music. "I don't think I've ever heard gospel music up in here," she said.

The music was soothing and a contrast to the choir that I'd just enjoyed at Trinity. Both appealed to my sensibilities.

By 1:00, the mosque was absolutely packed.

The telecast from Florida began.

The student minister, Ishmael Muhammad, began to speak.

"As Salaam Alaikum," he said

""Wa Alaikum Assaalam, Sir," everyone else replied.

This greeting and response happened often throughout the telecast and throughout the day.

The opening prayer appealed to all. The prayer leader referred to God as being, ". . . known by many names—some say Jehovah, some say Dios, we say Allah." He reminded us that there were, "prophets mentioned in the Bible and the Qur'an, and we make no distinction between them. As Muslims, we believe in all the prophets and the scriptures that they brought. We believe that all prophets are from one prophetic community."

Several prophets and their holy messages and books were mentioned: Moses and the Torah, the Israelite prophets and the Old Testament, Jesus and the Gospel, the Apostles and the New Testament, Muhammad and the Qur'an.

Allah.

Repeatedly I heard this:

There is one God, Allah.

All praise belongs to God.

All praises due to Allah.

God, Allah—two names for the same divine force?

Something to consider.

In the introduction before the Honorable Minister Louis Farrakhan appeared, we were reminded that many of us were polytheistic, and that really, we shouldn't worship anyone but God. The idea was that Allah would be displeased that we would choose to give love and praise to someone who has done nothing for us.

When I heard this, I thought of my ex, and all the time I'd spent missing him and wishing he was still around. He had left my side at what felt like my deepest time of need. Was God displeased that I still gave him space in my heart and in my head? Had he really done *nothing* for me? After all, we had many good times. He was there for me during some of the hardest parts of my father's illness, even though he was unable to walk the entire road with me. Should I devalue what we meant to each other because we were not meant to be in each other's lives forever?

Everyone has heard some version of the quote, "People come into your life for a reason, a season, or a lifetime. When you figure out which one it is, you'll know what to do."

Perhaps I shouldn't chastise myself for loving someone for the reason or the season he was in my life, just because he was not there for a lifetime.

In any case, it was something to consider.

There were more lessons that made me think of my ex.

"When you love deeply, you can suffer the abuse of those who don't love you like you love them," said the student minister.

You don't say.

"When God takes something from you, he gives you something in return that allows you to live bigger."

Well, I do hope so.

As the student minister wrapped up, the service continued. We heard from Farrakhan's wife, Mother Khadijah Farrakhan, and then, as in the Saviours' Day at the United Center, we heard from the Honorable Minister himself.

He spoke for a good amount of time, just as he had the last time I heard him speak. Many of the messages were the same, although there was a focus on sharing the story of the Million Man March, and on the message of atonement.

He encouraged us to seek knowledge, saying, "Ignorance is the enemy of God. Knowledge will make us the friend of God and will allow us to befriend one another. All the prophets encourage us to get knowledge." He reminded us that, "When you see ignorance, that's a teaching moment."

He emphasized that all have fallen short of the Glory of God, that we are the peacemakers, and that despite differences, we must gather to help heal.

He encouraged us to make ourselves the ideal church, and reminded us that, "Every human being has the possibility of reflecting God."

He referenced the Qur'an, saying, "The only way God can get a sincere prayer out of us is to put us into some sort of trouble. And after God delivers us, we set up other gods beside Him. Surely, man is ungrateful."

I felt as if I understood the point of this reference. We often ask for help when we are in trouble, but then forget to say thank you. Or, we worship other "gods" when the trouble has passed, whether those "gods" be money, power, other people, or something else.

In contemplating this reference to the Qur'an, I realized how little I still know about other religions and worship traditions. If you mention a book, chapter, and verse in the Bible, I might not be an expert on that book, chapter, and verse, but I'll know where it lives in the Bible. I have been to enough church services and completed enough Bible study classes that I probably will have heard it before. In contrast, I have never read the Qur'an, and wouldn't know where to find that reference. I would have no context within which to process it.

Research later yielded a few verses that he could have been referencing. Their English translations are:

Surah Yunus: Ayah 10:12

> When trouble toucheth a man, He crieth unto Us (in all postures)—lying down on his side, or sitting, or standing. But when We have solved his trouble, he passeth on his way as if he had never cried to Us for a trouble that touched him! Thus do the deeds of transgressors seem fair in their eyes![58]

Or, Surah Ibrahim: Ayah 14:34

> And He giveth you of all that ye ask for. But if ye count the favours of Allah, never will ye be able to number them. Verily, man is given up to injustice and ingratitude.[59]

I thought to myself, "I should read the Qur'an," but I wondered, with all my competing life tasks and responsibilities, when that might happen. I am interested in reading the holy books of other worship traditions, but I know that I also need to delve deeper into the study of the Holy Book of my own worship tradition.

As this was a celebration of the "Day of Atonement," an eight-step atonement process was mentioned throughout the message:

1) Point out the wrong
2) Admit the wrong
3) Confess to the wrong (1st to God, then to the person you wronged)
4) Repent
5) Atone (Make amends for the wrong)
6) Forgive
7) Reconcile/Restore
8) Perfect Union

This seemed like a worthwhile process. I thoughtfully considered the point that was made about how the first step was often the most difficult part of the process.

Having grown up in an African family in America, I was quite familiar with the difficulty of that first step. In many African cultures, the tact that is expected in western cultures is simply absent. Often, comments are made when wrong is detected that appear to be hurtful or unnecessarily harsh.

One of my favorite stories to illustrate this happened when I was visiting my family in Nigeria. I have never been a skinny woman. My weight falls somewhere between "normal" and obese. It has always been something that family members have freely and repeatedly reminded me I need to change. "When are you going to lose weight?" was a familiar question that was up for discussion, and not my favorite topic. On this particular trip, I was travelling with three aunts who wanted to make a point that I needed to be skinnier. On a trip to the market, they all told me to sit in the front seat—alone, because I was apparently enormous.

To highlight the point, the three of them chose to squeeze into the back seat. Tired of dealing with the same conversation repeatedly—and because it was oppressively hot and I had no desire to squeeze into the backseat—I swallowed the insult and truth of the intention of that action, and had a comfortable ride to the market, while three (skinnier) grown women squeezed in the back.

I'll never forget that day.

But during the message on this day at the mosque, I contemplated the usefulness of being open to hearing things that may be hurtful, but would help in the end to lead to self-improvement.

The minister reminded us that we should keep our ears open, and ". . . humble (ourselves) to listen to someone who wants to correct something in you."

Like my excessive weight?

The minister shared that, "No human should be afraid to know more," that, "To think right, the mind must feed on facts, truth, and reality," and that, "When you feed people lies and they believe you, you injure them—that's menticide."

I suppose I should have been happy that my beloved family was not trying to injure me.

Of course, I realize that there are many ways to look at this search for truth, and to balance how to communicate the truth with the feelings and the needs of the intended audience.

After all, as the Minister reminded us, "You can't find security in a liar, you can only find security in truth," and of course, "The truth will set you free."

More food for thought.

*　　*　　*

When things in your life don't go the way you had hoped or planned, it is normal to think about what you may have done wrong. This service brought back memories from years past, and gave me a chance to think about the theme of atonement, and what I could do to feel better about the regrets I had about my failed relationship, which contributed in its own way to the collective grief that I was feeling.

I can't say that I committed completely to the 8 step atonement process, but it was something that allowed me to think about how I would take responsibility for the experience that I had with my ex, and what I would do, or not do about it. As the saying goes—when you know better, you do better.

Week 43
Can I Get a Witness?
Discourse and Watchtower Study,
Kingdom Hall of Jehovah's Witnesses

9:30 a.m. Lincoln Park, Chicago, Illinois

As the year progressed, I started feeling very tired. I had not really taken a break from work or life after my father passed away. After months of grieving, and healing, and trying to drag myself back to being "my old self," I was exhausted.

Something had to change. After my emergency room visit on my father's birthday, I finally decided that I needed to take some time off. I looked forward to taking a month where I could sleep in if I wanted to, eat healthy, work out, cry if I needed to, and do little else.

So, of course, I get called to jury duty.

Jury duty is one of the things that, believe it or not, I'd always wanted to do. When we went through the jury selection, while others were trying to give answers to get out of jury duty, I cheerfully and dutifully answered honestly, hoping they would choose me.

The result was a jury duty stint that lasted three days. I was able to do my civic duty and learn a little about the judicial system in the process.

Yes, I know, it's not normal for me to be excited about this.

But I was.

During our lunch break on the jury selection day, as I sat in the courtroom cafeteria and looked out the window at the nearby Cook County Jail, I was taken back to a time when I volunteered in the Prison Ministry at my home church, Trinity. Weekly, we would visit men in a specific program within the prison. We were not allowed to ask them why they were in prison. Our purpose was to see these men as members of the community who were paying their debt to society for whatever transgressions they had made. We were there to help them as they were preparing to make a new start when they were released.

Every week, I visited the prison, went through the security procedures, left all my valuables with the guard, and participated in discussions with this subset of the prison population who had high promise for clean futures.

Until one day.

During our visit, a prisoner escaped from another section of the prison. A uniformed officer came to share with our group that we were "on lockdown," and there would be "no movement."

No movement?

Unsure of what that meant, I asked one of my fellow ministry partners, and found out that we wouldn't be able to leave until the situation with the escaped prisoner was under control.

Let's just say, I wasn't thrilled about that.

Our hour-long session turned into multiple hours, just sitting and talking with these individuals. I was scared that we would be in prison forever, and then mentally chided myself for feeling that way. No matter what, eventually we would go home, but—for the prisoners in this facility—there was no going home at the end of a nice chat session.

Hours later, we were allowed to leave. I went to my car, exhausted and a bit disappointed in myself—and that was my last visit to the Cook County Jail with our Prison Ministry.

I never said I was perfect.

I thought about this memory as I tried to choke down the poor excuse for food that was available at the courthouse lunchroom. Two individuals approached my table and asked if they could join me for lunch.

I invited them to sit, and we began talking about the jury selection process. I shared what I was thinking about the view of the prison's barbed wire outside the window. They shared that they had done some prison ministry with their church in the past.

Being ever mindful of opportunities to find new churches to visit, I asked the magic question, "What church do you attend?"

"We are Jehovah's Witnesses and we attend the Kingdom Hall in Lincoln Park," they shared. Lincoln Park is a well-known neighborhood on Chicago's North Side.

My eyes lit up.

Jackpot.

I had not yet visited a Jehovah's Witness worship service. I took this opportunity to get their contact information.

As I was having this conversation, I saw the humor in it. For better or worse, many spend a fair amount of time avoiding Jehovah's Witnesses. Here I was, soliciting information from these individuals so I could worship with them.

I'm a city dweller. I don't get the knock on the door from Jehovah's Witnesses these days. Only one memory of a personal solicitation stands out. I was living in a duplex that had a doorbell on street level. On a Saturday morning, I heard the doorbell. I looked out the window and saw a child standing there.

Well, who can say no to the children?

The child was no more than six or seven years old. I buzzed him in and he walked up the stairs to my door. The adult who was with him stayed at the bottom of the stairs, near the door to the duplex.

At this point, I was thinking, "Thank goodness I'm a good person, why is this child standing in front of my door all alone?"

In any case, I let the little guy give me his spiel. I don't really remember what he said, but I remember wondering about the adult who was with him, who apparently thought this was an appropriate way for a small child to spend his free time. After I heard the pitch, his young hand offered me a *Watchtower Magazine*. I did what I often do: I over-contributed. I gave the kid a $20 because I was really feeling for him. I wondered how much rejection he had received and didn't want to add to that number. He took the money, said thank you, and walked back downstairs to his chaperone.

A few minutes later, I heard my doorbell again. The same child was standing there. Although I was a little irritated, I buzzed him in again. He walked up the stairs to my door. When he reached the top, this time, in his outstretched hand was my $20.

"My father says that this is too much," he said.

Surprised, I said, "You tell your father I gave you that $20 on purpose. You are doing a very brave thing walking around and sharing this information with people. Please take care." The child looked at the $20, then looked at me. He decided that what I said made sense. (Or he thought I was a lunatic, hard to tell). He turned, walked down the stairs, and out the door again. That was my one experience with the active evangelism of the Jehovah's Witnesses.

One of my favorite stories, however, about my father, recounts what he finally did after visits from members of the same worship community.

Every weekend, for a long period of time, members of a local Kingdom Hall would show up at my parent's house in a suburb of Atlanta. They would ring the bell, and my father became tired of it.

Knowing my father, he had probably engaged in some philosophical discussion with the first few people who showed up. However, after repeated unsolicited visits, he lost his patience, and decided to take action.

He finally told one such group that when they had a *Watchtower Magazine* for him in his native language of Ibibio, they should come back and he would invite them into his house. From that day on, when they returned, they were greeted with a sign in the window saying just that: "For all members of the Jehovah's Witness faith, please do not ring the doorbell unless you have materials in the Ibibio language."

My father had given an assignment, and would participate in the discussion when his requirements were met. I guess he figured that if they wanted him to respect their religious perspective and traditions, then he expected them to respect his cultural perspective and traditions.

I thought of all these things on the Sunday morning after my jury duty was completed. I drove to the Kingdom Hall in Lincoln Park.

As I approached the building, I was conscious of the importance of blending in here—more than anywhere else I had been. I didn't want to stand out and then be forced into a one-on-one evangelical session. There are a few worship experiences where the "reputation" of the faith made me feel this way—and this was one of them (Scientology, Mormonism, Wicca—those were others). I always tried to be open minded, but it was sometimes challenging.

I sat in a chair and acted as if I knew what I was doing. People offered me the hymn book and a *Watchtower Magazine*. I accepted it, realizing that this act alone identified me as someone new. I wondered when I would get the pitch I was expecting.

In the meantime, I tried to focus on the service.

Very quickly, I learned that the sermon was called a discourse. The title of the discourse for that day was, "Does your thinking agree with God's?" The discourse focused on concepts of why it was important to follow God's thinking, what God's thinking was, and how we should ask ourselves where our thinking falls in comparison to God's thinking and the world's thinking.

I was very aware of the use of the term "Jehovah" to refer to God. I guess I should have expected this, but this was the first worship experience where that term was used consistently.

We were reminded to rely on Jehovah, both in the little things and in the big things. We were encouraged to be faithful in the little things. The idea was this: if we were faithful in the little things, then it would be easier to deal with the bigger trials if and when they came.

I agreed with the elder—those bigger trials always do come.

I continued to agree with the elder as he talked about having faith. He shared his perspective that if you do what is right and align your thinking with God's, then you'll be okay.

The elder encouraged us to, "Find out God's opinion on the matter, and let that guide you."

Sounded like solid advice.

I was thinking, "Well, I'm hearing relevant and useful information in this service with the Jehovah's Witnesses, just like I have every other week." I started to relax and stopped thinking so much about what others said I would find here, and decided to focus only on what I was actually finding.

Then, I had a moment.

I was nodding my head, agreeing, throughout a good chunk of the message, then the elder said something that made me say, "What in the world?" That moment came when the elder mentioned Matthew 4:8-10 (NIV):

> Again, the devil took him to a very high mountain and showed him all the kingdoms of the world and their splendor. All this

I will give you, he said, if you will bow down and worship me. Jesus said to him, Away from me, Satan! For it is written: "Worship the Lord your God, and serve him only."

The elder explained that voting in a United States election was an example of "bowing down" to someone other than God. He noted that this verse *clearly stated* the faithful shouldn't do this. The elder shared that, "In the Bible, mountains represent government," which is something I'd never heard. The elder reflected on how the 2008 United States election was historic: the first time, in his estimation, that an African-American and a woman were serious contenders to be President of the United States. While he understood that many of the faithful might have been tempted to vote, he reminded the congregation, "Voting in elections suggests that you are putting your faith in elected officials to make things better, rather than Jehovah."

I thought, "What? You really believe that?"

Luckily, I have the luxury in this journey of taking what makes sense and what feeds me, and leaving the rest.

Perhaps, we all have that luxury, always.

I continued to listen, but that portion of the discourse had affected my ability to be completely open.

More useful nuggets came. The elder talked about the importance of honoring our mothers and fathers, no matter what age we are. He talked about the importance of working with purpose, including "the preaching work," which I assumed referred to the door-to-door evangelism that has turned many off from hearing the Jehovah's Witness message.

A prayer and a song ended the discourse portion of the service. I looked around discreetly to see what would happen next. No one seemed to be moving to leave. I sat tight. What came next was the *Watchtower* study, which appeared to be an interactive study of a lesson in the *Watchtower* publication. The topic for the study was, "Who can deliver those crying for help?" There was a question-and-answer session led by a different elder.

Participation in the study came from all over the congregation, including the children. The elder called everyone by name whenever they answered a question, illustrating that this was a tight-knit community. I really do think that there is something to be said that everyone participated in the Watchtower study. Often, people go to service and hold down the pews (me included), but never really commit to focused study. This reminded me of my experience with the Mormons. In both situations, I saw the more intimate interactions. In this situation I chose to heed the lesson that I'd learned from the Mormon small-group experience—Just. Be. Quiet. And. Listen.

At some level, the whole visit was an enjoyable experience—but I was very aware of when the service ended. I wanted to leave without being detected. Before I was able to do that, my neighbor asked me if I was new. I decided to be honest and as open as I could be. I took a deep breath and told her I was. I told her how I'd met two members of the congregation during jury duty selection and they had invited me.

My heart skipped a beat when she told me that she had heard my story in their Wednesday night prayer meeting (I was being discussed in the Wednesday night prayer meeting?). It started again when she told me that my hosts were not, in fact, present on that day, confirming that I would likely be able to escape without offending anyone.

*   *   *

I believe that it's okay to come into a service, listen, and then leave without talking to a single soul. I tried, and failed to do that this week at the Kingdom Hall. But, overall, my experience at this service was a positive one. I don't think it was diminished by my lack of desire to continue interacting.

After all, I was not shopping for a new religion.

WEEK 44
HAPPY BIRTHDAY TO ME
ALL SAINTS DAY MASS, HOLY NAME CATHEDRAL

5:15 p.m. Mass, Chicago, Illinois

This day signified the end of my month off. I would be starting a new project the next day, so I wanted to relax as much as possible! I woke up, worked out, and went to the spa for a facial, massage, and mani-pedi. I treated myself to lunch, and thought about heading to Zumba later.

It was my birthday. All of my life, I have been intrigued by the fact that I was born on All Saints Day. I figured now was a good time to be in a Catholic Church and hear what the significance of the day was. I'd tried to make time to go to a Dia De Los Muertos service on Halloween, the day before, but couldn't make it happen. So, here I was on Monday, Googling around to find out where the closest Mass in the area was.

I settled on Holy Name Cathedral.

As I walked down Chicago city streets toward the church, I started to hear the church bells ringing. The cathedral was very close to a grocery store that I frequented. Amazingly, there are places of worship that you pass every day, in your comings and goings, but never think to stop or visit.

Everything about the church was dazzling. The bells played angelic tones; the heavy, ornate doors provided a magnificent entrance to the cathedral; and when I walked inside, the pulchritude of the sanctuary overwhelmed me.

I slid into a pew and opened my mind and my heart to hear about All Saints Day, a day where Catholics celebrate all the Saints, known and unknown.

*   *   *

Beauty inspires me. Sometimes, just finding and sitting quietly in such a place feeds my spirit. What a wonderful birthday present to be in a place such as this, enjoying the Mass, with all its now-familiar cadences, and focusing on all the blessings in my life.

WEEK 45
IS YOU IS OR IS YOU AIN'T . . . A CATHOLIC?
ST. MARY OF THE ANGELS

7:15 p.m. Mass, Chicago, Illinois

On this day, I was very aware that there were many worship experiences I still wanted to have before my year-long journey came to an end. I had grand plans for today. I'd thought about trying to visit a Hindu temple in the morning, but the time got away from me. Before I knew it, I was searching for an evening service.

I felt the Catholic experience calling me this week. I looked forward to the familiar cadence and liturgy of the service. However, I hoped to experience something a little different. I chose St. Mary's of the Angels, run by the priests of Opus Dei.

I'd only had two experiences with Opus Dei prior to this evening. For a year, I'd tutored in an after-school program sponsored by an organization called Midtown Educational Foundation (MEF). While MEF programs are non-denominational, the social teachings of the Catholic Church and Opus Dei inspire them.

The other experience I have had with Opus Dei was in reading *Angels and Demons*, by Dan Brown, a book that does not paint the most flattering picture of Opus Dei.

I didn't know what to expect when I approached the Cathedral on the North Side of Chicago. The church was enormous. A portion of it had scaffolding around it, as if there were repairs taking place.

I ascended the stairs, opened the door, and entered the dimly-lit sanctuary. I wondered what it would feel like and look like during the day, when it was flooded with light and the intricate decorations all over the sanctuary were more prominent.

I sat down and waited for the service to start. People lined up for confession on the side of the room.

I have never been to confession in the Catholic Church, and wondered what that would be like. I wondered how I would feel before and after unburdening my spirit to a priest behind the curtain.

I found the Book of Worship so that I could follow along, and let the ritual comfort me. Although I knew I wasn't shopping for a new method of worship, in the back of my mind I was beginning to think, "Maybe I should consider Catholicism." I was jolted from this line of thought by the words spoken a little later in the service.

The priest was a white-haired elderly man in a long robe. He moved slowly to the front of the church, where he would give his homily for the evening. I listened as he talked about certain virtues: prudence, justice, fortitude, and temperance. There was nothing particularly controversial about this portion of the homily. These were universal virtues valued by most people—whether religious, spiritual, or neither.

Then he started talking about the "dictatorship of relativism." He stated that, in this day and age, there was a popular push to suggest that there are no absolutes. On the other hand, he was very clear that absolutes absolutely existed. There were things that were right and things that were wrong. He listed some things we should remember were wrong:

- Stem cell research
- Abortion
- Divorce
- Contraception
- Pre-marital sex
- In-vitro fertilization

This list gave me pause.

I remembered the last time that I'd really believed in absolute right and absolute wrong. It was the summer before my freshman year in college, and I was working in corporate America for the first time. My close friend Marla and I were having a discussion on our lunch break.

I was sixteen years old then, had grown up in a relatively sheltered family environment, and had received a Christian preparatory education. I was absolutely sure that some things were just right and some things were just wrong.

Marla was incredulous. She couldn't believe the vigor with which I defended the idea that things were, in fact, black and white. I couldn't believe that she didn't hold the same views.

It was not long after that I headed to California for college and had all my simplistic views challenged. From that time until the moment I sat in the pew listening to the priest that evening, I had adjusted my thoughts. I didn't believe in complete relativism. I'd adopted a more moderate approach—believing that things were slightly more complicated than an absolute view of right and wrong.

The priest disagreed. He reminded us of the importance of keeping the rules of God regardless. He emphasized that God was counting on us, and that we should be prayerful, exhibiting strength to live in our lives and defend the faith.

Defending the faith sounded a whole lot like believing in certain absolutes, and I was not up for that.

I was reminded at that moment that visiting a Catholic church isn't the same as being Catholic. Indeed, being a visitor to any place of worship was just an infinitesimal slice of the experience of that worship tradition. It was fine to visit, and fine to be honored to be welcomed, but to truly be committed was something entirely different.

Being Catholic is more than the liturgy; it's more than the sitting down and getting up, and knowing when to do each. It's believing in a certain set of tenets and cultural points of view. Or doing the work to reconcile any views that are different from your personal views and figuring out how to be okay with all of it.

This all supported a realization that "being a Catholic" would be a complicated choice, and one that I couldn't take lightly, just because I enjoyed the cadence and the ritual of a Catholic Church service.

*　　*　　*

As a result of this service, I came to a conclusion that I could not, would not be a Catholic. Not really a surprise—but it was something that had been at the back of my mind as I became more familiar with Catholic worship services throughout my journey.

Nevertheless, as I listened to the benediction at the end of the service, I was blessed by the words that the priest used to send us back into the world:

"The mass has ended; go in the peace of Christ to serve the Lord. Thanks Be To God."

WEEK 46
GIVING THANKS
THE ZOROASTRIAN ASSOCIATION
OF METROPOLITAN CHICAGO

12:30 p.m. Burr Ridge, Illinois

After the relatively familiar experience of a Catholic church the previous week, I was ready to experience something new and different. While consulting the Harvard University site, The Pluralism project[60], I found out that there was a Zoroastrian Association of Metropolitan Chicago. I gave a call, and talked with someone who told me that there was a Thanksgiving celebration taking place during the upcoming weekend. The celebration was called Jashan, The Afringan Ceremony. When I asked if I could join in, I was welcomed.

As we talked, the voice on the phone told me he was a representative of the Zarathushti Learning Center of North America. He told me about the faith, which started in the Persian Empire, and shared that India had the largest Zoroastrian population. He mentioned that there were centers of worship in a few places in North America: Toronto, Texas, and Illinois.

He shared information about the primary deity for the religion, Zoroaster, clarifying for me one of the core beliefs: that we are coworkers of God. We are told to listen to God with an illumined mind, then decide. If what we hear makes sense, then we should follow God.

He shared that, in the faith, each day of each month is named after an attribute of God, so we remember.

We agreed on the importance of remembrance.

We hung up the phone, and I made plans to visit the next worship service.

The Zoroastrian Association of Metropolitan Chicago is located in Burr Ridge, Illinois, which is a suburb due west of the city. To get there, I had to drive on Highway 55, which leads from Chicago to St. Louis.

It's also the same highway that lead to my ex's house and I wasn't thrilled about driving down that road again—literally or figuratively. Although I hadn't seen or talked to him in months, the wound caused by his disappearance from my life was still quite raw. I didn't want to risk doing anything that would inspire me to keep driving past Burr Ridge and end up on his doorstep.

I had a conversation with myself as I contemplated attending this service in this particular location. This conversation continued as I drove to the service. I reminded myself of the importance of completing this journey with some sort of dignity and grace. I willed myself to drive ONLY the twenty-five miles to Burr Ridge, and NOT to continue the extra ten miles that would have me, pathetically, on my ex's doorstep.

I placed the address of the center in my GPS, being thankful for the freedom that comes from such a device. It seems like magic that, at any time, you can consult it, and it will tell you how to get to where you want to go. When I was a young girl, my father taught me how to read a map, sharing with me the low-tech way to figure out how to get somewhere you had never gone before. I thought of him, thankful that he had given me the tools I needed to make my way through the world.

As I drove down the highway, I coached myself the whole way. "Don't keep driving to the ex's house," I told myself.

Arrival at the center was a victory by itself.

Now, I just had to enter a completely different world, and do that with some grace and dignity.

Even after months of entering new worship services, there was still apprehension. I still had to figure out how to enter a new building and what to do when I got inside. I still had to figure out how not to look completely lost. Thankfully, every time, there was one person with whom I made eye contact, who reassured me that there was kindness here, and that I'd made the right choice.

I asked for the individual with whom I'd spoken on the phone earlier, and the kind "first eye contact person" told me he was busy, but that I was in the right place. Since I was late, I asked if the ceremony had started yet. I was assured that it hadn't. I was right on time.

I could see that there was an altar in the front of what looked like a recreational room of some sort. Members of the community were starting to put out folding chairs.

I sat down in the middle of the set of chairs, looking around to orient myself. I'd confirmed in my initial conversation that there were no special requirements for attire. Because I'd been told I didn't need one, I hadn't come prepared with a head covering. However, when I saw many of the women covering their heads, I covered my head in an impromptu fashion—pulling my sweater wrap over my head. I probably looked slightly ridiculous, but I chose looking ridiculous over being disrespectful.

In some ways, me being there at all was slightly ridiculous. I was again a chocolate chip, this time among a number of what looked like people of Indian, Pakistani, and Iranian descent.

As the ceremony started, four men in white approached the tablecloth-covered altar, where an assortment of fruit and flowers had been placed. They lit candles and incense on the table, and as they "set up," I could feel the room becoming a sacred space. Often on this journey, I was reminded that there were certain tasks and activities that could turn an ordinary space into a sacred space. I witnessed this now.

Later research described the ceremony that I was attending as:

> . . . a religious thanksgiving ceremony, or one that celebrates or commemorates an important event . . . Afringans are

dedications to God, God's creation, divine attributes and angels. An Afringan is also called a flower ceremony . . . . [61]

During the ceremony, four men worked in silence, tending to the ritual with precision. There was clearly a specific order to the ritual. Water, wine, and milk were present for use. Metal instruments were used to tend to a fire that was kept burning with sticks of sandalwood and different types of incense. One of the men tended to the fire, pouring ladles of liquid on it.

During the ceremony, prayers in Ancient Persian languages were used for this religious ritual. No part of the ceremony was in English. I learned later that most of those who attended probably didn't understand the actual words of the ceremony either, due to the use of these ancient, religious languages.

As I listened to the ceremony, I was reminded of a ritual that my father completed every year as the New Year started. From a cup of cognac that he carried, he would literally "pour out a little liquor," also known as pouring libations, on every doorstep and near every window in our house. Walking around, he prayed and spoke to the ancestors in his mother tongue, Ibibio. He thanked them for the blessings of the year that had ended, and asked for blessings and protection for the New Year. When he was done, he would approach me and each of my sisters. We would dip a finger in the cup, taste the bitter dark liquid, and in that way participate in the ritual.

There is something captivating about praying in the language of your ancestors.

On the side of the room where the Jashan took place, there was a banner that had a familiar image on it. It looked like the symbol of the Rosicrucian order, of which my father was a member. It looked like this:

The Rosicrucian Order website[62], in answering the question, "Is the Rosicrucian Order, AMORC, a religion?" says the following:

> AMORC, which stands for Ancient and Mystical Order Rosae Crucis, is not a religion and does not require a specific code of belief or conduct. Rosicrucian students come from a variety of cultural and religious backgrounds. Becoming a Rosicrucian student does not in any way require you to leave your church, join a church, or change your religious beliefs.
>
> Some Rosicrucian members do not subscribe to any specific religious beliefs at all. For students who do, we encourage them to participate in the religion of their choice. As a result, Rosicrucian students come from every religious denomination, and through our teachings, many find a greater appreciation of the mystical principles underlying their individual religious and philosophical beliefs.

For as long as I'd known my father, I'd known that he'd been a Rosicrucian. He was a philosopher, a mystic, and one who was not threatened by the challenge of worshipping as a Christian, while relentlessly seeking wisdom wherever he could find it. He encouraged me to do the same.

Upon further research, I learned that the Rosicrucian symbol was adapted from the Zoroastrian/Assyrian image—the one I saw in that cultural center. It is called the Wings of Jehovah.

When I saw that symbol, I was reminded once again that there was no spiritual ground that my father had not covered before me. That realization brought me comfort.

The ceremony was in full swing now. People had hand fans and covered their noses to protect them from the smoke that was coming from the offering fire.

Throughout the service, people approached the altar with bits of sandalwood, incense, and other sticks of different spices in their hands, ostensibly to contribute some sort of offering in thanksgiving. At one point, I watched a child approach the altar, guided by his father. In this gesture, I saw the father saying to the child, "This is our culture, this is our faith—here's your chance to participate." Hopefully, that child will use this experience and others to become multi-cultural and multi-lingual as he grows up in America, a country far away from the origins of the tradition of this religion.

*   *   *

Much of the Jashan ceremony was a mystery, but it reminded me that to live without some mystery of faith in your life is to live with something missing, I think.

On this day, I was able to experience a religious tradition that was different from my own. In the process, I was able to feel the presence of God and my father in a different way, in a different context.

Week 47
Psychedelic!
Young Adult Worship, Kensington Temple, London City Church

7:00 p.m. Notting Hill Gate, London, England

Along with a commitment to visit a different place of worship every week during this year, I also gave myself permission to travel wherever I wanted. I love travelling—it is a form of therapy for me, and I find a great peace in being in the air.

When I was given a reason to visit the United Kingdom in November, I decided to take it. I have many friends and family in that part of the world, and I knew it would do my soul good to see them. Mr. Friend Zone had moved to the UK to play rugby union in Lymm, a small village in the UK. I said I would come out and visit him to see him play.

I was going to London!

London is one of my favorite cities. Although it's very expensive, I enjoy the energy of the city, as well as the global nature of its denizens. I was looking forward to spending time in London with a close friend and sorority sister, Carla. We laughed, watched movies, and took cold medicine—as both of us were under the weather. There is nothing like having a friend who you can have fun with, even when both of you are stuffed up and sick, just sitting around laughing at the hijinks in our respective lives.

When trying to decide where my London-based worship experience would be, I considered trying to go to a service at Westminster Abbey, and also considered going to a Nigerian congregation, which ended up being very far out of the city limits. I also found a Spanish-Portuguese synagogue that held services in Spanish (Carla is fluent in the language, and I'm . . . functional). When I called, the person who answered the phone seemed confused about why I would want to visit. I decided not to fight about it, and crossed it off my list.

When it came down to it, I chose to visit the Kensington Temple, London City Church, in Notting Hill. Because I was heading to see Mr. Friend Zone in Lymm on Saturday, I ended up choosing to visit the Teen Worship service on Friday evening.

Early Friday evening, I had dinner with some of my UK-based cousins: Enimien, Omono, Lolia, and Oseyi. Afterwards, one cousin, Enimien, returned with me to Notting Hill to attend the Youth Ministry service at Kensington Temple.

I call myself lucky to have friends and family who thought my worship journey was worthwhile, rather than nutty or square. I thought about this as Enimien, Carla, and I found our way to a pew in the middle of the church.

On Friday night.

From the very beginning, the service was over-stimulating. Most of the worshippers looked to be in their late teens and early twenties. The energy of the service was extremely high.

I can only imagine that the experience was purposefully constructed so that young people would find it stimulating to be at a church on Friday night, instead of out running the streets looking for entertainment.

Machines filled the room with smoke. Laser beams and strobe lights shone light throughout the sanctuary, creating a display that was much like the show that I remember seeing when visiting Stone Mountain Park as a child.

Multiple flat screens hung throughout the church. I counted six before I gave up. These giant screens projected images and song lyrics, assaulting all of my senses with media.

One big screen showed what my father would have called a "psychedelic" display of colors—like one of the multicolored designs that mesmerize you as you listen to music on your Windows Media Player.

All of this was slightly incongruous, since the church was an old historic European temple. The church had memorable architecture that made you think about its history—until you were jolted back to the present by the overpowering technology and the high-fidelity speakers blasting the music for the evening.

There was plenty of music. To start the service, one very committed young saint sang for about thirty minutes. She projected a great deal of emotion, conviction, and commitment, in the way that only teenagers can do. It was clear she knew without of a shadow doubt that Jesus was her savior, and that was that.

The congregation was overwhelmingly African, which made me feel at home. This contrasted with the church literature. The bulletin, the magazine, and the programming was all multi-cultural. I saw notices of gatherings and presentations by different ethnic groups within the church: Indian, Nigerian, and others.

The youth pastor approached the altar and the service started.

Music played throughout the service, providing a background soundtrack. This amused me and reminded me of my time performing comedy or poetry. Performances often sound better when relevant music plays softly in the background.

The church was a Pentecostal Church. The pastor spent most of his time on this Friday night talking about the Holy Ghost, also known as the Holy Spirit.

During the sermon, the pastor referred to the Trinity, and spoke about how many churches and many Christians overlook the presence of the Holy Spirit. He stated that the focus is often on the Father (God) and the Son (Jesus Christ), and that people often forget the Holy Spirit, the third member of the Trinity. I heard more references to the Holy Ghost in this sermon than in all the Christian sermons I heard in the previous weeks.

The pastor referred to many people in the Bible who were in the middle of what appeared to be impossible situations. He shared that only the Holy Spirit resolved those situations.

One of those stories focused on Mary, the mother of Jesus, and how she was told that she would have a child. She, of course, being a virgin, asked God how. The answer, according to this pastor, was, "The Holy Spirit." In this situation, Mary was told not to look toward man. Rather, she was to look to the Holy Spirit.

That, according to the pastor, was a statement of faith. Mary was not questioning that it *would be*, but just asking *how it would be*.

As a woman in her thirties with no children, who had just ended a relationship, I could relate to Mary's question. I keep trying to have faith and telling myself, "It's not too late to have children with someone I love and respect," but the question, "How is that going to happen," often came up. I suppose, if I were to listen to the message from this service, the answer would be "The Holy Spirit."

The pastor went on to talk about how faith can heal doubt.

And that was the takeaway for me from the evening.

One unexpectedly memorable portion of the service came thanks to a young lady who, throughout the service, was making a startling high-pitched sound. She was yip-yipping with so much exuberance that her voice rose above all of the other Hallelujahs, Praise Gods, and Thank You Jesuses. She was so loud, in fact, that people turned around to find the source of the noise. She testified on, with no concern about feeling strange or out of place because of the noises she was making as she praised the Lord.

I thought to myself, "That, too, was apparently the Holy Spirit."

Heaven help us.

I really enjoyed my time throughout this service. It was extremely entertaining. Carla, Enimien, and I marveled at the spectacle of the service.

There is something decidedly different about going to church by yourself versus attending services with friends and family. We were able to focus on the message, but also enjoyed the abundant opportunities to find humor throughout the service.

As we all said our goodbyes for the evening, I had some time to reflect back on the service—specifically, how I truly feel about the Holy Spirit as part of my belief set.

My final thought was this: it's possible to go to church, to go to prayer meetings, and to not be open to the Holy Spirit. It will be important for me to think and pray on my true feelings about that third part of the Trinity, so when I end my prayers with "In the name of the Father, the Son, and the Holy Spirit," I'm clear who I'm calling upon.

* * *

As I left the service that evening, I found myself sending up a prayer thanking God for my spiritual journey, saying simply, "Thank you for all the weird and wonderful ways that people worship you."

Jesus and Rugby
Lymm Methodist Church

6:30 p.m. Café Church service, Lymm, United Kingdom

Early Saturday morning, I boarded a train travelling from the central train station in London, to Lymm, a picturesque village in the heart of Cheshire.

In August, Mr. Friend Zone had moved away from Chicago and came to this little village to play rugby for a local team.

Because I love travel, and because we had developed a solid friendship, I decided to make good on a promise I made before he left and come out to visit.

I spent all of Saturday watching rugby and rugby players—sometimes in the sun, and sometimes in the rain—in weather shifts that only the UK can provide.

Sunday morning when I woke up, I did some Googling, and located the few options for worship within the village limits. I decided that Lymm Methodist Church would be the place where I hung my worship hat this weekend. They had an evening service. After a lazy day exploring the village, that suited me just fine.

The service took place in the basement of the building next door to the main sanctuary. When I walked in, I was hesitant, because I wasn't sure where I was going or what I would find in that basement. When I opened the door to the room where service would occur, it was clear that I was in the right place. I made eye contact with one of the older ladies who was already seated in the room, and immediately I was put at ease. That eye contact felt like an invitation. I took a deep breath and walked in. I approached her, introduced myself, and let her know that I was a visitor.

She welcomed me warmly and led me to the kitchen in the back of the room to get some tea.

Of course. Tea.

We were, after all, in England.

That evening, a thousand miles from my home, I gathered with a small group in the basement of a church. Nevertheless, as I sipped my warm cup of tea, I felt very comfortable.

Light green and pastel yellow tablecloths covered the tables in the room. Many different families sat together. We drank tea and ate cakes and desserts together.

Everyone around my table introduced themselves. I learned that I was sitting at a table of local (lay) preachers. I sat next to my new friend. She explained to me that the service would start with singing, and warned me that she liked to stand up when she sang. She thought it showed honor and respect. "It's how she was raised," she shared.

We sang together, reading the lyrics that were being projected on a screen at the front of the room. Children from the community played instruments in accompaniment. It was a welcome change! I'd spent most of the weekend watching children playing rugby. But here, there were no ruggers in sight.

The focus of the sermon was on the concept of Jesus being King. There was an interactive discussion based on the question, "If Jesus is our King, what does that mean to us?"

First, we had an activity. We were asked to put together a jigsaw puzzle—answering that question. Each of us cut a puzzle piece out of a piece of paper, wrote our answer on it, and then we collectively put the puzzle back together at the front of the room. As we reassembled the puzzle, there was a Q&A and discussion period.

During the discussion, people shared their perspectives on what it meant to them to think of Jesus as their King:

- Being a king meant being a leader. Being a leader required humility.
- If Jesus is the son of God and he is a King, that makes us children of God, thus *we* too are royalty.
- Being a King meant doing the best for the subjects of the King.

Shortly before the service ended, a video played which explored that topic; it was called, *"That's My King."* When the video ended and the credits rolled, I found out, ironically, that it was a video from Willow Creek Community Church, a well-known church from my home state of Illinois. I told my friends at the table that I was from Chicago, home of this Willow Creek Community Church. A new friend at the table, an elderly gentleman, said, "That means you are in the right place at the right time."

At that moment, I agreed.

*   *   *

After this worship experience, I contemplated how you can find friendship and support in the most unexpected places. When I met Mr. Friend Zone at the beginning of the year, I thought I needed one thing. What I really needed, however, I got. Mr. Friend Zone provided a platonic shoulder for me to cry on throughout the year after my challenging year. He always listened to me talk about how I felt—even and especially when I felt terrible about the losses I was processing. The conversations we had contributed a great deal to my healing process.

Our friendship became strong enough that I could travel miles, and visit him in little village in England where rugby was part of the very fabric of life.

In that village, I had the opportunity to connect with a group of British people, drinking tea, eating biscuits, and discussing their faith.

Many of my worship experiences happened close to home, but those that happened far from home blessed me in an unforgettable way. Home is a good place to start, but out there is an amazing world full of people and places that can be blessings to you if you just let them be.

WEEK 48
DENIED, HUMBLED, ACCEPTED
ATLANTA MASJID OF AL-ISLAM

1:00 p.m. Jumu'ah service, Atlanta, Georgia

Up until this point in my journey, the only view of Islam I'd experienced was through the lens of the Nation of Islam. One of those services was at the United Center; the other was Mosque Maryam, where I went in, sat down in a pew, and heard a message. I was apprehensive about entering a non-NOI mosque without any idea about the order, rhythm, and vocabulary of a prayer service. This anxiety had prevented me from visiting a mosque during Ramadan, the holiest month of the Muslim calendar, and the month in which Muslims fast during the daylight hours to fulfill one of the five pillars of the faith.

While discussing my journey with a friend of mine, Aneesah, I shared that I'd only had an experience with the Nation of Islam. She had been raised Muslim and was skeptical:

"You have only been to the Nation of Islam?" she asked.

When I replied in the affirmative, she balked.

"You know that's not really Islam."

I let her speak her piece, not wanting to quibble about a worship community that would beg to differ, remembering the Honorable Minister Louis Farrakhan's thoughts on that particular matter.

"Are you going to visit a masjid when you go home to Atlanta?" she asked.

"I would rather go here in Chicago," I replied, "Would you be interested in coming with me?"

I shared my concerns about not knowing how to navigate around a mosque. In trying to explain to me what the experience would be like, she used the term "masjid" repeatedly.

I learned that the Arabic word "masjid" means "a place for prayer" or a "place for prostration" and that the English word mosque refers to all buildings dedicated to Islamic worship.

After she gave me a high-level overview of what happens in a mosque or a masjid, she agreed to accompany me to a service. I figured that, at the very least, she might remember how things went at the mosque, help me to navigate around, and be less conspicuous.

She had some reservations due to the fact that she was no longer a practicing Muslim, but agreed to accompany me to a 1:00 p.m. prayer service on the South Side of Chicago.

As I often did, I decided to wear traditional African attire to the service. I was mindful that I wanted to be modest. I brought a long piece of fabric—that would have served as a head tie if I was wearing the full matching outfit—so I could cover my head when I entered the place of prayer. I drove to the mosque, and waited in the car for Aneesah to arrive. When she arrived, I covered my head, exited the car, and we walked toward the entrance of the building together.

It was clear that Aneesah was anxious. She told me the first thing we would have to do was to "make wudu," which was a ritual ablution performed by Muslims prior to prayer and certain other acts of worship. She was concerned that she didn't remember the order of the washing, or the prayers that we should say while washing. I began to feel her anxiety. This appeared to be an important piece of the worship experience that I knew nothing about. I wondered if I should have done more research before coming, even with Aneesah as an escort.

Generally, before every visit to a new place of worship, I would call and talk to someone to ensure that it was okay for me to come and participate in the service. When I called this particular mosque, the phone just rang repeatedly.

The ever-ringing phone turned out to be a foreshadowing of problems to come.

We must have looked hesitant when we approached the door. A woman who was standing there greeted us in the expected way:

"As Salaam Alaikum," she said.

Peace be unto you.

"Wa Alaikum Assaalam," we replied.

And unto you peace.

After this exchange, it was apparent that we were not sure what to do next. The woman at the door sensed this, and asked if we were first time visitors.

Aneesah answered that this was not her first time to a mosque, but it was her first time to this mosque.

I answered that this was my first time to any mosque.

This is when the problems started.

The woman asked me what we were there to do, and when we replied that we were there for the afternoon prayer service, she asked if we were Muslims.

Both of us said no.

"Well, then you can't come in here," she said.

What ensued was a discussion that was somewhat surreal. She told us that this was a holy time of prayer, and that we were not able to come in unless we were Muslims. Aneesah challenged her.

"You mean we can't even come in and sit in the back to observe?" she asked.

The reply was no, followed by a long monologue about what it meant to be a Muslim, what was happening in the prayer service, and how we would be welcome to come if we were ready to recite the Shahadah, which is the Muslim declaration of faith.

Formally, someone becomes a Muslim by saying, in front of witnesses:

"There is no God but Allah, and Muhammad is a Messenger of Allah."

"If I'm not ready to convert, then I can't come in?" I asked.

She assured us that this was correct, and launched into a mini-sermon of her own about how the mosque was a holy place, and how not just anyone could go in. She told us that she had been around the world in her travels and there were some mosques even she couldn't enter, and she was a real Muslim. She explained that she used to be a Baptist, but then she started studying Islam, and after years and years of study, she was now able to tell us with certainty that we were not allowed to enter the prayer service.

Meanwhile, people were streaming in, walking by us as they entered the masjid.

By this point, I have to admit, I was getting a little irritated. I explained to her that I came in peace.

I may not have sounded or appeared very peaceful, however. I was unable to understand why this woman was barring us from this place of worship. I told her that I'd visited many different churches, synagogues, temples, and other worship services. I assured her that I just wanted to stand shoulder to shoulder with my Muslim brothers and sisters to pray and share peace and good intentions.

She was unmoved.

She mentioned that when Muslims stand shoulder to shoulder to pray, the energy of Allah flows through every member of the congregation. If I was standing in that number, the energy would stop at me, the unbeliever, and I would, in fact, block the blessing to the others in the room.

At that point, I was almost done. I had no intention of begging this woman to let me in, and certainly didn't plan to lie either. I asked her one last time, as earnestly as I could, "What if I'm standing here, truly interested in Islam, and you are telling me that I'm unable to come into this place of worship. Might you be blocking someone from learning more about the Allah you profess to love and worship?"

She replied by telling me that if I was truly interested in Islam, I should read some books about it, and then come back to speak to the elders. She also shared that if I sat on the bench outside of the mosque, I could probably hear some of the prayers said inside.

She mentioned that, honestly, she was not sure of our intentions, because we appeared to be "dressed like Muslims," and had she not asked us, she wouldn't have known that we were not supposed to be there.

I politely informed her that I was not "dressed like a Muslim." I was dressed in African attire because I was, in fact, African, and that I chose what I wore not so I could pretend to be a Muslim, but rather so that I could respectfully approach the mosque and participate with a modest appearance that wouldn't offend those who came to pray.

She seemed unconvinced.

Now, I was truly done. I apologized that I made her late for her prayer service, and I was ready to leave.

Aneesah, however, was not done.

It turns out that our cars were blocked in the parking lot. No doubt, everyone who had come to pray assumed that it would be okay to block us in, since we were likely there for service, as well.

Aneesah, who was very upset by the whole situation, began to explain to the woman in an agitated fashion that if she wouldn't let us come into the service, she needed to go in and find the people who had blocked us in, so they could move their cars and we could leave.

I thought that seemed unlikely, and the self-appointed gatekeeper agreed.

After watching Aneesah wrangling with this woman for a few minutes, in an effort to keep the peace, I suggested that we take a walk around the neighborhood until the prayer service was over and we could get our cars out of the parking lot.

Along the way, it was almost comical how many people waved and greeted us—me in my African attire and Aneesah in her head covering. People shouted to us, "As Salaam Alaikum," assuming that we had come from the service which we had not been allowed to enter.

As we walked and talked, I examined my feelings.

I was a little bit offended. Didn't this woman know how much time and effort I'd put into building bridges between worship communities by being open and praying with people of different faith traditions? How could she think that my intentions were anything but pure?

Then I had a very clear thought.

Be humble.

By not being able to just waltz into yet another place of worship, I was reminded that each place of worship is holy and sacred to those who come there regularly to pray, to find peace, to seek solace, to hear their holy words, and to be instructed by their religious teachers. Although it is nice to think that I could join in with that experience, I certainly was not entitled to do so. I had no *right* to enter a place that was set aside for Muslims to pray.

It was not a right to share in worship, it was a privilege.

In addition, given how much hatred is being directed at Muslims in the current political and cultural climate, I could certainly understand why someone would be hesitant to let a stranger come into their holy place.

Aneesah and I agreed that the woman was a self-appointed gatekeeper on that particular day, rather than a representative of the leadership of that particular mosque, or Islam in general. I was able to "settle down" and accept that I'd been denied entry into the first place of worship this year. I marveled that it had not happened before, and decided to be open to the lessons that I learned as result of that experience.

When I told friends about this experience, most people were outraged. Some friends said that I should call back and try to speak to an elder, let them know what happened, and find out if the self-appointed gatekeeper was accurate in her message that we were not able to come into the masjid until we had converted to Islam.

But I had no desire to return to that same mosque, although I may someday. Instead, I emailed another friend of mine, Taara, a practicing Muslim, and shared my story with her.

She was horrified.

She assured me that the words of the self-appointed gatekeeper we encountered didn't in any way represent the Islam that she knew, loved, and practiced. This confirmed my hypothesis that the woman we met was wielding power that she may or may not have had the authority to wield.

I told Taara that I would be travelling to Atlanta to spend Thanksgiving with my family, and that I would like to attend Jumu'ah at a masjid while I was there. She sprang into action. Having grown up in Atlanta, Taara knew the imam at the Atlanta Masjid of Al-Islam, and told me that she promised to contact him to let him know I was coming. She put me in contact with two of her childhood friends, Qadara and Nadiyah, who could serve as my hosts when I arrived.

I would try again to visit a masjid. I wouldn't let my initial experience deter me.

I asked Qadara and Nadiyah lots of questions: What should I wear? Would it truly be okay for me to visit? Did I need to cover my head?

I was told it was okay for me to visit, and I should not worry about wearing anything specific or covering my head. Nevertheless, I chose to wear a modest outfit, and brought a shawl, just in case.

The Atlanta Masjid of Al-Islam was in a section of Atlanta that was a good forty-five minutes away from my mother's house, and as I drove over, I wondered what my experience would be like.

It was fantastic.

After parking at the mosque, I called Qadara and Nadiyah. They met me and immediately put me at ease. They had heard the story of the self-appointed gatekeeper from Chicago, apologized for her, and let me know that I was welcome. They patiently answered every question that I had.

I followed them into the mosque. They both had children. A division of labor was necessary. One of them took all of the children into the main prayer room, and the other let me know that she would be going to perform the ritualistic washing.

Wudu.

This was the point in the last masjid experience where everything fell apart. I asked her if I needed to perform the washing, as well. She assured me that I was welcome to do so, or to just watch.

I chose to watch.

I was grateful for the company of new friends who were open to sharing their faith with me, along with all the different pieces and parts of the worship experience.

After she completed the washing and the prayers, we entered the inner room of the mosque. The majority of the worshippers in the room were African-American. The men sat toward the front of the room. The women and children were at the back. There was, however, no physical divider between the women and the men.

I sat down cross legged on the floor, and as I settled in, my host did two raka'hs, which was a multi-stepped process of bowing at the knees, kneeling, and prostrating, with her head to the ground. Again, I chose to watch rather than participate, and thought about the comforting nature of having a set of actions that would serve as a preparation for prayer.

Soon, the imam appeared and began to talk. I listened to his words. My new friends and hosts shared that there were two parts to the sermon. They let me know when the first part ended and the second part started. When I researched this later, I found this information:

> The khatib is supposed to deliver two speeches, stopping and sitting briefly between them. In practice, the first speech is longer and contains most of the content. The second speech is very brief and concludes with a dua, after which the muezzin calls the iqama. This signals the start of the main two rak'at prayer of Jumu'ah.[63]

After both parts of the sermon, one of my hosts informed me it was time for communal prayer. She indicated that it would be best for me to move toward the back, where there were a number of chairs. At her request, I walked to the back of the room, sat, listened, and watched as the prayer took place. I saw that everyone did stand shoulder to shoulder during the prayer, with synchronized movements, up and down. Together all the people in the mosque bowed, knelt, prostrated, and stood again. To participate in such a prayer, you would either need to be very observant, or you would need to know the order and sequence of the prayer movements.

As I watched this enthralling sight, I realized I was still trying to understand the perspective of the self-appointed gatekeeper from the

Chicago masjid. I still wanted to figure out her rationale for preventing me from experiencing this weeks before.

As the prayer concluded, I finally let it go with a shrug, figuring that, basically, the self-appointed gatekeeper had one thing that I didn't. She was a participating member in a worship community that I was merely visiting. It was her masjid, and she had a right to protect it however she saw fit. I could agree to disagree with her choices, so I did.

More importantly, I was thankful that I was able to have a positive, welcoming, enlightening experience with Islam during my visit to the Atlanta Masjid of Al-Islam.

*   *   *

Initially, I didn't tell people which faith tradition denied me entry into their prayer service. I had and have no intention of adding to the negative narrative about Islam in America. But this experience highlighted an important lesson for me: For every time you meet someone who does a disservice to their worship tradition, there are others who will help you to see the great things about that tradition. Don't judge a religion based only on the unkind people you may meet. Their lack of kindness and openness is probably based more on characteristics of their personality, or on challenges they are facing in their lives, than on their alignment with a particular faith tradition.

My experience with the mosque in Chicago humbled me and made me think about what can happen when the actions of one person (or a few people) serve as a negative representation of a particular religion. But my wonderful experience, engineered by my old friend Taara, and my new friends Qadara and Nadiya served as a flip side to that coin. At the mosque in Atlanta, I saw evidence of what happens when people can be open, welcoming, and share how they practice their beliefs.

As a result of my time at the Atlanta Masjid of Al-Islam, I looked forward to having other experiences with Islam in the weeks to come.

WHAT'S MY NAME?
TEMPLE SINAI

6:30 p.m. Shabbat service, Atlanta, Georgia

After I completed my visit to the masjid, I was ready for my second worship experience of the day.

One of the guiding principles of this journey was that if anyone invited me to their place of worship, then I had to go. Two friends of mine from high school, Kimberly and Liesl, invited me to be their guest and visit their temple, Temple Sinai in Atlanta.

After the service at the Atlanta Masjid of Al-Islam was over, I headed to Sandy Springs, a suburb north of Atlanta. Liesl was out of town, but I would meet Kimberly at her house, and accompany her to a Friday night Shabbat service at the temple.

When we entered the temple, there were snacks on a table in the atrium. My friend introduced me to the rabbi, and to some of her other friends, as we ate cookies and drank lemonade.

Kimberly mused that it had been a long time since she had been to the temple for something other than "Tot Shabbat" which was the service she attended with her young children. This was confirmed when we ran into some of her friends who expressed surprise at seeing her at the Friday night service.

I contemplated how children can often give us a gift of a second chance. We raise our children to learn the things they need to know to get through life, which sometimes includes spiritual and religious knowledge and principles. We get the opportunity, if we choose, to re-raise ourselves, learning what we may need to be reminded of as we teach them what they need to know.

By this time, I felt very comfortable in a Jewish worship service. I'd visited more than one over the span of this journey so far. Although I still had to look around, get my bearings, and ask questions to figure out how things might flow differently here, I looked forward to the service, the reading of the Torah, and the singing.

At one point, Kimberly leaned over and shared that she was impressed by my ability to follow along in the service and sing and read the phonetically-spelled Hebrew in the Torah, the Haftorah, and the prayer book. She commented that I had apparently done my homework.

I just smiled. It wasn't that I'd done my homework, per se, but that I'd walked through the year finding ways to participate in many different worship services. Each first experience held a touch of anxiety—not knowing how things were going to go, what I should do or not do. If there was a second visit, I was able to feel a little more comfortable and enjoy the similarities to the experience I'd had before, while also noting the differences. Any other services beyond that were enjoyable and joyful—as this one was. I felt comfortable and was able to participate and be blessed by the service.

One portion of this particular service I especially enjoyed was a baby-naming ritual. The new mother and father approached the altar and shared the name of their new child, explaining the meaning of the name chosen. In this case, the name selected was a family name.

This resonated deeply with me. The ceremony itself was similar to the hundreds of baby dedications I'd experienced at my home church over the years—an explicit showing of the importance of culture, family, and community, as well as faith and worship traditions. In many cultures, names are important and carefully selected with much love, based on the meaning of the name.

I know this well from personal experience. All of my life, I have had to explain to people how to pronounce my multi-syllabic Nigerian name and what it means, and what my nicknames are—and are not.

My full name, Ekpedeme Mfon Bassey, comes from my father's native tongue of Ibibio. The Ibibio people have a home in the southeastern part of the country of Nigeria, and if you go there, you'll find many people who have variations on my name. I grew up, however, in Stone Mountain, Georgia, where nobody had my name, and the mere sight of it caused people to stop in their tracks, uncertain how to pronounce it.

I would always dread the roll call that came at the beginning of a new school year, or with a new teacher. The teacher would invariably breeze through the "easier" names that preceded mine, then I would hear a silence. This would indicate that my name was next, and that my teacher had no idea how to pronounce it:

Anna Barnes?

Present.

John Bacon?

Present.

Jenna Barnwell?

Present.

Silence.

Me: "That's me, Ekpedeme, I'm here."

This would often be followed by a sigh of relief, and then a quick one on one tutoring session that resulted in the teacher asking me if I had a nickname, and what did my name mean and wow, was my name different!

How I longed for a simple interaction like many of my friends had.

What's your name?

Lisa.

Done.

But that was not my reality, and even though I had a nickname, Pamay, it was born out of the fact that my father and mother came from different ethnic groups: my father, Ibibio, and my mother, Esan.

Both my mother and father spoke several Nigerian languages, but my name came from my father's language, Ibibio, which my mother didn't speak fluently. As a result, my mother had a nickname for me that she used. I adopted the spoken nickname to help with the negotiations that occurred whenever people saw my name in print.

For years, this nickname was unwritten. A friend or teacher would see my full name, and I would pronounce it and then present my nickname as a peace offering.

I also tried having people call me by my middle name, Mfon, which seemed simple to me—four small letters! But the correct pronunciation of mm-fun eluded people. They called me Mufawn, or Mustapha, or mmmFUN!!!! which just sounded like an obscene bastardization of a carefully selected name that means "goodness." The final straw came when I was in third grade. I was trying out Mfon on this new class, but they began to call me "muffin," and then blackberry muffin, since I was the only Black child in the class.

I didn't enjoy that.

When I changed to the school where I would complete the majority of my junior high and high school education, I went back to the old approach, "My full name is Ekpedeme, but you can call me by my nickname."

311

But there was a wrinkle that I hadn't anticipated. Teachers at this school asked a question that nobody had ever asked me before.

They asked me how to spell my nickname.

I had no idea, because I'd never written it before.

Up until then, I would write my full name, people would call me by my nickname, and that was fine.

"Why were these people at this new school asking for more?" I wondered. At the beginning of the first day, when a teacher would ask how to spell my nickname, I just said, "Any way you want."

Thus, in records for that year, my name was documented with a decidedly French twist—Pémé, with the proper French accents.

As the day went on, however, I decided to take control of my destiny. By the time the fourth or fifth teacher had asked me how to spell my nickname, I provided a spelling:

P-A-M-A-Y.

And Pamay was born. Of course, due to the compressed time within which I was required to provide a spelling for my nickname, I was unable to do my due diligence. I didn't think about how my name rhymed with Camay, the soap, which came in handy for boys later, trying to flirt with a decidedly unattractive pick up line: "Pamay? That sounds like something I want to rub my body with."

Seriously?

I also didn't realize that my name gave people permission to call me Spamay, in an ode to the canned meat, or Pampers, or to call me simply Pam, and ignore the rest of my name, telling jokes such as my personal favorite, "Pam A? Where's Pam B?"

In any case, this continued, but as I grew older, I asked my father about my name. He explained that my full name expressed a thought or phrase in his language. It meant, in essence, "Who but God would share this gift of such a beautiful child with me?"

How could I not love and honor that name?

In one trip to Nigeria, my aunt even reminded me that in a culture where several family members or elders in the village often give a child many names, my name had been one given to my father when he was a young boy.

I tried to figure out how to become more comfortable asking people to call me by my full name. I went back to introducing myself as "My name is Ekpedeme, but my friends call me Pamay," giving people some history, and perhaps a choice.

This resulted in a memorable exchange with Attallah Shabazz, the daughter of Malcolm X. I was attending a summer program, the LEAD Program in Business, which took place at UCLA the summer before my senior year of high school. During the program, thirty young children of color forged friendships and prepared for the years ahead, which would include college, graduate school, and various careers in business and engineering. We invited business and community leaders to "fireside chats," where we could hear from and learn from these pillars in our community.

At every event, we were required to introduce ourselves. On the day that Ms. Shabazz attended, I did what I always did—I looked the guest straight in the eye and introduced myself.

"My name is Ekpedeme Bassey, but my friends call me Pamay."

As I prepared to launch into my spiel about my educational and career goals, she interrupted me.

"Why?" she said.

Confused, I said, "Excuse me?"

"Why do your friends call you Pamay if your name is Ekpedeme?" she said, pronouncing my full name properly, which I found impressive.

Unprepared to answer this question, I shared a short synopsis of the difficulties I had with my name: that people couldn't pronounce it, that they called me all manners of permutations and bastardizations of my name, and that a nickname was just easier.

She had her own spiel.

She shared that, as a child, her father, Malcolm X, wouldn't allow her or her siblings to use nicknames. They were instructed to tell people their name, and then tell them repeatedly until they were able to say it. She encouraged me to do the same.

As a fifteen-year-old, my response was part, "You can't tell me what to do because you don't know the stress this name has caused me," part, "Wow, that is powerful," and part, "Um, yeah, your father was Malcolm X." No disrespect to my beloved father, but I had to believe that simply being the child of such a strong revolutionary force had to carry some weight.

I wish I could say that, from that moment on, I made everyone call me by my full name—and probably for the rest of the summer I might have. However, the struggle continues, and now, some people call me by my full name, and some by my nickname. Still the question, "What is your name?" is far more complicated for me than for most people.

The piece of the puzzle that I found to be most helpful was when I knew what my name meant—this made a big difference. It stopped being a long name that always caused me grief when meeting new people, and started to be a symbol to me of my culture and my family. I also loved the extreme care taken by my parents to make sure I knew who I was, and what my history was. To this day, I feel that if you are going to give a child a unique name, make sure it means something. Sharing the meaning with them can help them navigate potential playground taunts if their peers find their name to be "weird" or "different."

As I watched the rabbi at Temple Sinai holding the baby and praying over him, I thought, "How nice that this child will know the meaning of his name, and will know the importance of his religious and cultural history." The baby naming was an important ritual that showed history meant something to the child's parents, and to this worship community. It would likely be important one day to the child.

After the baby naming, there was a candle-lighting ceremony, and the congregation sang a song. My friend told me it was a song commonly sung at Jewish weddings, as a musical way of wishing the couple well. She shared the name of the song, which was "Siman Tov u'Mazal Tov." Apparently, "Siman Tov" means "good sign" and "Mazal Tov" means good fortune.

The continuance of family and culture is indeed a good sign and a good fortune.

Given that it was the day after Thanksgiving, part of the rabbi's message talked about the "Jewish part of thanksgiving"—healing and repairing, and taking responsibility for community.

This was especially notable because a few hours earlier, the imam at the Atlanta Masjid of Al'Islam had mentioned the fact that Muslims were a thankful people, and spoke about similar themes: family, community, helping self, and helping others.

"What a blessing to be able to see bridges like this," I thought. No matter what the religion, isn't that the point—wanting to find a way to be of service to self, family, community, and the God you serve?

There was a portion of the rabbi's words about "making religion relevant within an American context," which was also something that had been mentioned in the prayer service at the masjid earlier. Both the rabbi and the imam mentioned this leave-taking from your home (whether it be a literal home or a religious or ancestral home) to build a better home elsewhere. They urged their congregations not to forget ancestors, customs, religion, and community.

It was the story of my parents, of the ancestors of those who I sat with during Shabbat service, and of those I'd prayed with earlier in the morning at the masjid. And it was a story I was honored to hear and experience on a very personal level.

*　　*　　*

Community and culture matters. I was reminded of this basic fact during my time at Temple Sinai.

The Power of Words
Trinity Center for Spiritual Living

10:30 a.m. Meditation, 11:00 a.m. service, Atlanta, Georgia

On my last Sunday in Atlanta before heading back home to Chicago post-Thanksgiving, I piled in a car with my sisters and my mother to visit my sister's home church, the Trinity Center for Spiritual Living in Atlanta, Georgia. Because I'd already been to my mother's home church several times during the year, I asked her to join us in worshipping at my sister's church. Because she loves her home church, she hesitated initially, but then agreed.

It was the first time my mother had been to my sister's church. I could tell that my sister was pleased that we were accompanying her to service that morning.

The church building was located on a wooded plot of land that was part of a personal estate. During the week, the gathering space was used by a school for children with disabilities. On the weekends, the church used it.

Before the service started, as people arrived, the church provided coffee, hot cider, and tea for us to enjoy during the service. My mother found this curious, as I suppose she had not been to a service where food and drink was provided to be enjoyed *during* the service.

Knowing about my journey, she turned to me and asked me if I had yet experienced a service where people ate during the service. Nodding yes, I told her about the popsicles that we received during the service at Missio Dei in Chicago. Unable to quite comprehend a church like that, she just looked at me and shook her head.

A woman played the piano and sang at the front of the room. She was very intent on her playing. She sang a song that appeared to be called "One Power." The song lyrics included the following[64]:

Call it God, Call it Spirit, Call it Jesus, Call it Lord, Call it Buddha, Ba'ha'ullah, Angels Wings or Heaven's Door . . .

The chorus followed:

The power of the love (one power . . . one power . . .)

Once Buddha was mentioned, I looked over to see my mother steadily praying under her breath. She calls on Jesus, and that's that.

I took it all in stride. Everyone experiences spirituality differently. I'm okay with that. By this time, I was quite comfortable with just letting worship happen how it was going to happen, and letting it all wash over me while I took it in.

Before I closed my eyes to participate in a guided meditation, I took a moment to take a deep breath while appreciating the sunshine streaming in the windows of the all-glass sanctuary. I gave thanks for the opportunity I had to meditate and worship with my sisters and my mother—the Bassey girls who my father loved so much.

After a refreshing meditation, it was time to sing one last song. It happened to be, "I'd like to teach the world to sing." All I could think of was the Coca-Cola commercial from the late '70s.

What can I say? I'm from Atlanta, home and headquarters to the Coca Cola Company. Everybody in Atlanta drinks Coke.

Suddenly, I began to hear applause. I turned around in time to see the pastor running down the church aisle to the front of the room, like a *Price is Right* contestant. When he reached the front of the room, he bowed, and then gave the hang loose sign.

Enthusiastically, he made some brief announcements, then it was time for the sermon.

As the pastor began the message for the day, he shared how he came to be a man of the cloth. He told a story about an aptitude test he took when he was in high school. The results of the test said he should be a minister. First, he laughed it off, but over time, he stopped laughing at the image. He began asking himself what that would look like.

What it looked like, apparently, was leading a learning center like the Trinity Center for Spiritual Living—a place for spiritual lessons.

Before the pastor launched into his message, he took some time to recognize visitors, which, of course, included most of my family. As we stood, I remembered the last time I'd seen the Reverend was at my father's funeral. It had been some time since that day, but the memories were still quite strong. I took a moment to compose myself, and prepared for the sermon.

The sermon's theme was, "The power of your word." The pastor shared that, "Every word you speak is a life form unto itself." He referred to the creation story in Genesis, specifically the portion where God said, "Let there be Light," and there was. He provided a different perspective on that directive, stating that likely the command was, "Light. Be."

Simple. But powerful.

He reminded us that our words are packed with the same energy as in Genesis, and need to be spoken with clarity.

"Your words of prayer are always alive," he said. "Every good thought you have is a positive force of nature in the Universe."

He reminded us that, when we speak, words become seeds, and seeds represent what we are yet to experience. Once a seed is planted in the soil of the infinite mind, we need to nurture it, shield it, and allow it to grow.

Nurturing comes in the form of treatment as affirmative prayer.

He urged us to nurture these word-seeds until the idea becomes the experience.

He asked the following questions:

- How many days before a rose seed becomes a stalk?
- How many days before that stalk becomes a bush?
- How many days before that bush grows a rose bloom?

Of course, the answer to these questions is nobody knows. You just have to have faith and patience until the desired result appears.

He reminded us that the process takes as long as it takes, and that we should let go of any artificial time frames that we have created for ourselves.

He shared one of my favorite Marianne Williamson quotes:

> Our deepest fear is not that we are inadequate. Our deepest fear is that we are powerful beyond measure. It is our light, not our darkness, that most frightens us. We ask ourselves, Who am I to be brilliant, gorgeous, talented, fabulous? Actually, who are you *not* to be? You are a child of God. Your playing small does not serve the world. There is nothing enlightened about shrinking so that other people won't feel insecure around you. We are all meant to shine, as children do. We were born to make manifest the glory of God that is within us. It's not just in some of us; it's in everyone. And as we let our own light shine, we unconsciously give other people permission to do the same. As we are liberated from our own fear, our presence automatically liberates others.[65]

This quote hit home, because it really gets to the heart of the matter. In order for this whole power-packed approach to work, we really need to be comfortable with the idea that we are really so powerful we can "speak our experience into existence" with our words.

320

And this is no small thing.

As I listened to this sermon, I thought about my own beliefs. I told myself, "I need to really work on speaking *only* words that create experiences I want to manifest."

The pastor agreed.

He emphasized a number of things that should be our focus:

Don't engage in self-deprecating speech or useless tasks!

Let the nonsense go!

No more going into our closets and praying in secret!

Focus instead on creating the reality that we want to create!

Weed out what does not serve us!

Never stop and never give up!

Know that the universe supports us!

He reminded us that every time we say the words, "I am," and follow that by anything, we are claiming that thing. He challenged us to take extreme care to make sure we only claimed that which we actually wanted in our lives. He urged us to believe in the power of our words, and stand on the side of our words.

He provided powerful imagery, saying, "If you dip a bucket out of the ocean, that water would still include all of the attributes of the ocean. So are you, a bucket of spirit." Powerful spirit.

As the message continued, one specific thought filled my mind: This is exactly what I needed to hear today.

He addressed any issues with the process, quoting Yoda from *The Empire Strikes Back:*

Do or do not. There is no try.

That is to say, we shouldn't *try* to believe in the power of our own words, we *should just believe.*

* * *

One final, powerful quote stuck with me as I contemplated how hopeful I felt at the end of this service: "Your final emancipation will be written with your own hand. Or it won't be written at all."

My healing was in my own hands, and that inspired me.

WEEK 49
THE SIMPLE LIFE
ROSEWOOD FELLOWSHIP

9:30 a.m. service, Shipshewana, Indiana

What would a spiritual journey be without spending time with the Amish?

This Sunday would be the day.

I researched on the Internet to find the Amish or Mennonite communities that were closest to me in Chicago. I found many, most in downstate Illinois. But when I was researching, I found some information that suggested if I did visit an Amish community, I would be able to drive around and see the community in action, but that I likely wouldn't be able to worship in an Amish church. Throughout this whole process, I was learning about the different communities, all with Anabaptist roots: the Mennonites, the Amish, and the Beachy Amish Mennonites. I made an initial plan to drive to downstate Illinois on a Saturday, take a tour through Amish country, and then attend a Mennonite church on Sunday.

As with my experience researching the Mormons before I visited, I Googled around to see exactly how intense of a chocolate chip experience I would have if I visited any of these congregations.

I found the following questions on a discussion board run by an Amish woman[66]:

The questions:

> What do you think about the Beachy Amish . . . I was recently
> on the Beachy Amish website and saw a picture of an African-
> American girl on it. How do the Old Order feel about people
> of different races and ethnicities?

The answer was long and detailed, but a portion of it answered these
questions:

> Because the Amish rely on retaining their young to ensure the
> survival of their religion and way of life, they have not had to
> confront issues of race and ethnicity. For the most part they
> see themselves as separate from not only "English" people, but
> anyone else who isn't Amish. Though, your question raises an
> interesting issue: Would they allow someone of color to join?
> They will occasionally accept someone willing to join their
> religion and way of life to become members of their faith. Just
> as the Amish have separate beliefs from the outside world in
> matters of religion, my guess is, if pressed, their values on this
> issue would also be different than the outside world—in other
> words they may not share our value of being all-inclusive,
> especially in matters that would concern their culture. One of
> the things that holds their culture together is shared experiences
> and shared ancestry. This makes it hard for anyone from the
> outside to join the Amish from both the Amish point of view,
> and that of the person joining. My guess is that the Amish
> resistance to someone of color joining the church would make it
> uncomfortable enough for the person thinking of joining that it
> probably wouldn't happen. At least I never saw anyone of color
> among the Amish.

> As for the question of how Amish feel about people of other races
> and cultures in general, I would say they probably don't have
> enough exposure to have strong feelings one way or another.

> It does not surprise me that you found a picture of an African-
> American girl on a Beachy Amish website because they believe
> in going out and saving as many people as they can. They
> are open to all races and ethnicities receiving their essential

message—that Jesus Christ is one's personal Lord and Savior. They believe that one must hold this as one's central tenet, otherwise salvation cannot be achieved. In fact, those who are born-again Christian, whether they are Beachy, Mennonite, or from any other denomination, see it as their mission that everyone in the world find out about the gospel. Most often coupled with this belief is the one that because God created everyone, it applies to all, no matter what race, ethnicity, or culture they are from.

After reading this, I did some additional research about the Beachy Amish Mennonites. I found another website dedicated to them. The website included information about the denomination and a form that you could fill out if you were looking for a congregation nearby.[67]

I filled out the form and waited.

Not too long later, I received a response letting me know that there were no churches in the Chicago area that would match what I was looking for. The closest was two hours east in north-central Indiana.

Well, after having visited worship spaces all over the world, a two-hour drive to north-central Indiana would be a piece of cake. I responded, requesting the name and address of the church, and received a detailed email including directions to the church, and letting me know that I didn't need to contact the church in advance of attending. I did anyway. I spoke to the bishop, who was warm and reassuring. He extended an open invitation and told me a little about what I might expect when I came. I asked about what I should wear, and he said I should come as I was, explaining that most of the congregation would be dressed modestly. I decided that I would dress modestly as well.

He also mentioned that I was welcome to stay for as long as I wanted. It was customary for visitors to be welcomed into the homes of church members for a meal and an overnight stay. I thought I would take it one step at a time, and first just attend the service, but I was touched by the openness and welcome of the bishop and his congregation—even before seeing or knowing me.

I also asked him the race question, letting him know that I was African-American. Some might wonder why I thought that would matter, but after a lifetime of being Black, I find that eliminating surprises always works in my favor. He assured me that I was welcome, and then let me know that, in fact, he had Black friends and knew of some Black members of the church.

I made plans to visit Rosewood. As luck would have it, on the morning that I was to drive to Shipshewana, Indiana, there was a spectacular snowstorm. Although I questioned the wisdom of going to the service on that day, I realized that the year was fast coming to an end, and that this might be the last opportunity I had to visit the church before the Christmas holidays came and I found myself travelling to be with my family.

The detailed directions that I had received showed that the trip should take about two hours. For this southern girl driving in the snow, the two-hour trip took about four hours. I was driving forty miles an hour the entire way. There wasn't much visibility, especially as I drove deeper into Indiana. My comfort level wasn't very high as I drove in the snow, even though I was driving a four wheel drive vehicle.

A white car drove in front of me on the highway. It was driving pretty slowly, and although I considered trying to pass it, I ended up happily resolving to drive slowly behind it. It provided me with a cover—I was able to drive in its tracks, and didn't have to worry as much about the snow. I just focused on the vehicle.

The car had Michigan license plates. After driving behind it for three hours, I saw the exit for Shipshewana, Indiana. Amazingly, the car exited on the same exit, and then, before I knew it, the car was gone.

It disappeared into the snow.

Being so close to my final destination, I was thankful. That little white car was like an escort delivering me safely to the Rosewood Church in Shipshewana, Indiana.

An angel car.

As I navigated the final few miles to the church, I felt a little giddy when I saw my first horse-drawn carriage.

Amish country.

After driving down a long dirt road, I saw the church sign, pulled into the parking lot, took a deep breath, and walked into the building. I was nervous. I picked a pew and sat down.

Not only was I a chocolate chip, I was also the only one not in Amish clothing. My modest outfit was a long melon-colored skirt that went past my ankles and a black sweater. Everyone else was wearing white. All the women wore plainclothes and buns; they all had the same hair coverings. Most if not all of the men had distinctive Abraham Lincoln looking beards. I didn't cover my head, heeding the advice of the bishop. Even if I had, I would still have looked significantly different from everyone else. There was no way I was going to blend with the members of this church.

In many worship experiences that I've had, the women and children sat separately from the men. I noted that in this congregation, although the women and men did sit on different sides of the church, there were just as many kids sitting with the men as with the women.

The service started with three songs. As I fumbled with the song book, my neighbors kindly and silently pointed out the place in the song book where the lyrics resided. Smiles were exchanged, and that helped. Nevertheless, I was still nervous.

My soul was soothed by the *a cappella* sounds that were coming from the pews as everyone joined in song. Perfect harmonies and melodies blended as if I was in a congregation of professional singers.

I sang softly, so as not to disturb the perfect harmony of the music. A young girl in a pew in front of me kept turning around and staring at me. She was about six years old. I smiled at her, but she just looked at me.

I was happy to let her look—sometimes kids just get right to the point. It was clear that I was not someone she expected to see in her church. Her look said, "I just need to know who you are and why you're here."

After the singing, there was a brief message. The bishop, who I assumed was the man I'd spoken to on the phone, reminded us that, "The human soul has a place within where only God fits, even when we are stubborn and our hearts are hardened."

A few scriptural selections followed. The first was Matthew 7:3 (NIV):

> Why do you look at the speck of sawdust in your brother's eye and pay no attention to the plank in your own eye?

This is one of my favorite verses because it really focuses on the fact that we need not judge others—rather, we should worry about our own sins and shortcomings.

This was followed by Mark 8:38 (NIV):

> If anyone is ashamed of me and my words in this adulterous and sinful generation, the Son of Man will be ashamed of them when he comes in his Father's glory with the holy angels.

This took me back to the day before. I was not having a particularly great day, but pulled it together to go to a going-away party for a friend who was leaving Chicago to move to Los Angeles. After the party was over, I walked back to my car with my friend Mina. As we walked and talked about how we were really doing, I let loose with a flood of tears, letting her know that I was still grieving, and wondering if I would ever feel better. She, being a devout Christian, reassured me with her words. She offered to pray with me, and I accepted.

There, on the snowy Chicago street, we stood, she and I, and we prayed.

I didn't care if anyone looked at us crazy, or wondered why I was crying, or why we were praying in the middle of the street. I focused on her words and on my belief that there was healing for my spirit.

I marveled that I'd come so far in my spiritual journey that I could pray on Chicago's streets and not bat an eye.

"Don't be ashamed of God," said the bishop—and I knew what that meant.

The bishop went on to talk about prayer. He told us that we should pray with expectation, that we should trust God, and know that God wants to answer our prayers. Further, he reminded us that sometimes God doesn't always answer in the way we ask.

Sometimes he answers in a better way.

After reciting 1 Thessalonians 5:17: "Pray without ceasing," the minister shared that it was time for prayer, and told us to kneel.

Everyone moved to kneel—but not in the way that I would expect from my experiences with Catholicism. Here, everyone turned around to face the pew, rather than the front of the church. Elbows went up on the pews, heads bowed, and prayer began.

This was a new prayer stance for me, but I just followed the lead of my new Amish sisters who were sitting around me.

Later, I did some research and found that this was a way of focusing not on the leader at the front of the room, but on God and the prayer.

After the brief message and prayer, it was time to split up into smaller groups. One of my neighbors shyly asked me if I was married, and when I said no, they invited me to join the Single Ladies Sunday School. I accepted, remembering my Mormon small-group experience, and followed my new friend to a different part of the church.

At the beginning of the Single Ladies Sunday School, all of us introduced ourselves. When it was my turn, I let them know that I was from Chicago and that I was honored to worship with them this Sunday. The group was a mixed group: very young women, older women, and then people in between like me.

We focused on Hebrew 11, the faith chapter. The leader of the Sunday School read the chapter and then we all discussed the topic, "What is faith?"

Different answers were part of our discussion:

- We show faith by the way we act.
- A reference to part of the chapter: 11:6 "Without faith, it is impossible to please God."
- The attitude of your heart is important; you need to make your offerings with faith mixed in.
- Faith comes in when I don't really know, but I believe. Trust that God knows.
- Faith means I don't have to worry; I just have to be faithful to God today. Then repeat tomorrow. God will show you the way.
- Faith allows me to experience the pleasure of the Lord in my life through love, peace, and joy.
- It's not just about how I feel. If I feel badly, I have to ask myself why? Then I make the choice to focus on God, and have faith that everything is going to be okay.

The focus on faith is just what I needed to hear.

After Sunday School, my single friends and I headed back to congregation and sat in the pews. There were more songs, then an offering, then it was time for scripture. Different groups had been assigned memory verses, and when we came back together as a group, they shared. The preschool children shared their verse, Matthew 5:8 (NIV):

Blessed are the pure in heart, for they shall see God

Then came the primary-school children, who shared their verse, Proverbs 15:3 (KJV):

> The eyes of the LORD are in every place, beholding the evil and the good.

The intermediate youth, single women, single men, and then the married men and women followed them. Each group contributed their assigned verse to a chorus of scripture that bridged the transition from the small groups to the sermon.

During the sermon, the bishop covered many different topics.

He shared a portion of the verse, Zechariah 4:6 (NIV):

> Not by might nor by power, but by my Spirit, says the Lord Almighty.

He reminded us that God didn't just provide in the past, we have to believe that He will provide and does provide today. He reminded us that we should share our stories about when our backs were against the wall, we prayed, and God worked in our lives. This was confirmation, a request really, that I should share this journey with others.

Referring to the medical pain threshold questions that doctors will often use to ask us how much something hurts, he challenged us to ask ourselves, "On a chart from 1 to 10, where is your relationship with God?"

What would we say?

What would God say?

Would the numbers match?

He asked us to contemplate the difference between believing and trusting, sharing that the two are intertwined—trust is the action that illustrates belief.

He challenged us to think about what we are contributing to the kingdom, to ask ourselves not just what we are getting out of each church service, or out of our communities, but what are we giving? What are we contributing?

Most memorable to me was a thought-provoking question that the bishop posed. Referring to various scriptures, he stated that many of us like to take part in a bountiful harvest, but he asked, "How many of us like to take part in the plowing, the hard work that comes before the harvest?"

For those of us, like myself, who might have been thinking about how difficult plowing actually is, he said, "Dig out the roots, and you will see fruitfulness again."

By this point, we were past the two-hour mark, which—over the months—I had learned is my cutoff. At two hours, I start to fidget and it becomes much more difficult to focus on the message and true meaning of what's happening, as I'm fighting not to focus on when the service would end.

I consider this a valuable piece of information as I go forward and try to make my worship experiences as effective as possible. Wherever my next church home will be—service will be less than two hours!

After the service ended, I took some time to chit chat with the different members of the congregation who welcomed me and asked me questions about who I was and what I was doing there. As expected, I was invited to stay for a meal, or even spend the night. But as I looked out at the snow coming down, I decided that it was time for me to get back on the road to Chicago.

Surprisingly, one of my new friends asked if we could exchange email addresses so we could keep in touch. Many do know the Amish to be people who shun different types of technology, but apparently the Beachy Amish Mennonites have no such restrictions. I took the offered email addresses gladly and smiled as my new friend reminded me that I could access the service and the sermon online, as well.

As I prepared to leave and head back home, I promised my new Beachy friends that I would be back.

And I will be.

*   *   *

During the Sunday school portion of the service, I thought of my friend Mina, who asked me the day before if I would continue this spiritual journey after the year was over. Her concern was that if I went from worship experience to worship experience, I would have a nomadic religious experience, and that potentially I could become a worship tourist.

"Don't forget, *you* have to be fed," she said.

Driving home to Chicago, as I contemplated my time at Rosewood Fellowship, I thought:

"I *am* being fed."

Wisdom comes clothed in many different ways. This week, I was glad to experience a special brand of wisdom—clothed in the simple garb of the Beachy Amish Mennonites.

Destination, Merita
The Earth Center

7:00 a.m., Zen Zem Ceremony, Kemetic holy day of prayer, Chicago, Illinois

When I initially contacted the Zen Zem center, I discovered that they were a center dedicated to, ". . . preserving Kemetic knowledge, culture, spirituality, philosophy, and healing." They hold classes teaching different elements of Kemetic beliefs and practices. Further information about the Earth Center included this explanation:

> The Earth Center was born because the elders of the traditional Kemetic priesthood decided that it is necessary in this time to provide an alternative to the destructive/self-destructive lifestyle that the modern, colonial, political, educational, and religious systems have maintained for the last two thousand years.

> The Earth Center was founded and is directed by Master Naba Lamoussa Morodenibig. Master Naba was a Dogon High Priest in the traditional priesthood of Kemet. The purpose of The Earth Center is to inspire and support education and research into the original, ancestral culture of humanity, for the health and well-being of all people. The Earth Center is unique in the fact that it is connected to the initiation systems (Mystery Schools) of ethnic groups of Merita (traditional Africa) that have maintained the same initiation process as was done in Kemet during the times of the Pharaohs.[68]

When I made the phone call to the center and asked if I could participate in a service, the man who answered the phone let me know that there were classes in meditation and Kemetic history. Additionally, if I wanted to, I could participate in the Zen Zem ceremony, which took place periodically during the month on a holy day of Prayer.

Today was the day. The time was 7:00 a.m. I woke early just to make sure that I didn't oversleep. I was really excited to visit The Earth Center in Chicago. African Christians raised me. I had little exposure to ancient African religions, and I looked forward to the experience.

Not knowing what to expect, I put on some African attire, bundled up in my winter coat and headed to the North Kenwood neighborhood in Chicago, where the Center was located.

When I arrived, I saw what looked like an unassuming, two-flat apartment building. I would have thought it was a residence, except for a passenger van that was parked out front. On the side of the van "The Kemetic Center" was written. I sat in my car for a moment, not sure what I was going to experience. I took a deep breath, walked up the stairs, and entered the building.

When I entered the Center, I saw a room to my right where many were already sitting in quiet meditation. Not knowing where to go or what to do, I first removed my shoes, and then stood there in the foyer of the building looking kind of stupid and feeling a little out of place.

One of the women in the room came to my aid. I whispered to her that I was there for the Zen Zem ceremony, and she gestured to the room to my right, whispering back to me that I should sit in the back quietly.

Around the room were symbols, wall paintings, and artwork inspired by what we know in the modern day as Egypt—pictures of pharaohs, pyramids, hieroglyphics, and ankhs.

Participants knelt on colored, beaded prayer mats. All were of African descent, and all had natural hairstyles—short afros or locks. Everyone was wearing white except me. Everyone seemed to know what was going on; I had no idea.

I knelt in the back behind the mats, mimicking those who were kneeling in front of me. I sat quietly and observed.

It was clear from the energy in the room that this was a close community of faith. The ceremony began with a few words—a short sermon of sorts. The rest of the ceremony was meditative, mostly silent and serene. There were prayers and chants, meditation and incense burning. Peace filled the room. Sometimes words were spoken in English, and sometimes words were spoken in another language that I later learned was Medu, the language of Ancient Kemet. During the ceremony, there was a time where offerings were given, and a time where participants shared their concerns. Prayers were said for those concerns.

After the ceremony was over, we all sat in a circle and there were introductions. They welcomed me as a guest and asked me if I had any questions. I shared how I'd found them and told them of my spiritual journey. They told me of the commitment that many of them had made to the ancient Kemetic way of life—so much so that they lived in dorms next to the center, and were committed to learning Kemetic teachings, as an alternative to the philosophical and religious frameworks they had experienced before.

*   *   *

At the Earth Center, I enjoyed the feeling of peace and oneness with the others in the room. I took that peace with me into the rest of my day, and into my week.

WEEK 50
COMPLETELY OUT OF MY ELEMENT
HINDU TEMPLE OF GREATER CHICAGO

10:30 a.m., Sri Rama Maha Abhishekam, Lemont, Illinois

There is a reason why it took me so long to get to a Hindu temple during this year-long journey.

This religion is complicated. There are many stories, many gods, and much information that my Judeo–Christian sensibilities had a hard time understanding. Several times during this journey, I planned to go to a Hindu temple or a Hindi service. I always ended up rescheduling, diverting my attention, or attending a different worship service entirely. Even writing this chapter was a bit difficult.

But the year was coming to an end. I felt it would not be acceptable to go through a whole year's odyssey of worship, and not spend any time at a Hindu temple.

When I visited the website for the temple, I saw a number of events scheduled on that day which apparently took place periodically throughout the year. I decided to arrive in time to witness the Sri Rama Maha Abhishekam. I hoped that by spending a few hours at the temple I would learn something.

In order for me to have any idea what I was in for, I had to do some research, and this is what I found:

- Sri: Typically, Sree or Shree or Sri or Shri is a honorific prefixed with the Indian/Hindu title of respect and esteem. It is an Indian title applied to people and Hindu gods in various languages, derived from Sanskrit.[69]

- Rama: Lord Rama is the seventh incarnation of Lord Vishnu. The worship of Lord Rama is very popular among all Hindus . . . Rama represents an ideal man, as conceived by the Hindu mind . . . Rama's personality depicts him as the perfect son, devoted brother, true husband, trusted friend, ideal king, and a noble adversary.[70]
- Maha: In Sanskrit, the name Maha means "great."[71]
- Abhishekam: An abhisheka is a religious bathing ceremony . . . (during which), a Deity is bathed not only in water, but also with milk, yogurt, butter milk, honey, clarified butter, sugar, and all kinds of fruit juices. After this bathing, the sacred image is dressed, ornamented, fed, and praised with hymns accompanied with bells, drums, and other instruments.[72]

On a very snowy Chicago morning in December, I woke up, put on some of my favorite white and gold African attire under a large winter coat, and drove to the Hindu Temple of Greater Chicago, in Lemont, Illinois. Based on my research, I expected that I would witness a ritual washing of one of the great Hindu deities, and then a dressing and decoration of that deity after the washing was done.

The ceremony took place in one of the many temples on the grounds, the Rama temple. As I entered, I saw signs that asked me to take off my shoes. I did, placing them on one of the many shoe racks in the building. As I walked through the temple, I noted the delicious smells of Indian food that wafted into the hallways from a kitchen and cafeteria area that was to the right of the stairs leading to the room where the ceremony would take place. The delicacies being prepared smelled inviting.

Following signs that I saw on the wall, I approached and ascended a number of stairs and entered into an enormous room covered in rich red carpets. White columns were positioned throughout the room, and intricate patterns decorated the ceilings. There was one main room, and a few rooms off to the side from the main room. In all the rooms were a number of statues of various Hindu deities. Near one, I saw the sign, "Please no pictures of the deities," and I noted that this was a sacred space.

When I entered the room, it was mostly empty.

Before the ritual began, I wandered around the temple, visited the different deities that were there and watched people interact with them. Some deities were swathed in colorful robes, some with leis of flowers around their necks. Some appeared to be sitting on thrones surrounded by pillows covered with intricate embroidery.

There were single adults, families and children. Often it appeared that they were visiting with and praying with or to different gods. Some left gifts at the feet of some of the gods.

I had very little idea what was happening, and felt exceedingly out of place. I went from statue to statue, read the names of each deity, and reflected on the fact that, without a great deal of immersion in the cultural and religious stories of Hinduism, I would never fully understand the worship traditions of those who I saw walking around me.

There is something amazing about being in a place where you have very little idea what is going on. To just be humble and silent and watch the ritual, and respect the fact that you are in someone else's sacred space is a unique experience.

In one of the side rooms of the temple, on the walls were plaques with verses from the Bhagavad Gita, a religious text that summarizes the core beliefs in Hinduism:

First, Chapter 9, verse 26:

> If one offers Me with love and devotion—a leaf, a flower, a fruit or water—I will accept it.[73]

Then, Chapter 18, verse 66:

Abandon all varieties of religion and just surrender unto Me. I shall deliver you from all sinful reaction. Do not fear.[74]

It was with thoughts of love and with a heart free of fear that I walked back to the main room to experience something new.

As the room filled with the faithful, there was a great diversity in the appearance of the people who joined me for the ceremony. Many of the women and children were wearing beautiful saris—gold, maroon, and sapphire. Some of the men were wearing polo shirts, Bill Cosby sweaters, and khakis. I even saw one gentleman wearing a Chicago Bears sweatshirt and jeans.

Two teenage girls, wearing skinny jeans and fashionable tops, approached one of the statues chatting and catching up. When they arrived in front of the deity, they became silent—standing and praying in front of it. I was struck by the balance they found between being modern and hip, but at the same time being respectful of their centuries-old faith tradition.

Although there was a community feel in the temple, with some younger children running around and playing with friends, most of the adults gathered at the back of the room where there were ornate black, red, and gold embroidered velvet curtains. It was clear that this would be the focal point for the ceremony.

When those curtains opened, I saw two sets of gold doors. In the innermost room were three statues. In both the innermost and the outer room, between the two sets of golden doors, a number of men sat and worked, wearing white and gold robes.

Some of them burned incense—preparing the sacred space, I surmised, for the ceremony to come. Before long, a sweet, smoky smell filled the temple. Throughout the ceremony, one of the men waved incense throughout the inner space, around the statues of the deities within.

One man in the outer room rang a bell throughout the ceremony. These men, and others who participated, outside the second set of gold doors, chanted mantras throughout the ritual. I sat silently among the number, taking in the whole picture unfolding before me.

I witnessed a washing of the statues within the inner section beyond the second set of gold doors. Systematically, the men inside poured different liquids on the deities.

Lining the inner section were cartons and bottles of milk, apple juice, and other liquids I didn't immediately recognize. In what I assumed was an act of respect, before any of the liquids touched the deities, they were first poured into ornate silver bowls and vases, and then onto the deities. At one point, liquid was poured from a vessel shaped like a violin; later it was transferred to a pan with holes in it above the head of the deities as if they were simulating a rain shower.

After what seemed like the majority of the washing was complete, platters of fruit were held toward the deities, as if a sacrifice was being offered.

Then, it appeared to be time for us to participate. Those who were watching stood up, as did I. The robed men who had been conducting the ritual came out to share portions of it with us. First, fruit and nuts from the altar space were distributed. Some people ate these fruits and nuts. Then one of the men came out and put what looked like a white milky substance in the hands of each of the participants, who drank it. I bowed my head every time something was offered and put my hand up to say, "I respect this portion of the ceremony, but choose not to eat of what is being shared."

Then, one of the robed men brought out incense in an incense holder on a velvet-covered silver platter. Participants waved the smoke from the incense over their faces and their heads, sharing in a portion of the sacred atmosphere. Some placed money on the platter; it appeared to be offering time. Water from the ritual was sprinkled on us.

Then, the embroidered velvet curtains were drawn. Most of those watching left, spreading to different parts of the temple. A few adults and children stayed and chanted mantras in unison—some reading from a small book, some reciting by heart, and one scrolling along and reading from an iPad. The chanting went on and on and on. I thought it would never end.

Until it did.

At the end of the service, the curtains were opened, and we saw the deities—draped in finery, and in leis of flowers, "dressed" after the Abhishekam, or washing.

I stayed for hours in that temple, soaking up what bits and pieces of the worship experience I could, given my limited knowledge of Hindu worship traditions. I talked to some of the people who were there, and they told me I was welcome to come back one day when it wasn't snowing and when the weather was not preventing people from coming out.

I figured that is something I would and should do.

*   *   *

One of the realities of this journey was that there was no way for me to learn everything about a religion, it's beliefs, practices, and traditions, in a few hours spent in a place of worship each week. My experience at the temple reinforced this. I still strive to learn more about Hindu religions—I know I have much to learn.

That said, I learned something by just being in a place where I understood very little of what was going on. Everyone should, at some point in life, go to a place where they totally stick out, and they have no idea what the rules are. Why not have a wild, humbling and unforgettable experience?

One of the great gifts of my 52-week journey was the development of this spirit of openness within me. In life, you don't always know what is going on. But if you approach everything with a spirit of wanting to learn, things usually work out.

COMMUNITY AND HOSPITALITY
ANSHE SHOLOM B'NAI ISRAEL CONGREGATION

3:50 p.m., Mincha/Kabbalat Shabbat service, Chicago, Illinois

By this time in my journey, I'd been to a few different types of Jewish services, but I had not yet been to worship with Orthodox Jews. As a result of my research, I finally found a place where I could experience a service with a modern orthodox community—Anshe Sholom B'nai Israel Congregation.

When I called, I was told that the service started at 3:50 p.m. on Friday afternoon, which was perplexing to me until I did a little research. What I found was this:

> Jews are bidden to pray three times daily to God. The Shacharit prayer takes place in the morning. It is the longest of the three daily prayers and contains within it the basic affirmations of Judaism: the Shema, the Amidah, and the ideas of repentance, self-improvement, and loyalty to God and Israel.
>
> The Maariv prayer takes place at night, after sunset. It is much shorter in length than Shacharit, but nevertheless includes again within it the basic Shema and Amidah prayers.
>
> The shortest prayer service of the day takes place in the afternoon, or at least just before sunset, and is called Mincha. It is composed of the recitation of Psalm 145, the Amidah, a prayer of repentance and the concluding prayer to all Jewish prayer services, Aleynu. Aleynu is a reaffirmation of Jewish goals and a hope for the better world for all humankind.[75]

343

Because the Chicago winter sunset took place early in the day, so did the Mincha.

That Friday afternoon, along with the Mincha, there was to be a lighting of candles at 4:03 p.m., and the Kabbalat Shabbat would take place at 4:05 p.m.

> Kabbalat Shabbat ("Reception of the Sabbath") is a term designating the inauguration of the Sabbath in general and, in a more specifically liturgical sense, that part of the Friday evening service which precedes the regular evening prayer and solemnly welcomes the Sabbath.[76]

On this Friday, we were in the thick of winter. I pulled into the parking lot behind the shul, I wedged my car into a snowdrift and made my way toward the sanctuary.

Heavy, ornate wood doors led to the entrance of the shul. Each door had a Star of David on it.

The sanctuary's cream colored brick walls were punctuated with green textured columns. Stained glass windows of varying sizes and gold light fixtures lined the walls. Each light fixture bore a Star of David. One in particular stood out. It was called "Six Branches in Mountain Flames." A plaque below it explained that it commemorated the "six million Jewish martyrs"—referring to those who died in the Holocaust. Other plaques on the walls, on the pews, and all over the shul honored mothers, fathers, siblings, friends, graduations, marriages, anniversaries, promotions, and other life milestones. The words and names on the plaques were in both English and Hebrew—highlighting not only the importance of community, but also of the community's shared history. Bookshelves lined the back of the sanctuary. Stacks of copies of the Torah and the Siddur were available for the faithful to use during worship.

On the stage at the front of the sanctuary were Star of David-decorated velvet drapes and podiums covered in blue; they matched the blue plush chairs in which the worshippers sat. The stage was also adorned with candles, flowers, and plants. An American flag stood to one side of the podium; Israel's flag to the other side.

Men sat on one side of the sanctuary. Women sat on the other side. The partitions between each side housed flower boxes with greenery growing in them; prayer shawls draped the partitions—available for those who might need them during the service.

The men wore yarmulkes or other types of hats. Some covered their heads with prayer shawls. I covered my head with a scarf although I learned later that this wasn't required of unmarried women. I picked a seat on the women's side of the sanctuary and made myself comfortable.

On the back of the chair in front of me was a hinged book stand—a place, I gathered, where worshippers could store the holy books they would refer to during the service. It reminded me of a school, which made sense, as it was clear this was a place of community-based learning.

Before the service began, the rabbi travelled around the sanctuary, shaking everyone's hand and making small talk with the congregants. When he came to me, he welcomed me, acknowledging that this was my first visit to the shul.

Although I held a Torah in my hand, I was unable to really follow along, because most of the spoken words in the service were in Hebrew. There was some translation into English in the Siddur that I held, but aside from the rabbi calling out page numbers every once in a while, it was hard for me to follow. Instead of trying, I just settled in to the rhythm of the service. I did try to stand when others stood, bow when they bowed, and sit when they sat. At one point in the service, everyone turned around in the pews and faced the back of the sanctuary. I'm not sure why. I turned as well.

I was aware that I was in the presence of much history and culture. Somehow, the fact that I couldn't understand anything made the experience even more profound. I imagined that they were saying the words, praying the prayers, and singing the songs that their ancestors had prayed and sung for generations.

After the service, there was food provided. I found out that 4:55pm marked the end of a fast that had begun at 6:00 a.m. that morning. People were excited about the food that was before them.

*   *   *

Although I didn't eat, I did take some time to talk to some of the faithful, all of whom were very kind, respectful, and interested in how I'd chosen to visit their shul on that Friday night. I received more than one invitation to Shabbat dinner. It was customary to make sure that everyone who came to service would have somewhere to break bread with others.

It struck me that *that* was the true meaning of community—coming together to worship, and making sure everyone had someone to share their cares, joys, and a little Shabbat dinner.

WEEK 51
MODERN MYSTICS
CENTERS OF LIGHT

9:30 a.m. meditation, 10:00 a.m. service, Chicago, Illinois

When I saw the Rosicrucian symbol during the service I attended at the Zoroastrian Association of Metropolitan Chicago, I was reminded of my father's studies as a mystic. This motivated me to investigate if there were any Christian mystic churches in the Chicagoland area.

What I found was the Centers of Light, a non-denominational mystical Christian church.

The Centers of Light website answers the question "What is Christian Mysticism" with the following explanation:

> The word "mystical" means a spiritual reality or experience that is not perceived by the five physical senses. A mystical experience is different than having a belief because a mystical experience involves coming into a direct relationship with God. Feeling God, seeing God, and knowing God cannot be accomplished by belief alone. Belief in something may nudge you in the direction of finding out something or inspire you to hope for something. A belief in God may move a person toward having a relationship with God. A direct, personal experience of God is what every mystic strives to attain. Christian mysticism is the process of coming into the experience of God at the center of one's being. A mystic meditates and prays and strives to be in close relationship with God throughout the day and throughout their life. Only through a direct experience can you say you know anything for certain.[77]

I remember talking to my parents about mysticism. They had both been part of different mystical communities—my father was a Rosicrucian, and both of my parents had studied with the Mayan order. Of course, now my father was gone, and my mother is a bona fide, born-again Christian, with a vociferous love for Jesus Christ.

I knew I needed to investigate the Centers of Light for myself. I told my sister, Idara that this worship experience was next on the agenda. She shared that she had visited the Centers of Light in Atlanta, years before. When I asked her how it went, she said simply: "It was intense."

On the morning of the service, I was driving to the Center, which was in an unfamiliar part of town. I exited from the highway and, following the directions from the GPS on my iPhone, made a right turn onto a city street.

Almost immediately, I saw police lights flashing behind me and heard sirens.

"Damn it!" I shouted in my car.

When the police pulled me over, I was not happy, nor did I feel particularly holy.

See, I was driving a car with expired Georgia plates, and I didn't have a valid driver license.

Why, you might ask?

Well, in my frequent travels, my license had simply gotten lost. I figured it was probably in some remote pocket of a suitcase somewhere. I knew it was still valid, but had no idea where it was. And I had neither the time nor the energy to replace it. Still, after all this time, my energy was low. Grief takes from you what it takes, and you do your best to live your life with whatever energy it leaves for you.

Also, I hadn't switched my vehicle registration because I was driving my father's car. It had become mine after he passed away. I hadn't wanted to change the plates from Georgia to Illinois, as that felt like yet another acknowledgement that my father was gone and wasn't coming back.

Well, now I would have to face the music.

I'd learned during my jury duty stint what happens to people who drive without their license and registration. I knew a trip to the police station was in my near future.

As the police officer peered in my window, I handed him my state ID and my insurance, knowing that was not what he asked for. He took them to his vehicle, and when he came back he asked, "This is your state ID, do you have your license?"

I came clean and admitted, "No, I lost it."

He then asked, "Are you aware that your license plates are expired?"

I nodded yes.

He looked at me with a bit of pity in his eyes, and said, "I'm going to need you to follow me to the station."

With a sigh, I indicated that was fine, and I pulled out behind him in traffic and followed him to the station.

I am generally fascinated by having different experiences; this time, being the person in trouble was intriguing. I parked across from the police station, went in, and sat at a table across from the police officer. He confirmed that my license was not expired. He was going to write me three tickets: one for driving with no license, one for driving with an expired registration, and one for turning right where there was a no turn on red sign.

When I told him I didn't see the sign, he told me that it had been there for years. It seemed futile to tell him that this was the first time for me in this neighborhood because I was visiting a new church.

I just watched him write out three expensive tickets, and tried to neutralize any thoughts of anger with meditation, since I knew I was currently missing the meditation that preceded the service at Centers of Light.

It wasn't really working. I was angry and grumpy. At this point, I was thinking, "If I wasn't traipsing around the city going to churches in neighborhoods I didn't know, I wouldn't be in this predicament."

Oh well.

Finally, my time with Chicago's finest ended. I was able to leave the station and make my way to the church.

When I walked into the church building, one of the Deacons met me. I took my shoes off and entered the sanctuary, where there was incense burning and meditation under way. Because of the cop business, I'd missed a good deal of the meditation, which made me sad, because I was looking forward to that part of the service.

At this point, I remembered that Christmas was near.

This year, I was largely ignoring Christmas—which was not much of a stretch, because I'm not someone who goes overboard with this particular holiday. My father and my sister, Emuata, were the ones who loved the whole ritual around putting up the Christmas tree and the decorations. For years, I'd never really cared.

But on this morning, I was unable to ignore Christmas because I was forced to sing Christmas carols.

When the first song, "O Holy Night," began, I immediately started to cry. With a rush of emotion, I found myself remembering my mother and father singing this song during my childhood when Christmas still meant something to me. Tears continued to fall from my eyes as the songs continued: "Hark the Herald Angels Sing," "Silent Night," and "What Child Is This."

I was grateful that there were boxes of Kleenex in the pews. I grabbed a handful and wiped away my tears.

Following the songs, there were announcements, then one member came to the front of the sanctuary to share her testimony.

In a heartfelt manner, she shared stories of the relationships that she had with women in general, and with her mother in particular, and how studying the heart and the life of Mary had impacted her. A main focus of the teachings here were focused on Mary—a place where I have not spent much religious energy.

After the woman's testimony, she shared a reading from a book about Mary. As I listened to this story, I had one of those, "So, you say you are a Christian?" moments. I thought: "If I say I'm a Christian, then this Christmas story—Jesus, Mary, and the virgin birth—I should believe with my whole heart. How can I be a Christian who only believes in this fuzzy fashion?"

I call myself a Christian. I'm not looking for another religion. It would be scary to leave my Christian religious home, and I didn't think it was necessary. But, would it be more authentic of me to consider it? This whole worship experience was calling me to task. As the service continued, I was asking myself, "What do I really believe and to what depth?" It was clear that there was a challenge on the table that I should try to be a better, clearer Christian if I'm going to claim that title.

I was reminded of a time, many years ago, when my father was visiting me in Chicago. I'd just finished reading *Conversations with God*, by Neale Donald Walsch, and was questioning some core beliefs I had.

The sun was shining brightly as I drove down Chicago's Lake Shore Drive on that day. Lake Michigan was a bright, deep blue. I asked my father some very basic questions about his Christian faith.

"Dad, if you call yourself a Christian," I said, "there are some very specific beliefs that you should have. Do you believe that Jesus Christ is the *only* way to heaven, and that everyone who doesn't go through him goes to hell?"

He, in his typical fashion, replied by asking rhetorical questions about different stories in the Bible. Was the burning bush really burning? When Jesus went to the top of the mountain, was it a literal or figurative mountain? And so on.

I knew my father well and appreciated the opportunity to talk to him about spirituality and philosophy, but on that day, I wanted a specific answer.

"I know, I know, Dad," I said, but I didn't let him off the hook.

I tried to pin him down to have him say that he believed that Jesus Christ was the only way, but he kept dodging and weaving with philosophical and rhetorical flourishes.

I smile now, knowing that he was giving me a huge gift—the gift of the freedom to search for my own truth. To follow his footsteps and worship within a Christian context, but to also have my own religious experiences, explore my own spiritual connections, and decide what I thought and believed based on those experiences and connections.

It was a fond memory, even as I remembered it within the context of this very intense experience in the Centers of Light.

By this time, the pastor began to speak. She discussed the importance of trusting and following God's word like Mary had.

"When you follow God, the logic comes after you follow the steps, not before," she said.

She asked an important question: "In one day, how often is your mind considering God's word, as opposed to your concerns, your worries, your plans?"

As I contemplated the answer to that question, it was clear to me that still, I was spending far more time considering my concerns, worries and plans, rather than God's word.

She encouraged us by saying that in our biggest trials, we have to trust God more. She reminded us that when we encounter truth, and when truth is revealed to us, we should hold on to that truth. There's no need to doubt it and try to make it untrue, to obsess about it and worry about it. Just hold on to it.

Her message ended, and we knelt to pray and prepare for communion. At the end of the prayer, there was a unique conclusion.

Instead of saying, as many churches do: "In the name of the Father, the Son, and the Holy Spirit," this prayer ended with the pastor saying, "In the name of the Creator, the Mediator, and the Holy Spirit."

In addition, instead of making the sign of a cross, they made the sign of a triangle or a pyramid. Triangles and pyramids are spiritually powerful shapes, but this was the first time I'd experienced a prayer ending with these words, or with that sign being made.

A second prayer before communion ended with the words, "In the name of Jesus and Mary this is done."

*   *   *

The entire experience was, as my sister warned me, intense. It seemed like Catholicism turned up 1,000 percent.

I was glad I came to the entire service, and not just the communion, as I'd considered due to a busy schedule. I learned to look at Christianity in a different way, and question the very foundations of the religious tradition that I call my own.

PEACE BE STILL
ALL SAINTS CHURCH

6:00 p.m. Taizé Prayer Service, Prayers around the Cross, Pasadena, California

Since my family decided to gather in Los Angeles to avoid the cold in December, I found myself in California for Christmas.

In preparation for the trip, and realizing that I only had a few more opportunities to experience a few different worship traditions before my year ended, I researched and found a few locations for worship experiences that I wanted to have while I was in Los Angeles.

I contacted a preacher at a church in Pasadena. I was looking for a Taizé service, and through email communications, she confirmed that there was a service held every fourth Thursday—which happened to fall within the time I was going to be in Los Angeles.

Gathering as a family can provide certain stresses, and our family was no different. After a long day of last minute Christmas shopping, my sister and I engaged dueling GPS systems to try to get from West Hollywood in time for the Taizé prayer service at All Saints Church in Pasadena, California. Although the GPS duo gave us a travel time of about thirty minutes, it turned out that was an estimate of how long it would take if we were actually moving. The 101 was in gridlock, and my sister and I were trying to determine if we should trade this gridlock for the suggestion made by her fancier GPS, which gave options for "avoiding the traffic."

Los Angeles traffic can turn anyone from a saint into a sinner.

I knew the service was only an hour. I really didn't want to miss a minute of it. I decided to go with her option, which of course, traded the more direct route for one with side streets and unfamiliar turns. Somehow, I always found myself in the far right lane when it was time to turn left, and in the far left lane when it was time to turn right! As a result, I was getting stressed out and grumpy with my sister and my family and considered just going home as it became clear that we wouldn't be on time.

The majority of my worship experiences have been solo—not just in this year's journey, but in my life in general. In the years when I was an active member of my home church, ninety percent of the time I attended by myself. I sat in a folding chair in the aisle in the same section of the church every Sunday. I like aisle seats.

If I was feeling particularly inspired by the service, I could praise loudly and cry. If I was feeling disconnected, I had the option to leave. Although I became familiar with those who sat in the seats around my favorite seat, I didn't know them well. In the early years of my church experience, I joined a ministry and worked in small groups, but it had been years since I had done that.

I had a great relationship with my pastor, whom I affectionately call Daddy J. I knew I could count on him if I needed anything—but rarely did I ask. When my father passed away, he sent a very thoughtful letter to my mother and my sisters. I knew he prayed for me, and I appreciated it.

If I had to think deeply about my experience at Trinity, even though my church home is indeed a home, I was basically worshipping with people who just happened to gather with me in the same place every Sunday.

But I was okay with that. I was able to control each worship experience. I could make sure that I arrived early so I didn't have to rush, and could only blame myself if I was late or otherwise unprepared for some aspect of a service.

In the times where others joined me, I realized that I still had much to learn about "playing well with others."

I had to seriously think about the benefits of sharing an experience with people who knew me. I had to be flexible about their adherence to strict time schedules. I also knew myself. I was much more likely to participate in a running commentary if I was in a service with someone I knew. And because I process things through humor, I was more likely to make jokey comments with a friend, rather than focusing more on the service if I was by myself.

I had lessons to learn, apparently, about sharing my life with others. This was an especially sobering realization as I navigated through Los Angeles traffic toward the Taizé service, and thought of my ex, who no doubt was spending Christmas with his family, and probably not thinking of me.

When we arrived at the church, it was huge.

It was not immediately apparent where we should go for the service. We asked a congregant who was milling about the church entrance where it was. She led us to a basement room that was empty and obviously not the location for the service.

Meanwhile, we were getting later. I was getting more anxious.

I fished out my iPhone, checked the email I'd sent to the pastor in charge of the service, and realized that the service had moved to a different room. We hustled to that location, already fifteen minutes late for an hour-long service.

When we arrived, we saw a semicircle of people who were facing an altar decorated with Christmas poinsettias and trees on both sides. Candles were lined up across the altar. A decorative cross lay in the middle of the semicircle, with a candle on it.

The energy was so peaceful I immediately and thankfully felt the melting away of all the stress and anxiety that had built up on the way to the service.

Those who were already there were singing a contemplative tune, but silently rose to go and get chairs for me and my family. They rearranged the semicircle so we were part of it.

It was so seamless, that in that moment, I was treated to a lesson of what to do when things don't go exactly as you had planned. Don't make a big stink. Keep doing what you're doing, but quietly and peacefully incorporate the new information. If someone is late or disruptive, no need to go bananas. Just open the circle.

There is a lesson to be learned in going with the flow.

In addition to the chairs, the worship leader quietly picked up folders and handed them to me, my mother, and my sisters. The folders included the order of worship, as well as all the songs, which gave us a chance to find our place in the service and begin to participate ourselves. As the readings and songs continued, those around us silently showed us what was being read, and sung. Their help was much appreciated.

Finally, I was able to take a deep breath and actually try to feel the deep feeling of relaxation that a Taizé service affords. The service was minimalistic—we sang, with the accompaniment of a pastor who played a guitar and another musician with a flute. There were a few scriptures read, and a unison reading, including the Lord's Prayer. Near the end of the service, we were able to approach the cross, touch our head to the cross, and say personal prayers.

I kept peeking at my family throughout the service to see how they were experiencing it—especially my mother, who had heard about my journey often, but was now experiencing a worship tradition that was quite different than her home church.

When I saw her approach and touch her head to the cross, I thought about all that she had been through that year. My life had been difficult because I lost my father, my grandmother, and the man that I'd loved for a few rocky years. But my mother had lost her husband, the man who had been her life partner for fifty years. And she had lost her mother. She too had survived the first year of living a new reality, figuring out what her life would be like after enormous change, grief, and loss.

As I watched her pray, I saw in her a strength that I knew was in me as well. I was thankful that I was able to share this experience with her.

*   *   *

At the Taizé service, even after the hustle and bustle of urban traffic and holiday family dynamics, there was time for a little peace, a little remembrance, and some focus on the reason for the season. For this, I was grateful.

Liberal Minds
Unitarian Universalist
Church of Studio City

9:00 p.m. service, Christmas Eve, Studio City, California

Throughout the year, many times, I'd made plans to visit a Unitarian Universalist church. Each time, something came up. On this Christmas Eve, I decided to visit one that was not too far away from where I was staying, at my sister's house in Los Angeles.

I was exhausted from travel. I was jet-lagged and was fighting sleep from the beginning of the service. But I was committed to experiencing a Unitarian worship service.

Timber beams lined the ceiling of the inside of the church—it had a feel like a barn or a loft space. Poinsettias covered the altar. Some were dressed up in their Christmas finery; some were wearing traditional Christmas-themed sweaters.

The congregation made me feel like we were in the Midwest, not in fabulous L.A. It felt more inviting, homey, and family oriented. I was once again a chocolate chip—the congregation was mostly older adults, and all were Caucasian.

There were Christmas carols. We sang, "O Come All Ye Faithful"—in Latin. The lyrics started with "Adeste Fidelis," and as I sang along, I was reminded of my father, who was well versed in both Latin and Greek. As I sang aloud in my own voice, I heard his voice in my head and in my heart.

After the song, there was the lighting of the chalice—a symbol of hope and faith, affirming light against the darkness. We each had our own candles, and filed to the front of the room to light them. They remained lit for a good part of the service.

Because I was so sleepy, I found myself focusing on not dropping the candle and burning the church down.

After the lighting of the chalice, the next song was also in Latin: "Gloria," by Antonio Vivaldi. There was a small orchestra to the right of the pulpit, at the front of the church. There were violins and cellos, and a shiny Baby Grand. The musicians were very talented and I enjoyed it, but the classical music was unexpected. I guess in my mind the Unitarians were more granola-earthy-types—and classical music seemed so traditional.

There were several readings from Isaiah. Some of them reminded me of the lyrics of *Handel's Messiah,* which then reminded me of my high school years.

Every year when I was in high school, the chorus did a *Messiah* sing along during the Christmas season. Members of the choir and of the community would practice, prepare, and perform *The Messiah.* I came to love the presentation, and now try to experience it every December.

When I heard Isaiah 9:6 (KJV), I felt like I was at home.

> For unto us a child is born, unto us a son is given: and the government shall be upon his shoulder: and his name shall be called Wonderful, Counsellor, The mighty God, The everlasting Father, The Prince of Peace.

I got a taste of the belief structure of the Unitarian Universalist church as the pastor referred to the Bible. He referred to the Unitarians as "liberal-minded Christians." During his message, he said, "These are not stories of history, but stories of faith."

During the service, there were several inspirational readings. One focused on the message: "Christmas returns with the assurance that life goes on." This was especially poignant. The assurance that life goes on was comforting to me, and I contemplated these words throughout the remainder of the holiday season.

Afterwards, members of the congregation met for wassail and holiday goodies.

I slipped out, exhausted, to go to my sister's house and rest.

*   *   *

Although I was physically tired throughout this service, I was well aware of the emotional and spiritual strength that I had developed throughout my 52-week journey.

I did not underestimate how much I had been affected by the stories of faith I had heard at this church, and all the other places of worship I had visited throughout the year. I wondered what blessings I would receive as I made my last worship stop of the year.

WEEK 52
LAST WORSHIP STOP OF THE YEAR
MUSLIM COMMUNITY CENTER

1:05 p.m., Jumu'ah prayers, Chicago, Illinois

New Year's Eve.

The end of my spiritual journey after my year of loss.

I knew that I would be spending the final day of the year having a memorable last worship stop.

As it was Friday, I chose to visit Friday Jumu'ah prayers at the Muslim Community Center on Chicago's North Side.

I'd planned to visit this mosque during Ramadan, but at that time, the structure of a Muslim prayer service still confused me. I saw prayer times listed on the website for the community center, but I still didn't really understand what they meant, when I should show up, and what I should do.

Because of my positive experience at the Atlanta Masjid of Al-Islam, I felt a little more comfortable about the idea of going, for the first time, to a mosque that was in no way related to the Nation of Islam, and was not a majority African-American congregation.

As in my exploration of other religions, I wanted to visit different communities within a worship tradition. After my experience in Atlanta, I'd made a mental note to visit a mosque that had members who appeared to have been born outside of the United States, primarily in Northern Africa and the Middle East.

I was especially nervous going to this service because, believe it or not, I still had anxiety remaining from my experience where I was denied entry into a mosque.

When I drove up to the community center, I saw a parking lot across the street from the actual building. I slowed down, with the intention of turning into the lot. But I soon realized that the lot was roped off. Standing in front of the rope was a man in a white flowing gown and hat. He just looked at me, no doubt wondering what I was doing. When I realized my error, I kept driving and drove around the corner.

I parked a few blocks away and walked toward the mosque. I was apprehensive, but trying to be brave and act as if I knew what I was doing.

Miraculously enough, as I approached the front door, the same man who had been standing in front of the parking lot was standing in front of the front door.

I hesitated before I entered the front door because I wasn't sure if maybe there was an entrance for the women and a different one for the men, like on Saviours' Day.

When I hesitated, he looked at me puzzled, unsure why I'd stopped, then he gestured toward the door, inviting me in. With that act, I gained a level of confidence and thanked him internally for helping me to feel "invited" to worship.

Say what you want. To me, it was clear that this man was there to help me walk through my fear and into the mosque.

I silently thanked God for the assistance.

As I entered the mosque, I followed the women. I left my shoes in the place where the women left their shoes. I then followed a woman who entered in front of me as she went into what looked like it might be the women's bathroom.

And it was, kind of. There were bathroom stalls and a mirror, but there were also several washing stations.

Wudu.

Here, the women were doing the ritualistic washing that had kept me out of the first mosque and that I'd watched in the second.

I washed my hands and feet as best I could, mimicking the others around me, and said my own prayers. Nobody seemed to be concerned if I was doing it right or wrong.

I breathed a sigh of relief, and exited the Wudu room.

There was indeed a women's entrance and a men's entrance to the prayer space. I followed the women and children through the correct door, like Simon Says.

The women and children were all together in what looked like the back part of the mosque. We were behind a partition and the men were in front. We could hear them, but we couldn't see them.

Now it was time to prepare for the service.

I was armed with the good advice from my worship neighbor from Mosque Maryam. She had told me months ago that I should just watch and do what the others did.

She had also suggested that I get on the Internet and do some research so I could have a sense for how things flowed. I'd done just that, and I remembered my experience from the Atlanta Masjid of Al-Islam. Armed with that information, and focusing on a young lady who was in front of me in the mosque, I prepared for prayer.

The man standing by the parking lot and then at the door was the first angel who helped guide me through this experience. The woman in front of me would be my second.

364

Two raka'hs.

I followed her steps, first putting my hands to the side of my head, then bowing, then fully prostrating with my head to the floor. I tried to balance my desire to focus on entering into a worship stance with my need to make sure that I had my second angel guide in front of me and I was doing what she was doing.

After the first raka'h, I was able to do a second, and a third without having to be as concerned about the woman in front of me.

I felt slightly better, but still apprehensive. This feeling didn't really leave me throughout the whole service.

The experience was different than my previous experience with Jumu'ah because I was by myself. I did the best I could. I marveled that after visiting so many other places of worship prior to this one, the experience of worshipping in a new place could still humble me so thoroughly.

The service was in Arabic. I didn't understand what was being said. I just tried to soak in the rhythmic cadence of the message. As I looked around, I saw a diverse set of women and children—only one other woman appeared to be African-American.

Then, while I was lost in observing the different women in their dresses and various head coverings, my third angel guide gave me a nudge.

There were two small children next to me. They were well behaved throughout the entire prayer service, but at this moment, one of them tapped me on the shoulder, and looked straight at me and said: "Everyone is praying."

I smiled at him, realizing that he gave me a cue as to the content and cadence of the next part of the service. I silently thanked the kid!

As everyone prepared for final prayer, again I remembered my previous experiences with Islam.

Since I'd watched the prayer from the back when I went to the Atlanta Masjid of Al-Islam, I prepared to move to the back on this day as well.

But my final angel, an elderly Muslim woman, grabbed the edge of my shirt, and pulled me towards her. It felt like she was insisting that I join the prayer line.

Far be it from me to refuse her.

We stood shoulder to shoulder, tight. I kneeled when everyone kneeled, prostrated when everyone prostrated, and thanked God for the blessings and mystery of the last stop on my journey.

*   *   *   *   *   *   *

In Closing . . .

My journey ended where it started. On New Year's Eve, I attended the 7:00 p.m. watch service at Trinity. It was a homecoming of sorts for me. Before the service began, I contemplated the lessons I learned over my 52-week journey.

So, what happened after 52 Weeks of Worship?

Two or three hours at a time, every week, for one year, my life changed.

I faced my grief and pain head on, and came out on the other side grateful, strong, and prepared to live a life where I see evidence of goodness and divinity all around me. Healing came through my journey.

Each experience gave me a chance to learn about a new community of worship and the people in that community. Through different lenses, I experienced God, culture, family, and love. Connection came through multiple, memorable interactions with strangers, who over the course of a worship service, left an indelible imprint on my heart, my life, and my story. I will never forget the countless acts of kindness I received.

Gifts of remembrance were sprinkled through my journey. Through a song here, and a memory there, I remembered the loved ones I had lost. I was able to say goodbye to my grandmother and my father, although I still miss them. I draw solace from the realization that the best parts of them are in me.

Life now is not perfect. I have not turned magically into someone who feels no pain, who always sees the silver lining, and never has a moment of doubt. I'm not holier-than-thou, and haven't become an insufferable evangelist. Every now and then I throw a pity party, although they are shorter and less dramatic than they used to be.

My 52 Weeks of Worship rebooted my experience as a woman of faith. When I started my journey, I was looking for a life vest. What I found was an anchor. I developed a strong spiritual foundation that helps me every day. It keeps me centered as I weather life's storms.

In my blog, www.my52wow.com, I share 52 things that I learned from my 52 weeks of worship. Number 52 is:

Sometimes when you start a journey, you have very little idea where you are going to end up. But with a little faith, you can end up having a more amazing experience than you ever imagined.

It happened to me.

NOTES

Dedication Page

[1] Quote originally heard on The Oprah Winfrey Show: http://www.oprah.com/oprahs-lifeclass/Oprahs-Forgiveness-Aha-Moment-Video

Introduction

[2] The Pluralism project at Harvard University: http://www.pluralism.org

[3] The 15 Greatest Black Preachers: http://findarticles.com/p/articles/mi_m1077/is_n1_v49/ai_14258251/

Week 5

[4] Lyrics, "To God Be the Glory": http://www.hymnsite.com/lyrics/umh098.sht

Week 7

[5] The Spirit of New Orleans: http://www.wyntonmarsalis.org/2010/02/07/the-spirit-of-new-orleans/

[6] An alternate benediction by the Rev. Dr. William Sloane Coffin, Jr., pastor and peace activist.

Week 9

[7] Lyrics, "It is Well with My Soul." http://library.timelesstruths.org/music/It_Is_Well_with_My_Soul/

[8] Horatio Spafford's story: http://www.faithclipart.com/guide/Christian-Music/hymns-the-songs-and-the-stories/it-is-well-with-my-soul-the-song-and-the-story.html

Week 12

[9] Wards in the Mormon church: http://www.mormonwiki.com/Wards

[10] A website dedicated to Black members of the Church of Jesus Christ of Latter-day Saints: http://www.blacklds.org

[11] Lyrics, "Help Pour Out The Rain," by Buddy Joel: http://www.cowboylyrics.com/lyrics/jewell-buddy/help-pour-out-the-rain-laceys-song-2157.html

Week 13

[12] What is the Baha'i faith? http://www.bahai.org/faq/facts/bahai_faith

Week 15

[13] What is a Church Warden? http://edmonton.anglican.org/resources/wardens-handbook/what-is-a-church-warden/

[14] Perspectives on cults on Nigerian college campuses: http://www.campuscults.net/index.html

[15] Lyrics, "Christ the Lord is Risen Today" http://www.hymnsite.com/lyrics/umh302.sht

Week 16

[16] Information about Okrika: http://www.riversstate.gov.ng/

[17] High School Handbook, The Westminster Schools, Atlanta, Georgia http://www.westminster.net/academics/handbooks/HighSchoolHandbook.pdf, page 6

[18] The parable of the talents: Matthew 25:14-30 (NIV)

Week 18

[19] Walt Whitman's Soul Children of Chicago: http://www.soulchildrenchicago.com/

Week 19

20 The Creed of the Church of Scientology: http://www.scientology.
org/what-is-scientology/the-scientology-creeds-and-codes/
the-creed-of-the-church.html

21 "What is Greatness" by L. Ron Hubbard: http://www.lronhubbard.
org/articles-and-essays/what-is-greatness.html

22 The Scientology Prayer for Total Freedom: http://www.freetobelieve.
org/pg014.html

23 What is Scientology Auditing?: http://www.auditing.org/

24 Scientology's 'Suppressive Person' (SP) doctrine: http://www.
xenu-directory.net/practices/sp.html

Week 20

25 Lyrics, "Lord of the Dance": http://www.celtic-lyrics.com/forum/
index.php?autocom=tclc&code=lyrics&id=309

26 Blue Mountain Center of Meditation: www.passagemeditation.com

27 Saint Teresa of Avila, Let Nothing Upset You: http://www.
easwaran.org/saint-teresa-of-avila-let-nothing-upset-you.html

28 The Prayer of St. Francis: http://www.easwaran.org/
the-prayer-of-st-francis.html

29 Lyrics, Day by Day: http://www.stlyrics.com/lyrics/godspell/
daybydayreprise.htm

Week 21

30 The Story of Pentecost: Acts 2:1-41

Week 22

31 Lyrics, Siyahamba http://ingeb.org/spiritua/siyahamb.html

32 Lyrics, Woke Up This Morning With My Mind Stayin' on
Jesus: http://www.stlyrics.com/songs/f/fredmcdowell26298/
wokeupthismorningwithmymindonjesus1173673.html

33 Lyrics, Oyaheya: http://www.lyrics59.com/RICKI-BYARS-
BECKWITH-OYAHEYA-LYRICS/448058/

Week 23

[34] Lyrics, In the Waiting: http://www.christianlyricsonline.com/artists/greg-long/in-the-waiting.html

Week 24

[35] The Mountain of Fire & Miracles Ministries International Headquarters: http://www.mountainoffire.org/
[36] The Mountain of Fire & Miracles Ministries International Headquarters: http://www.mountain-of-fire.com/

Week 25

[37] Hector Pietersen Memorial: http://www.joburg.org.za/culture/museums-galleries/hector-pieterson-memorial-a-museum
[38] The Nicene Creed: http://www.reformed.org/documents/nicene.html
[39] Lyrics, Kyrie Eleison, http://www.metrolyrics.com/kyrie-eleison-lyrics-mr-mister.html

Week 26

[40] Lyrics, For the Fruit of All Creation: http://www.oremus.org/hymnal/f/f211.html

Week 27

[41] http://www.anandapaloalto.org/index.html

Week 28

[42] William P. Young, *The Shack* (Newbury Park, CA: Windblown Media, 2007), page 185 (paperback)

Week 29

[43] Chögyam Trungpa, *Shambhala: The Sacred Path of the Warrior* (Boston, MA: Shambhala Publications, 1984), back cover

Week 30

[44] Reference to Ephesians 5:19(KJV)

[45] Harvey Church of Christ, *How many Churches Did Christ Build* (Pasadena, Texas: Haun Publishing Company), page 7

[46] Lyrics, Let it Rise by Holland Davis, http://www.nligc.org/songs/letisrise.html

Week 31

[47] WBEZ Article, Dr. King Comes to Marquette Park, by John R. Schmidt: http://www.wbez.org/blog/john-r-schmidt/2011-08-05/dr-king-comes-marquette-park-89583

[48] Judaism 101:Synagogues, Shuls, and Temples: http://www.jewfaq.org/shul.htm

Week 34

[49] Krishna Lounge, A Community for Spiritual Revolution: http://www.krishnalounge.com

[50] Krishna Lounge, A Community for Spiritual Revolution: http://www.krishnalounge.com

Week 36

[51] Website, KAM Isaiah Israel: http://www.kamii.org/

[52] Jewish Outreach Institute: http://www.joi.org/qa/denom.shtml

[53] Jewish Virtual Library http://www.jewishvirtuallibrary.org/jsource/Judaism/kaddish.html

Week 38

[54] What is Yom Kippur? http://judaism.about.com/od/holidays/a/yomkippur.htm

[55] The Wiccan Rule of Behavior, The Wiccan Rede: http://www.religioustolerance.org/wicrede.htm

[56] What is Kirtan?: http://www.gauravani.com/download/kirtan

Week 40

[57] Website, Indo-Pak United Methodist Church, http://www.indopakfellowship.org/

Week 42

[58] The Holy Qur'an, Yusuf Ali Translation, Surah 10. Yunus (Jonah) http://www.harunyahya.com/Quran_translation/Quran_translation10.php

[59] The Holy Qur'an, Yusuf Ali Translation, Surah 10. Ibrahim (Abraham) http://www.harunyahya.com/Quran_translation/Quran_translation14.php

Week 46

[60] The Pluralism project at Harvard University: http://www.pluralism.org

[61] Definition of a Jashan: http://heritageinstitute.com/zoroastrianism/jashan/index.htm#afringan

[62] AMORC Rosicrucian Order: http://www.rosicrucian.org

Week 48

[63] Islamic Society of Michiana: http://michianamuslims.org/fridaysermons.html

[64] Lyrics, One Power by Daniel Nahmod, http://www.danielnahmodlyrics.com/op-one-power.html

[65] Marianne Williamson, *A Return to Love* (New York: HarperCollins Publishers, 1992), Chapter 7, Section 3. http://www.marianne.com/

Week 49

66 About Amish: http://aboutamish.blogspot.com/2010/06/amish-and-beachy-amish.html
67 The Beachy Amish Mennonites: http://www.beachyam.org
68 The Earth Center: http://www.theearthcenter.com/index.php

Week 50

69 Meaning of Sree/Sri/Shree/Shri: http://teck.in/meaning-of-sree-sri-shree-shri.html
70 Kashmir Hindu Deities: http://www.koausa.org/Gods/God4.html
71 Glossary of Sanskrit Terms: http://www.selfdiscoveryportal.com/cmSanskrit.htm
72 A Hindu Primer: http://www.sanskrit.org/www/Hindu Primer/abhishekam.html
73 Excerpts from the Bhavagad Gita taken from the English Translation from His Divine Grace A.C. Bhaktivedanta Swami Prabhupada: http://www.asitis.com/9/26.html
74 Excerpts from the Bhavagad Gita taken from the English Translation from His Divine Grace A.C. Bhaktivedanta Swami Prabhupada http://www.asitis.com/18/66.html
75 Mincha, the Afternoon Prayer, by Rabbi Berel Wein: http://www.aish.com/jl/m/pb/48950221.html
76 Kabbalat Shabbat: http://www.jewishvirtuallibrary.org/jsource/judaica/ejud_0002_0011_0_10515.html

Week 51

77 What is Christian Mysticism: http://www.centersoflight.org/what_is_christian_mysticism.html

Made in the USA
Monee, IL
22 July 2020